National
Security
Planning

National Security Planning

ROOSEVELT through REAGAN

MICHAEL M. BOLL

THE UNIVERSITY PRESS OF KENTUCKY

Copyright © 1988 by The University Press of Kentucky

Scholarly publisher for the Commonwealth,
serving Bellarmine College, Berea College, Centre
College of Kentucky, Eastern Kentucky University,
The Filson Club, Georgetown College, Kentucky
Historical Society, Kentucky State University,
Morehead State University, Murray State University,
Northern Kentucky University, Transylvania University,
University of Kentucky, University of Louisville,
and Western Kentucky University.

Editorial and Sales Offices: Lexington, Kentucky 40506-0336

Library of Congress Cataloging-in-Publication Data

Boll, Michael M., 1938-
    National security planning : Roosevelt through Reagan

        p. cm.
    Bibliography: p.
    Includes index.
    ISBN 0-8131-1645-7
    1. United States—National security. 2. Military planning—United
States—History—20th century. 3. United States—Foreign
relations—1933-1945. 4. United States—Foreign relations—1945-
I. Title.
UA23.B58   1988
355'.0335'73—dc19   88-43

This book is printed on acid-free paper meeting
the requirements of the American National Standard
for Permanence of Paper for Printed Library Materials. ⊖

To ROBERT W. MEYER—
friend, teacher, colleague

Contents

Tables

Preface

The idea for this study of national security planning arose in 1981 when I was a member of the policy-planning staff of the Pentagon. This being the first year of the Reagan administration, our offices were besieged with papers suggesting new policy positions and seeking concurrence for ideas originating from new appointees in other bureaucracies. After one particularly long review session, a colleague commented that the most recent position paper was totally illogical, an opinion I fully shared. But this started me to thinking. What was "illogical" in the policy suggestions we had read? Surely it was not the absence of an internal consistency, for each section of the document fully revealed the author's position. What was lacking was a coherence between the proposed action and the notions my colleague and I held about both our allies and our enemies. It was then that I realized how different the new administration's assumptions were from those of the preceding administration during which the two of us had been hired. Several years later, after returning to my university, the realization that policy only made sense in terms of some set of assumptions was reinforced when students raised questions as to why America possessed 1,054 ICBMs and not, for instance, 1,122. The answer to the question could not be found by analyzing the concept of security itself nor in the facile assertions that America sought overwhelming nuclear superiority. National security was not a subject susceptible to scientific precision in which awareness of a few "first" principles produced common conclusions among practitioners and students alike. What was required was an understanding of the specific assumptions of the defense planners whose decisions had produced this specific missile deployment. Yet even here much more than bare assumptions was required, since defense planners had to judge the nature and magnitude of the threat before selecting a given response to meet it. And since defense planning occurs within a highly politic atmosphere, the bargaining and trade-offs between the executive and legislative branches, as well as between the various departments of the bureaucracy, needed to be factored into the explanation. In short, an understanding of America's defense posture required an account of the historical process in which various security planners provided diverse assessments of dangers facing the nation and debated ways in which these threats might best be met. And all this occurred within a dynamic political process in which beliefs about both the enemy and the very nature of American society frequently found significant divergence.

A study of national planning offers a number of important lessons aside from providing insight as to why our current military posture is as it is. Each policy has been premised upon a certain view of our main enemy, largely the USSR. By making these views explicit, the reader can judge for himself how well these assumptions have stood the test of time. Predictions made about the probable constraints upon Soviet behavior in the immediate postwar period undoubtedly require reexamination. Certainly, the USSR is a very different country under Gorbachev's leadership than it was under Stalin's. Policies justified by appeals to the unchanging essence of communism or to Soviet behavior of decades past need careful review. A historical assessment of security planning also provides some insight into the working of agencies normally shielded from public view—those dealing with intelligence. The specific threat to which past planners have responded was usually sketched in fullest detail by the diverse branches of the intelligence establishment. The correctness or incorrectness of our views of the enemy through time should allow us to judge how well these agencies have served us. One can also gain insight into how well various administrations have balanced means and goals in the interest of efficient as well as adequate defense. The dramatic expansion of alliances with third world states during the Eisenhower administration at the very time when military budgets were subject to intense scrutiny augured ill if America's resolve were tested. Lyndon Johnson's refusal to demand either military mobilization or a major tax increase when faced with unanticipated Vietnamese resistance demonstrated an inability to balance means and goals—an inability that helped produce domestic inflation in the next decade. The lessons of the past might help future administrations to be more aware of the potential gap between the type of world we seek and the amount of resources and commitment we are willing to make.

Finally, a historical analysis of national security planning offers a unique perspective on the tenacity with which American leaders have held to their most cherished ideals. Franklin Roosevelt, for example, wished to avoid the full domestic strains of war so as to preserve as many of the New Deal's assistance programs as possible. This, in turn, could be achieved only if the allied manpower requirements identified in Washington as early as 1941 were met by continued contributions of Soviet troops. Thus, Roosevelt worked to assure Moscow's active participation in the conflict up to the bloody end. It is against this background that the concessions granted our wartime Soviet ally find explanation within Roosevelt's overall set of priorities. In sharp contrast President Eisenhower's main concern was to limit the federal role in domestic, economic, and social development and to preserve the values of thrift and individual initiative that he perceived as the source of America's strength and worth. The result was a consistent refusal to abandon a frugal defense strategy despite growing evidence that new global challenges required major reconsideration. Indeed, in the last resort, national security planning has always focused upon defense of the values and institutions that make up the American way of life. In the difficult defense choices made, each postwar administration has revealed which aspects of this way of life it has held most dear.

This study would have been impossible without the assistance of individuals far too numerous to mention. I would, however, like to thank Art Plank of San Jose, California, for his suggestion that a book such as this might be worthwhile and Mrs. Joan Block, a virtual virtuoso at the computer keyboard without whose help this book would not have been possible.

National
Security
Planning

Introduction

Few phrases sound more familiar to the modern ear than those embodying the term *national security*. From pulpit and podium, individuals with a specific political or social platform to discuss add weight to their remarks with references to this concept. Given the diverse meanings current in contemporary society, some definition of the way this term is employed in the following pages is in order. While a definitive explanation of the various meanings of national security will not be attempted, a "working definition" is necessary if only to clarify why some topics have been included in the discussion and others omitted. As the reader will soon learn, the numerous policymakers and practitioners of national security doctrine in the forty some years since World War II have themselves used diverse interpretations of this term as they struggled to identify both the changing threat and the basic values they wished to protect.

It ought to be made clear at once that national security is not equivalent to the protection of a state's territorial boundaries nor to the repulsion of foreign attack. This truism becomes clear if one examines a key episode in the modern history of contemporary America's main enemy, the Soviet Union. In the spring of 1918, four months after the Communist Revolution of the preceding November, the Soviet leader, Lenin, faced a dilemma that threatened to split his movement and imperil his newly won revolution. Taking advantage of the disorder that the revolution had created, the German army made deep advances into Russia and appeared poised to capture the Russian capital itself. The inability of Lenin's government to face such an onslaught would surely have undermined the slight confidence that his revolution had inspired, perhaps ending the fledgling communist government prior to its consolidation. The alternative, which many in Lenin's government thought unpatriotic and unthinkable, was to accept a humiliating peace that would detach fully one-third of the prewar European part of Russia. To Lenin the choice was clear. The national security of communist Russia lay not in its territorial boundaries but in the ideals of Marxism, which only a functioning communist government could nurture and maintain. In March 1918 Lenin's government signed the Carthaginian peace of Brest-Litovsk and left the war. Had Lenin followed the advice of many of his comrades, including his foreign minister, Leon Trotsky, and rejected this loss of frontiers, the German army might well have crushed the new communist regime. In such a case, what would the meaning of national security have been?

As the above example suggests, national security, at its most basic level, concerns neither foreign nor military policy but rather the values and ways of life a given society considers as its most important heritage. As early as the seventeenth century, the English political philosopher Thomas Hobbes argued that the protection of a way of life was the most important task confronting any government. As he noted, without such security "there is no place for Industry, because the fruit thereof is uncertain; and consequently no Culture of the Earth, no Navigation, nor use of the commodities that may be imported by sea; no commodious Buildings; no Instruments of moving and removing such things as require much force, no Knowledge of the face of the Earth; no account of Time, no Arts; no Letters, no Society; and which is worst of all, continuall feare, and danger of violent death; And the life of man, solitary, poore, nasty, brutish and short."[1] To Hobbes, writing at a time when England was engaged in bloody civil war, little difference was accorded the distinction between external or internal threat to English society. A city was just as ruined whether the torch that fired it was held by a foreign or a domestic rebel army. If Hobbes's notions of national security were applied to contemporary America, they would imply that threats to our national security may emerge from such internal events as pollution, racial war, and class struggle, as well as from some foreign enemy. Indeed, one can cogently argue that the greatest threat to the traditional American way of life in this century arose from the economic collapse of the Great Depression and the resulting despair that engendered movements to abolish both private property and the regular functions of American democracy.

Despite the conclusion that internal threats can be of equal importance, the conventional understanding of the term *national security* tends to restrict its application to challenges that arise beyond our borders. Yet whether the threats are foreign or domestic, one point ought to be clear: The goal of national security exclusively concerns a domestic phenomenon, a way of life that must be protected. Two contemporary sources, both men who played a key role in the postwar development of U.S. national security

policy, can be quoted in support of this definition: George Kennan and Paul
Nitze. Kennan, a key figure in the postwar State Department, wrote that a
central purpose of U.S. foreign policy must be the protection of the security
of the nation "by which is meant the continued ability of this country to
pursue the development of its internal life without serious interference, or
threat of interference, from foreign powers; and to advance the welfare of its
people, by promoting a world order in which this nation can make the
maximum contribution to the peaceful and orderly development of other
nations and derive maximum benefit from their experiences and abilities."[2]
Paul Nitze, Kennan's replacement as head of the State Department's Policy
Planning Staff and architect of a crucial national security plan entitled
NSC-68, was equally clear as to the domestic roots of security planning.
Attempting to explain America's role in the postwar world, Nitze focused
upon America's "purpose," the fundamental American values that inspired
security planning.

One way in which that purpose can be stated is found in the constitution. It is ". . .
to form a more perfect union, establish justice, insure domestic tranquillity, provide
for the common defense, promote the general welfare, and secure the blessings of
liberty to ourselves and our posterity."

Four corollaries flow from this purpose: (1) our resolve to establish and preserve a
system based on the concept of human dignity; (2) our determination to promote
and secure conditions at home and abroad under which this system can live and
prosper; (3) our willingness to cooperate with others in any action, however costly or
challenging, needed to achieve this purpose by peaceful means; and (4) our readiness to fight, if necessary, to defend this system for ourselves and for our children.[3]

While it is agreed that national values are to be protected by creation of
a favorable external and internal environment, some other, less abstract,
notion is required if one is to calculate how national security policy is
formulated. If one relates national values to the domestic and foreign
environment, the concept of national interests arises, goals toward which
national security planners strive in order to construct a world in which
American values are secure. In the period since World War II, it has been
the international arena in which the primary threats to America's security
have occurred, and it has been there that America has identified most
specifically its national interests. In the immediate postwar period, the
notion of "containment," with its assumption that America's national interests would be jeopardized by the expansion of communism into the more
industrialized portions of the world, functioned as a comprehensive worldview facilitating the choice of means to protect America's national security.
In the Nixon administration, the idea of containment was replaced by a

more flexible notion of consensus and competition that promised better use of America's economic and military resources in blunting the Soviet threat of that decade.

Regardless of the overriding assumptions as to the nature of the international threat to national interests, the responses available to security planners in Washington are selected as to the degree of danger perceived and the likelihood that a given response may change the behavior of the threatening state. Diplomatic, economic, and military pressure are the main responses available, with the proper selection of the correct mixture of each means depending upon the nature and extent of the perceived threat. Application of diplomatic pressure may take the form of creating an alliance of like-minded nations pledged to resist encroachment from outside. It may include negotiated agreements such as the Strategic Arms Limitation Talks (SALT) designed to reduce the likelihood of nuclear war. The use of economic constraints normally indicates an increase in pressure aimed at modifying the behavior of a threatening nation. Restrictions upon the exchange of technology or upon trade in agricultural products may penalize a state enough to prompt a change in its policies. In the Nixon administration, for example, the United States refused to allow open access to American markets for Soviet goods without pledges to permit unlimited Jewish emigration from the USSR. In the early eighties, the Carter administration embargoed agricultural shipments to the Soviet Union pending the withdrawal of Soviet troops from Afghanistan. Direct application of military force against an offending nation is the highest form of coercion a nation can apply, and its use must always be closely guided by the political objectives and national interests that prompted its use.

National security planning as a practical activity and as a proper object of historical examination consists of three distinct but interrelated functions. First, a consensus must be achieved as to what forms the basic national values to be defended. This normally occurs through the process of national election in which various candidates espouse differing views as to what America stands for and how such values will be protected and advanced by a given candidate's term in office. Second, the international environment is surveyed with an eye toward relating national values and foreign threat in such a way as to identify goals to be achieved and national interests to be protected. Normally, the identification of national interests in the international arena is facilitated by the construction of a worldview such as containment that allows a plausible integration of what at firsthand appears to be a world of diverse dangers and perils. Third, a judicious selection of measures to meet the threat must be made, keeping in mind that diplomatic, economic, and military responses are part of a continuum in which one response may soon shade into another.

In the postwar world, there has been a high degree of accord as to the basic national values at stake but less consensus as to the nature of the threat and where and how national interests must be defended. It is the changing nature of these views about the world and of the means selected to promote our security that makes a study such as this one both possible and important. Each worldview and each combination of means confront a real world imperfectly known by the security planners, and the historical pattern of confrontations and cooperations that dot the postwar world reveals how adequate to reality the planners' plans in fact were. The history of America's postwar national security efforts is a study of which efforts have been mounted and which have succeeded or failed.

While the very concept of national security functions as a means of integrating policy outputs from the various branches of government, the historian's task of assessing the record of the past half century is facilitated by proceeding in the opposite direction, by dividing, however arbitrarily, these policy debates and decisions into simpler groupings. The present study attempts to understand this period through the use of five analytical categories through which the various presidential administrations are examined. These categories are (1) the changing perception of the threat; (2) strategic planning; (3) tactical planning, especially as it concerned general purpose forces; (4) efforts to promote arms control; and (5) the shifting institutional structure of the national security establishment. Conceptualized within the broad limits of the dominant consensus of national values and tempered with more or less coherent perceptions of a changing world, policy decisions in these five important areas dominated the postwar search for national security.

While this account of national security planning begins with the Roosevelt administration on the eve of World War II, it would be wrong to assume that prior administrations were unconcerned about threats against the American way of life. America's emergence as a world power even prior to the advent of World War I prompted consideration of a global strategy in defense of American interests. To the traditional goals of the defense of the continental United States and the protection of the Western Hemisphere was added the defense of America's possessions gained in the Spanish-American conflict. Thus, America's empire in the new century stretched seven thousand miles westward from San Francisco to the exposed islands of the Philippines. In 1903 a Joint Army-Navy Board consisting of four members representing the Army General Staff and four from the General Board of the Navy drafted common plans to ensure coordination of the two services in case of war. With Japan's surprising victory in the Russo-Japanese War that began the following year, the Japanese Empire quickly became the primary potential enemy in terms of which plans had to be prepared. Such plans were identified by a color code, and while the Army-Navy Board did draft a dozen or so diverse color schemes—green for a war with Mexico, red for a war with Great Britain—the majority of attention fell to Plan Orange which was predicated upon war with Japan.[4]

As early as 1913, the main outlines of Plan Orange had been determined. Following then conventional doctrine, any future war would be met by rapid American offensive action. Since it was assumed that Japan would strike without warning—an assumption drawn from Japanese behavior in the recent Russo-Japanese conflict—the Philippines were projected as Japan's first target. Upon the outbreak of war, the U.S. fleet would sail from its Atlantic ports, using the incomplete facilities at Pearl Harbor on its way to the western Pacific. Until its arrival the army defenders of the Philippines would resist Japanese attacks to ensure the use of Philippine bases in the subsequent attacks upon Japanese shipping and the Japanese home islands.

World War I and the postwar territorial settlements that awarded Japan former German island possessions in the central Pacific required modification of Plan Orange since Japan now sat astride of the navy's planned reinforcement routes to the Philippines. Since Japanese forces would first have to be cleared, doubts were raised as to the army's ability to hold the Philippines until the navy's arrival. The Washington Naval Conference of 1921 posed further problems for Plan Orange since its prohibitions on further fortifications of possessions west of Hawaii precluded plans to strengthen Manila or to begin fortifications on Guam and in the Atlantic. Despite naval protests the Harding administration agreed to such restrictions, indicating the near total lack of coordination between the political and military branches of the U.S. government in determining the principles and means of national security. The absence of political guidance was to bedevil U.S. military planning for the next two decades.

While the results of the Washington conference hindered army-navy planning, they in no way affected the choice of the most probable enemy. In 1922 the reorganization of the fleet and the location of the navy's twelve most modern battleships in its Pacific component reconfirmed the fear of a future Japanese attack. Plan Orange was further refined to note that war with Japan would be primarily naval and that America would quickly take the offensive to isolate and harass the Japanese home islands. This would be accomplished by gaining control of the vital Japanese sea lanes and through air and naval attack against Japan's economic lifelines. Since bases in the western Pacific from which the continued naval strikes could be mounted were crucial, the American army had as its task the defense of Manila until reinforcements could arrive with the fleet. Since only 15,000 men existed in the entire military within the Philippines, Plan Orange called for the rapid dispatch of 50,000 U.S. troops from the West Coast upon the outbreak of war, a number exceeding one-third of the authorized regular army of 1922.[5] An additional problem that remained was the incomplete nature of fortifications and post facilities at Manila itself. As might be imagined, the details, although not the basic assumptions of Plan Orange, were to be revised numerous times in the years ahead.

In 1926 the assumption of rapid reinforcements sent from the West Coast was abandoned with the navy acknowledging the need to capture the Japanese bases on the Marshall, Caroline, and Mariana Islands prior to arrival at Manila. The army calculated that due to its geographical closeness to the Philippines, the Japanese could land 300,000 troops within thirty days of the outbreak of war. To meet this force, the United States would have 11,000 troops of which 7,000 were Filipinos plus a native constabulary of 6,000. Nevertheless, the army's mission remained tied to holding the fort. With Congress debating the possible freeing of the Philippines in the early thirties, the army requested a modification of Plan Orange that would allow a retirement of U.S. forces from the islands and from China upon the outbreak of conflict. For the army, granting independence to the Philippines would allow a return to the priority of defending the continental United States in case of conflict. In 1935 when Japan denounced the limitation upon naval construction contained in the Washington Naval Treaty, army demands for the modification of Plan Orange and a new objective of defending an Alaska-Hawaii-Panama perimeter became more strident, conflicting with the continued naval emphasis upon taking the offensive early in the war. When Japan joined the Germans and Italians in the Anti-Comintern Pact in 1936, army fears were further exacerbated by concern over a two-front war for which plans had not been drafted. Not until 1938 was a compromise attained between the army's wish to focus initially upon defense and the navy's continued emphasis upon an offensive doctrine.[6]

The 1938 revision of Plan Orange foresaw the defeat of Japan by a combination of military and economic pressures but omitted former emphasis upon an immediate offensive action. Initial operations would be primarily naval but in combination with measures designed to secure the continental United States, Alaska, Hawaii, and Panama. While the notion of a progressive advance across the Pacific was retained, the absence of a definite timetable confirmed the army-insisted primacy of initial perimeter defense. The plan assumed that a period of tension would precede the outbreak of hostilities and that a surprise attack was the likely means by which war would come. America would mobilize three-quarters of a million men for the army, and the navy and marines would expand in similar fashion. Provisions for the defense of Manila Bay were retained, but the absence of details as to reinforcements or the anticipated arrival time of the navy implied a military foreboding that the area, in fact, could not be held.[7]

1

Prewar and Wartime Planning

Until the late thirties, U.S. planning focused primarily upon the Japanese threat in the Pacific, relying upon the American fleet to perform its traditional defensive role. Plan Orange foresaw little possibility of coalition warfare, placing the burden for meeting Japanese expansionism squarely upon American forces. Yet even here Plan Orange was never completed, never fleshed out to include timetables for mobilization of men and materials required to fight a determined enemy. Fortunately, in the Army War College then located in Washington, D.C., some rudimentary thought had been given to the possibility that the next war would embrace combatants far in excess of just the United States and Japan and that potential American allies must be accounted for in any long-range assumptions. In 1934 members of the War College drafted a contingent war plan that assumed Orange (Japan) and Carnation (Japanese-controlled Manchuria) would engage in war with Pink (Russia), Yellow (China), and, eventually, Red (the British Empire) and Blue (America). As a harbinger of things to come, this plan included provisions for joint naval and ground attacks by America and its allies, a notion of coalition warfare that was still considered anathema by the army-navy planners in Washington.[1]

The cause for America's eventual shift to plans foreseeing a future war in which America would have to fight side by side with several allies can be located in the emergence of Nazi Germany in the mid-thirties. Following his appointment as chancellor in 1933, Adolf Hitler withdrew Germany from the League of Nations and refused to participate in any future discussions of arms control. Two years later Germany announced it would no longer abide by the limitations on armaments in the Versailles treaty, which had concluded World War I. In 1936 German troops advanced into the demilitarized zone between France and Germany, the Rhineland, created at the end of the war to preclude a future sneak attack by resurgent German forces. That same year Germany and Japan signed the Anti-Comintern Pact, which was aimed at containing the spread of communism. With these two militaristic nations increasingly linking their fate, plans predicated upon an American-Japanese conflict limited to the Pacific became increasingly unrealistic.

In 1938 Germany began its relentless drive for domination in Europe, annexing Austria in the spring of that year and gaining a large portion of Czechoslovakia (the Sudetenland) in the fall. Faced with an increasingly complex and unstable world, the Joint Army-Navy Board in November tasked its Planning Committee to create a defense plan designed to repel an attack upon the Western Hemisphere by one or more European powers and a second plan to take account of a simultaneous assault by Japan against the Philippines. With several potential threats now to be weighed, the planners assessed the likelihood that in the event of war America would have assistance from future allies. The resulting plans, named *Rainbow* to symbolize the diverse threats and various enemies and potential allies, assumed that British and French assistance against Germany, Italy, and Japan would be forthcoming. At the end of June 1939, five Rainbow plans were approved by the Joint Army-Navy Board.[2]

Rainbow One was designed to guard the Western Hemisphere against any threat to the traditional Monroe Doctrine and was essentially defensive. The area to be protected was defined as any part of the New World north of latitude ten degrees south, roughly the bulge of Brazil. Greenland, but not Iceland, was included in the defensive perimeter to the east, and Hawaii, but not Guam or the Philippines, to the west. No account was taken of coordinated efforts with potential American allies.

Rainbow Two provided for securing the areas identified as crucial in Rainbow One but extended the defense perimeter to the western Pacific. It assumed that British and French forces would engage fascist troops in Europe and that America's contribution to the global conflict would lie in the Pacific.

Rainbow Three reiterated the defense perimeter identified in Rainbow Two, confirmed that America's main efforts would be focused upon the western Pacific, but made no assumptions about aid from future U.S. allies.

Rainbow Four also omitted assumptions about coalition warfare but extended the American defense perimeter to include all of South America and foresaw the projection of U.S. forces as required to the southern portions of the New World or to the eastern Atlantic.

Rainbow Five, the most realistic of the plans, provided for the protection of the Western Hemisphere as defined in Rainbow One and the possible projection of American forces to either or both Africa and Europe as rapidly as possible with the aim of defeating Germany and Italy. This plan assumed "concerted action between the United States, Great Britain, and France." With the various contingencies identified, all of which placed defense of the Western Hemisphere in primary position and two of which anticipated that America would coordinate its efforts with European allies, the planners possessed a framework that they could develop as the world situation changed.[3]

Germany's invasion of Poland in September 1939 prompted U.S. planners to concentrate their attention upon updating Rainbow Two to fit the existing conditions. It was now assumed that France and Britain would prosecute the war vigorously, controlling the Atlantic with their combined fleets and restricting the movement of Hitler's armies with their ground and air forces. In such a situation, invasion of the Western Hemisphere by Axis forces appeared unlikely, and Japan remained the sole serious threat to American interests. Detailed studies were produced concerning the defense of the Philippines and Guam by American forces acting alone.

In the spring of 1940, a drastic change in the military fortunes of the anti-German forces required U.S. defense planners once again to reconsider their assumptions about the future. In April German forces invaded Denmark and Norway, thus securing further naval bases from which the Western Hemisphere could be threatened. In May Winston Churchill became prime minister of Britain, promising continuation of "blood, sweat and tears," while in mid-May German forces rolled west and south, forcing the capitulation of Belgium before the month was out and the surrender of France in mid-June. These events undercut America's reliance upon the continuation of British-French efforts in Europe contained in Rainbow Two and shifted American attention instead to Rainbow Four. Fearing that Germany might soon neutralize opposing British forces, perhaps gaining control of the British and French fleets, the American military now focused upon protecting the Western Hemisphere from a possible future invasion from victorious Axis forces. Concluding that America did not possess sufficient resources to ward off such an invasion and to prosecute an offensive war in the Pacific, planners called for a move to a defensive posture with respect to Japan. Yet before these drastic alterations in U.S. planning could be completed, President Roosevelt, commander in chief of U.S. forces, intervened. In June 1940 Roosevelt informed representatives of the military that he had confidence in the survival of Great Britain and that for the next six months he foresaw Britain and its empire intact. More important, Roosevelt suggested that by the expiration of this period America itself would be at war.[4]

With such new "instructions" as to the type of future anticipated, army and navy planners, with reservations and doubts, shifted attention again, turning to the outlines of Rainbow Five as the basis of plans. In September 1940 U.S. planners were briefed in London by British officers, further tying the fate of the two nations together.

In November the first detailed army-navy plan based upon the premise of concerted U.S.–British cooperation was drafted. Drawn up by the naval commander in chief, Adm. Harold Stark, *Plan Dog* argued for a Europe-first strategy, maintaining that the defeat or disruption of Britain and its empire would greatly weaken U.S. defense efforts. "If Britain wins decisively against Germany, we could win everywhere; but if she loses, the problem confronting us would be very great; and, while we might not *lose everywhere*, we might, possibly, not *win* anywhere."[5] Although the British themselves appeared to believe that a combination of continental blockade and directed propaganda would eventually undermine nazi rule, *Plan Dog* took a more conventional approach. It argued that the United States must prepare for great land operations across the Atlantic and that certain German defeat lay only in "military successes on shore." "I believe," Stark wrote, "that the United States, in addition to sending naval assistance, would also need to send large air and land forces to Europe or Africa or both, and to participate strongly in this land offensive."[6]

Concomitant with planning for an offensive in the Atlantic, Stark recommended a defensive posture in the Pacific. The broad outlines of American policy were beginning to emerge, with the navy itself now downplaying the heretofore key role of naval offensive action against Japan, so long an essential part of Plan Orange. Stark's plan was forwarded to Roosevelt in November, but no record of an official response has survived. Consistent with *Plan Dog*, however, Roosevelt promptly authorized high-level staff talks between American and British officers to explore the forms of coalition warfare suggested by Stark. In late January 1941, the ABC Talks (American-British Conversations) opened in Washington.

As the official report of the ABC Talks noted, the objective was "to determine the best method by which the armed forces of the United States and the British Commonwealth, with its present Allies, would defeat Germany and the Powers allied with her, should the United States be compelled to resort to war."[7] Three common defense principles were quickly approved: (1) that America's paramount interest would be in defending the Western Hemisphere; (2) that the security of Great Britain would be maintained in all circumstances and disposition made for the security of the Commonwealth; and (3) that security of sea communications would remain essential to the general purpose of common defense. The Atlantic and European theaters were deemed as decisive, with both powers to adopt a defensive strategy in the Pacific if war erupted there. America indicated no plans to strengthen its Pacific fleet in the event of conflict but would employ its existing assets in a fashion best calculated to weaken Japan's economic power.

Besides identifying common principles and tactics of future joint operations, the ABC Talks emphasized Britain's increasingly critical need for war materials, especially planes. By early 1941 U.S. army planners, still basing their future requirements upon the possibility that America might one day stand alone in defense of the Western Hemisphere, estimated air needs at 54 trained combat groups plus personnel and facilities for rapid expansion to 100 combat groups. The British position, however, argued that first priority for American planes ought to go to Britain to reduce the disparity between German and British air forces. Recognizing the importance of ensuring that Britain remain in the conflict, the Americans conceded that Britain ought to have priority on American plane production while the United States remained at peace, a priority that would retard army plans to create the desired 54 combat groups. If or when America entered the war, U.S. output would be equally divided. In addition, America would begin training 30,000 pilots a year and 100,000 technicians, the basic requirements for an eventual expansion of American air forces to the proposed 100 combat groups. Until America entered the war, however, the entire U.S. plane output would be available to Britain.[8]

Once the ABC discussions had been approved by the U.S. military chiefs, a directive was issued to adapt future planning to its requirements and assumptions, using as a basis Rainbow Five, which provided for coalition warfare. The resulting plan, submitted for Joint Board approval in April, contained the explicit premise that the United States and its allies were at war with Germany and its supporters. This by no means meant that the United States would seek to promote such a conflict but rather that a realistic analysis of future developments required sober evaluation of such strong possibilities. In such an event, the Allies would follow the objectives identified in the ABC agreements. The defeat of Germany would be the main Allied objective, and protecting the Western Hemisphere and Atlantic shipping routes would be America's initial assignment. Specific goals were organized around the day America would mobilize (M-Day), with such mobilization being deemed possible even prior to the entry of the United States into the war. Within the first several months after M-Day, America would dispatch some 220,000 troops to overseas posts, including Hawaii, Panama, the Caribbean, and Iceland. Continuing American mobilization of men and materials would allow the assignment of air and antiair defense units to the British Isles. In the Pacific the new draft of Rainbow

Five assigned responsibility for protecting Allied territory and securing sea routes of communication to America in conjunction with Allied assistance. The American army would protect the frontiers of the Philippines, but no additional forces were earmarked for such duty. In June 1941 this plan was forwarded for presidential approval but was returned without Roosevelt's signature, an event justified by Roosevelt as due to the fact that the British had yet to grant full approval to the earlier ABC discussions that formed much of the underpinnings for the revised Rainbow Five. Army Chief of Staff George Marshall, however, interpreted Roosevelt's action as equivalent to approval, and this Rainbow Five plan formed the basis for U.S. military activity from this point through the attack on Pearl Harbor six months later.[9]

While American planners discussed the most expeditious means of defeating Germany if and when the United States entered the war, Germany itself continued a relentless advance in Europe and threatened to take a major role in the struggle for North Africa. In February 1941 German troops landed in Africa, entering Libya the next month. In April the Germans invaded the Balkans, and two months later, to the surprise of many including Joseph Stalin, Germany's forces attacked their former ally, the Soviet Union. By late summer Soviet troops were in disorganized retreat along the extensive battle lines, and the prospects for a new German victory appeared high. With such a fluid conflict, American and British planners sought an opportunity to meet at the highest levels to coordinate revisions of their projected strategies. The opportunity was provided by the meeting between Winston Churchill and Franklin Roosevelt, complete with their military advisers, in the waters off the Newfoundland coast in early August.

On the eve of the meeting subsequently named the Atlantic Conference, the British chiefs of staff had undertaken a full review of their own strategy in preparation for the anticipated discussions with their American counterparts. The British aim, this review confirmed, was the eventual destruction of Germany's war-making potential. The methods best applied to this objective, however, excluded a direct ground assault upon the continent itself in favor of an indirect approach emphasizing blockade, bombing, subversions, and propaganda. Hand in hand with Winston Churchill, the British military leaders believed that the obvious tyrannical nature of Nazi rule in combination with economic privation aided and abetted by blockade would suffice to undermine German dominion on the continent. If these tactics were well applied, the British review concluded, "whatever their present strength, the armed forces of Germany will suffer such a radical decline in fighting value and mobility that a direct attack would once more become possible. . . . It may be that the methods described above will by themselves be enough to make Germany sue for peace."[10]

Such sentiments coincided with the anxieties of many British citizens who recalled the loss of the best of their young men in the trenches of World War I just two decades before. These recollections, and the strong desire to avoid such direct, bloody confrontation, were especially powerful in Churchill's mind. "We do not foresee vast armies of infantry as in 1914–18. The forces we employ will be armored divisions with the most modern equipment. . . . When our armored forces had dominated an area, it would be handed over to the patriotic forces to garrison."[11] Consistent with this indirect approach, the British suggested that a joint operation against North Africa ought to be considered. Clearly, the prospect of America entering the war was assuming increasing importance in British planning, with the British staff concluding that "the intervention of the United States would revolutionize the whole situation."[12] Unfortunately, the British apparently took little account of the fact that such intervention would dramatically increase America's desire to influence strategy, often in directions far different than London wished. From the Atlantic Conference onward, America found its own voice in suggesting preferred alternatives.

To American planners the British strategy, as annunciated in August, appeared far too optimistic. As the U.S. Joint Board concluded, even the entry of American combat forces would not support the rosy British view since "the potential combat strength of [U.S.] land and air elements has not yet been sufficiently developed to provide much more than a moral effort."[13]

Equally questionable was the British notion that Germany's defeat could be purchased "on the cheap," without the direct application of massive ground forces in an invasion of Europe. Such a plan had already received consideration in Washington. In July, undoubtedly anticipating further British demands for war supplies, President Roosevelt requested an estimate of the munitions needed by the armed forces in an effort to set the outlines for a comprehensive industrial mobilization plan. To meet this request, the army concluded that some understanding of the likely manpower needs of a future war would be required in addition to a general survey of likely scenarios of troop engagements. If, for example, not enough pilots could be trained to conduct effective raids over Germany until 1943, then industry would not have to produce as many planes in 1941 and 1942; such "freed" industrial capacity could be used for more time-sensitive objectives. Thus, the planning for industrial mobilization set in motion a new analysis of U.S. strategy and tactics for the future conflict. As the chief of Army War Plans stated, "We must first evolve a strategic concept of how to defeat our potential enemies and then determine the major military units (Air, Ground and Navy) required to carry out the strategic operations."[14] The army's "Brief of Strategic Concept of Operations Required to Defeat Our Potential Enemies" was the result.

In its new estimate, the army identified five main U.S. goals. First, America would be prepared to resist by all means Axis penetration into the Western Hemisphere. Second, assistance would be given to Britain, limited only by U.S. needs and the British ability to use the flood of anticipated supplies. Third, aid to other anti-Axis forces would be limited only by the first priority assigned to American and British forces. Fourth, in the Far East, America would show strong disapproval of any Japanese expansion but would avoid major naval and military commitments in this theater for the present. Fifth, no abridgment of freedom of the seas would be allowed.[15]

The stages of U.S. participation in the war were also identified. The first stage would last until either hostilities against America began or until America felt compelled to mobilize its forces (M-Day). During this period the primary objective would be delivery of supplies to Britain and other Allied powers and the preparation of U.S. troops for battle. The second stage would run from Mobilization Day until preparations for the final assault against the European enemies. Its main characteristics would be active participation in the conflict and the progressive weakening of the foe. The third stage would be the total defeat of Germany with the target date for the grand offensive tentatively set for mid-1943. By this date it was assumed that Germany and its allies would possess 400 divisions in Europe compared with the estimates of 300 divisions and 11 million men under Axis arms in 1941. Since the fate of the Soviet Union lay in the balance even as the American strategy was under debate, army planners concluded that the United States would have to supply the needed troops to equalize German resources. On the likely assumption that the Soviet Union would be rendered impotent by 1943, this meant that the United States would need close to 300 divisions since the estimated strength of Britain and other allies was projected at only 100 divisions two years hence.[16]

The manpower studies appended to this projection of American war strategy took into account the nation's total able-bodied manpower available for service by 1943. The estimates for industrial workers and for deferred classes of young men were appropriately deducted as were the number of men required for naval duty. The results suggested that over 8,795,000 men would be available for army and air force duty by mid-1943. Interestingly, these estimates proved quite accurate. On May 31, 1943, the army and air force totals were, in fact, 8,291,000. The distribution of these men, however, was far off the mark.

Assuming that America had to provide divisions needed to balance the disparity between British and German forces, the army foresaw a need for

215 by mid-1943, 61 of which would be armored. In fact, only 91 divisions existed when the target date of mid-1943 was reached, and just 16 of them were armored. By then the initial pessimistic assumption about future Russian impotence had proven wrong, with the Soviets contributing the essential divisions otherwise required from the United States. In late September the completed estimate of forces needed and scenarios projected was delivered by the secretaries of navy and war to the White House. The document was entitled "Victory Program" and was the culmination of three years of planning for coalition warfare.[17]

The unanticipated Japanese attack upon Pearl Harbor on December 7, 1941, once and for all removed the uncertainties from America's participation in the global conflict, especially since Germany and Italy declared war upon the United States four days later. For the British, who had stood virtually alone against Germany from the fall of France until the June 1941 German invasion of Russia, America's entry into the conflict was heartening news. With his military staff, Winston Churchill hastened to Washington to renew discussions of joint strategy and to bring the Americans up to date on British near- and far-term planning. By December 1941 the Europe-first strategy was accepted on both sides of the Atlantic, and it was the anticipated stages of Germany's defeat that now required discussion.

Consistent with earlier hopes of combining air and sea efforts with uprisings of subjugated European peoples, the British plans looked to landings of Allied forces in Europe as early as the summer of 1943. Such assaults would not require large American-British forces, would rely heavily upon local populations for support, and would be dispersed among a number of landing sites. Highly mobile and armored forces would enter the continent at numerous places, with Norway, the Balkans, Italy, Denmark, Holland, Belgium, and France all being listed by Churchill. Germany's defeat would be accomplished by a three-phased strategy. Initially, the ring of anti-German forces around the continent would be tightened through ensuring Soviet participation in the conflict, arming Turkey, and establishing Allied control in North Africa. Stage two, which would commence in 1942 or, perhaps, 1943, would include reentering the continent through the Mediterranean, via Turkey and into the Balkans, and perhaps landings in northwest Europe. Stage three would be the direct assault upon Germany, although the precise date of such operations could not be predicted.[18]

Churchill's emphasis upon encircling German-dominated Europe reflected Britain's continuing commitment to a Mediterranean strategy, and on December 23 Churchill proposed a joint British-American invasion of North Africa. For Roosevelt such an operation had distinct advantages. It would allow U.S. troops early entrance into combat in the European theater and, if successful, promised to elevate morale that Japanese advances in the Pacific had depressed. Roosevelt thus ordered an immediate study of the plan's feasibility. Yet the opposition of American military planners to what they perceived as an indirect and unwise use of forces plus the need to divert all available shipping to the Pacific eventually overrode Roosevelt's initial enthusiasm.[19]

If this initial wartime meeting between British and American planners revealed that serious differences of strategy remained, it also showed the superior wartime organization of the former and their ability to coordinate all branches of the British government on behalf of a given plan. In the British wartime government, Churchill formed the apex of military and political planning. As prime minister he presided over the War Cabinet, which considered both political and military topics. Holding the position of defense minister as well, Churchill ruled over the Defense Committee in which representatives most involved in the war held seats. These included the British minister of foreign affairs, the minister of production, three civilian cabinet ministers in charge of the War Office, the Admiralty, and the Air Ministry, and the three military chiefs of the British armed services: the chief of the Imperial General Staff, the first sea lord, and the chief of the Air Staff. These last three officers formed a Chief-of-Staff Committee that held corporate authority for issuing instructions to the armed forces. Each chief had a special staff of his own, including a strategic planning section. By contrast, the corporate structure of the American Joint Chiefs of Staff was not officially established until 1947, and the president, as commander in chief of the American armed forces, did not appoint his own chief of staff until the summer of 1942. No parallel to the British Defense Committee ever evolved, and the American secretary of war continued to be a presidential appointee. The precise coordination of British military-political efforts would be a source of amazement to the Americans throughout the war.

In an effort to promote closer cooperation between the British and the Americans, a Combined Chiefs-of-Staff Committee was created, consisting of high-ranking British military representatives who would meet regularly with the heads of the American army, navy, and air force. Their task would be to settle the broad issues of requirements and to provide general direction for the distribution of available war materials. By the summer of 1942, Roosevelt, in an effort to lend coordination to these meetings, appointed Adm. William Leahy as his own chief of staff. Henceforth, Leahy would meet with the chiefs of the army, navy, and air force to form the American Joint Chiefs of Staff. No executive order was provided as a legal basis for this combination; the Joint Chiefs were simply constituted as an ad hoc committee.[20]

In late February 1942, the War Plans Department completed a study significantly at odds with the British preference for an encircling strategy of German-occupied Europe. While economic assistance and the continued shipment of war goods to Britain were perceived as crucial to the war effort, a direct assault upon German-dominated Europe occupied first place in the American strategy. Army Chief of Staff George Marshall and War Secretary Henry Stimson supported this conclusion, arguing before Roosevelt that America ought to spare no effort in concentrating required invasion forces in the British Isles.

In April 1942 Roosevelt approved the army plan, and Marshall and Roosevelt's special friend and envoy, Harry Hopkins, departed for London to acquaint the British with American reasoning. The plan, entitled *Roundup*, called for a combined attack of 48 divisions supported by nearly 6,000 combat aircraft. The target would be western Europe, and the suggested date would be April 1943. In the preparatory phase, America would contribute approximately 1 million men in 30 divisions plus support to be paired with 18 British divisions. About three-fifths of the required aircraft would be American as well. The assembling of this invasion force in Britain would be code-named *Bolero*, and the specific objective would be the creation of a six-division front in western France. Since one of the "necessary" objectives for eventual victory in the war was continuation of the Russian front, Bolero-Roundup contained an emergency plan that would come into play if Russia appeared to be on the verge of collapse. In such an event, a smaller invasion force would be in place by the fall of 1942 and would go by the code name *Sledgehammer*. Its use would be tied to any urgent need to draw German forces from the Russian front as the sole means of preventing a German victory or in the event that Germany appeared on the verge of defeat itself at this early date. In mid-April 1942 the British formally accepted the American plan, and the preparations for the 1943 invasion became the order of the day. Unknown to the Americans, however, even at this stage the British were preparing studies that would show the infeasibility of the proposed American invasion timetables.[21]

In June 1942 the British War Cabinet, in a reverse of promises recently extended, concluded that no invasion of the continent (Sledgehammer) should be made that year unless prospects were favorable for establishing a permanent European front. Since a crucial aspect of Sledgehammer was its potential use to relieve pressure on the Russian front independent of Allied ability to maintain any immediate gains, such restrictions made the invasions less and less likely. That same month Churchill noted that no substantial landings in France ought to be attempted unless German troops were demoralized by defeats on the Russian front, a total reversal of the goals Sledgehammer was designed to achieve. By month's end, British planners concluded that mounting a continental invasion later that year would tie up all available landing craft in the British Isles, terminate preparations for the more important large-scale landings foreseen for 1943 in Roundup, and require postponement of any subsequent assault on fortress Europe. On July 8, 1942, the British served notice on Washington that Sledgehammer no longer constituted a viable option for 1942, proposing instead joint planning for an invasion of North Africa.[22]

The British refusal to sanction continued planning for Sledgehammer gave new impetus to several American military leaders already dissatisfied with the predominance of Europe in Allied planning. In March 1942 Adm. Harold Stark, a firm advocate of the Europe-first strategy, was replaced by Pacific-directed Adm. Ernest King as chief of naval operations (equivalent to army chief of staff). By early summer the navy had achieved two major Pacific victories at the battles of the Coral Sea and Midway, and there were plans for an invasion of Guadalcanal. Even the army had concluded that failure to mount an invasion of Europe in the fall of 1942 would probably end Russian participation in the conflict and thus make a future return to the continent by Allied forces extremely difficult. In such a situation, the principle of concentration of force might call for a Pacific-first strategy. In early July Army Chief of Staff Marshall formally proposed to his fellow Joint Chiefs that if the British rejected Sledgehammer, the United States should concentrate upon a decisive struggle against the Japanese. A memorandum signed by Marshall and King was dispatched for Roosevelt's consideration.[23]

While subsequent historical investigation suggests that Marshall's approval of this alternative contained significant elements of bluff in an ongoing attempt to gain revision of the British rejection, Roosevelt himself decided to probe the seriousness of the proposed American strategy. Upon receipt of the memorandum, he requested immediate plans for the Pacific campaign, only to be informed by the Joint Chiefs that such plans had yet to be designed. As Marshall now admitted, "My objective is again to force the British into acceptance of a concentrated effort against Germany, and if this proves impossible, to turn immediately to the Pacific with strong forces for a decision against Japan."[24] Marshall's "bluff," however, clearly indicated that important American military leaders stood ready to change the focus of war activities in the face of British recalcitrance.

Roosevelt's response to the growing split between U.S. and British planners consisted of two elements: a rejection of the Pacific-first strategy and a reconfirmation of the importance of Sledgehammer despite the British objections. Recognizing that Britain would have to provide the bulk of forces for any invasion of the continent in 1942, Roosevelt now dispatched Marshall, King, and Hopkins to London to argue for retention of Sledgehammer. If arguments proved impotent, Roosevelt authorized his representatives to approve joint action in North Africa later that year. Britain's firm arguments against Sledgehammer, supported with convincing statistics and shortages of landing craft, provided further support for a North African campaign. If Sledgehammer were excluded and if Russia fell due to the mighty German summer offensive, prospects for an early invasion of Europe would be dim indeed. Thus, a reversion to a Mediterranean strategy long advocated by the British—an attempt to secure the European periphery—appeared logical. The U.S.–Britain discussions concluded that a final decision on a proposed North African invasion code-named *Torch* would be made by September 15. Even if accepted, however, the plans for a 1943 invasion of the continent (Roundup) would continue. Shortly thereafter, Roosevelt gave the green light for Torch, and in November American troops swarmed ashore at several places on the North African coast. By mid-May 1943 organized German resistance in North Africa ended.[25]

The selection of North Africa as the concentration point for America's first effort determined to a large degree the course of the fighting thereafter. At the Moroccan city of Casablanca, Roosevelt, Churchill, and their staffs met in mid-January 1943 to plan future actions. By now it was clear that Russia would not be knocked out of the war and that the possibility of future continental invasion appeared good. America and Britain agreed to maintain pressure along the Mediterranean and agreed to a summer invasion of Sicily code-named *Husky*. The Mediterranean strategy, however, was not to detract from continued planning for Roundup, and the destruction of the German air force through concerted Allied air action over Europe (*Point Blank*) was authorized as preparation for the invasion.[26]

At the next major conference between U.S. and British political and military leaders held in Washington in May 1943 (code-named *Trident*), world conditions seemed even more propitious for future planning. By now North Africa had been cleared of Axis troops, and in the East the Soviets were in the midst of a successful counteroffensive, rolling up German troops in a westward direction. In such conditions Roosevelt and his military planners proposed emphasis upon Bolero-Roundup with a realistic date for invasion of the continent to be set for 1944. To avoid a drawdown on Allied preparations, the United States recommended only limited operations in the Mediterranean. In contrast, the British pushed for a renewed Mediterranean strategy, with the invasion of Sicily to be followed by an assault upon Italy. In the compromise reached, further action designed to eliminate Italy from the war was approved. Efforts to drive German aircraft from the sky were to be expanded, with the last stage to be completed by April 1944. The invasion of the continent would follow with May 1 designated as the preferred date. With agreement now reached, the invasion plan was renamed *Overlord*.[27]

In mid-August 1943 the two Allies reconvened in the Canadian city of Quebec (*Quadrant*). By now Sicily had surrendered, and the way to Italy was open. Nevertheless, Overlord was reconfirmed as the crucial offensive of 1944, and action against Italy was to be planned with this in mind. If a dispute should occur in allocation of military supplies, Overlord would take full precedence. At Tehran, in November 1943, Roosevelt, Churchill, and Soviet leader Joseph Stalin confirmed the priority of the spring 1944 continental invasion. Soviet offensive plans would be coordinated to put maximum pressure upon Germany at that time. On June 4, 1944, Allied troops stormed ashore on the beaches of Normandy. The major tasks of planning for the invasion of Europe had been successfully completed.[28]

With the 1942 rejection of a Pacific-first alternative, planning for the war in the East lacked clear focus until relatively late in the conflict. As Ray Cline perceptively noted: "American strategy in the war against Japan necessarily remained shapeless and vague long after the crystallization of the main lines of thought about defeating Germany. Through 1942 and early 1943, long-range strategic planning for the Pacific and Far Eastern operations were compounded of approximately equal parts of tactical opportunism and abstract geopolitical theory."[29] This was true despite the fact that in both years, America had more fighting men assigned to the Pacific theater than to the Atlantic.

In the fall of 1943, the combined Chiefs reached agreement that the defeat of Japan would not proceed by way of invasion launched from China but rather would proceed across and up the Pacific. In March 1944 the Joint Chiefs approved such a dual approach with Gen. Douglas MacArthur to move toward the southern Philippines and Adm. Chester Nimitz to proceed westward against the Marianas and Palau. These two forces would meet in a major combined operation against the Formosa-Luzon area in February 1945. By the summer of 1944, a three-step invasion plan of Japan itself had been drafted, culminating with an October 1945 assault upon the Japanese island of Kyushu and a landing on the Tokyo plains of Honshu in late December. This plan was approved at the September 1944 Quebec meeting (*Octagon*) of Roosevelt, Churchill, and their staffs. Yet some six months later, this plan, too, was modified to take account of the persistence of Japanese defense efforts. It was now assumed that the invasion of the Tokyo plains would not occur before March 1946, with the end of Japanese resistance not anticipated until November of that year.[30] Needless to say, the potential effects of the atomic bomb—a weapon whose existence few in the military were privy to and that had yet to be tested—were not factored into the new plans. The dropping of two bombs on Japan on August 6 and 9 and the entrance of the Soviet Union into the Pacific war undercut all assumptions of Allied planners and produced a rapid Japanese surrender.

2

FDR and U.S. Wartime Participation

Up to this point, the analysis of U.S. national security planning in the prewar and wartime period has focused primarily upon wise selection of the means by which vital American interests might best be protected. The logic of such planning naturally lay within the military establishment where such plans as Orange and Rainbow Five were drafted and modified as the perceived threat varied. But as the case of U.S. confusion as to whether British rejection of Sledgehammer ought to prompt a redirection of military efforts to the Pacific clearly showed, the ultimate arbiter of overall strategic thinking was President Roosevelt himself. Within the White House resided the central source of rules and objectives that the military planners sought to realize. And yet, unlike the well-coordinated British system that united both military and civilian strategists within common War and Defense committees, relations between the American president and his subordinates were haphazard and frequently incomplete.

President Roosevelt delighted in discussing differing points of view with various people, so that each believed he alone knew what the president wanted. As a further hindrance to effective coordination, Roosevelt frequently failed to inform his key subordinates of important policy decisions until after an announcement had been made. The January 1943 Casablanca proclamation that the Allies would settle for nothing less than the unconditional surrender of Germany was not cleared first with the State Department. In the late spring of 1944, Roosevelt reversed his past policy of not authorizing the use of American troops to occupy postwar central Europe outside of Germany in a private discussion with the American representative to the ongoing Three Powers discussions in London, clearing the way for an American occupation zone in Austria. The State Department, which was formally charged with preparing instructions for this American delegation, continued to issue guidelines premised upon the absence of such occupation troops long after the matter had been settled.

For the student of national security planning, the absence of a clear overall plan, well coordinated and frequently debated, makes it most difficult to state with assurance just what principles President Roosevelt felt were vital to America's wartime participation. Since Roosevelt was one of only two presidents to die in office in the past fifty years and thus bequeathed no final memoirs affirming his basic goals, the student of this period must construct as best as he can the principles that guided both FDR and his military in the conflict. Fortunately, the available documents and memoirs of the period do provide considerable evidence as to what these principles in fact were.[1]

Basic to Roosevelt's worldview was the belief that America's national security and its vital interests were tied to the preservation of a Europe in which democracy and a balance of power prevailed. As head of a nation that had experienced all the despair of the Great Depression, Roosevelt believed that increased international trade and the growth of common interests that such trade would promote lay at the foundation of a peaceful postwar Europe and world. It had been the disruption of economic intercourse between states and the resulting economic hardships that had produced fascism, and it was hoped that a reinstatement of the rules of free trade would preclude the emergence of such systems of rule in the future. A world of freer trade and investment would also benefit America, which had surmounted its own economic difficulties only through expanded war production. By the end of 1944, a series of international agreements sponsored by the United States would create such institutions as the International Monetary Fund and the World Bank to ensure the coordinated expansion of world economic development and to further economic cooperation between states.

A second determining principle of America's wartime participation was the notion that supplies, not men, would be the main contribution to Allied victory. As early as December 1940, prior to America's entry into the war, Roosevelt proclaimed that the United States would be the great "Arsenal of Democracy." Three months later, still at peace, the White House proposed the Lend-Lease System that would eventually send billions of dollars of U.S. war supplies to our European allies. The "Victory Program," a study of the manpower needs to defeat the Axis, was ordered in 1941 but never officially approved by the president. This program, drafted by the army, called for 215 U.S. divisions to be ready by the time of the future continental invasion. To Roosevelt, who had served as assistant secretary of navy in World War I and who knew of the horrors of trench warfare, a mass expenditure of American manpower was repulsive. Such a force could only be prepared if the total fruits of American industry were assigned to equipping the American forces. Yet throughout the war, Lend-Lease continued to flow to the Allies, while the total number of American divisions never exceeded 100. The principle of furnishing supplies in preference to providing brute manpower prevailed to the end. As a result, when the war was over, America sustained less than 400,000 dead. For every American who died, 15 Germans and 50 Russians died, many of them civilians.

The belief in supplies and not manpower as America's most important contribution put important limitations upon Roosevelt's negotiations with the Allies. An alternate source of manpower was urgently required, and only the Soviet Union possessed young men in near endless quantity. Thus, the U.S. preference for supplies forced Roosevelt to maintain Russia in the war at all costs. In the spring of 1942, a solemn Franklin Roosevelt promised Soviet foreign minister Vyacheslav Molotov that Allied troops would launch an invasion of Western Europe before the year was out. Without such action the fate of the beleaguered Russian troops then fighting the bulk of the German army would be in serious doubt. When British objections eventually doomed any opening of a second front in 1942, Roosevelt felt impelled to stress that a cross-channel landing must come as soon as possible. After the Soviet army had turned the tide on the eastern front following the battle of Stalingrad in early 1943, Roosevelt's fears shifted to the possibility of a separate Soviet-German peace. From that point onward, burdened perhaps by a sense of guilt over nonfulfillment of his second-front pledge, Roosevelt took pains to show Stalin that America was a trusted friend.

The third key principle underlying America's wartime participation concerned the type of postwar world Roosevelt wished to create above and beyond his plans for greater economic interdependence and trade. In the political realm, Roosevelt slowly developed the idea of a world body that would guarantee peace and stability. A former advocate of President Wilson's notion of a League of Nations, Roosevelt, by the end of the thirties, had concluded that neither the world nor the American people were yet ready for such an institution. At the first meeting with Churchill in the North Atlantic in August 1941, FDR pointedly opposed British suggestions for a postwar international body, favoring instead continuing cooperation between Washington and London.[2] By 1942 Roosevelt came to support a modified balance-of-power arrangement for the postwar world based upon the idea of four world "policemen." These policemen, to include America, Britain, the Soviet Union, and China, would be the predominant powers in their respective areas.

The year 1942 was a time when the British were developing their idea of a postwar world composed of federations of smaller states, and the policemen proposals fit well with such plans. Each policeman would be the leading state in its own geographical area, providing guidance for the separate federations. The regular meetings of the policemen themselves would provide stability for the entire globe. By the fall of 1943, however, the Soviet Union had registered a decisive objection to the idea of European federations, fearing that they aimed at restricting Soviet expansion in Eastern Europe.[3] In addition, China's meager showing in its war against Japan cast doubt upon the ability of postwar Peking to function in a supervisory fashion in Asia.

At the Tehran Conference of the Big Three held in November 1943, Roosevelt proposed creation of a three-part postwar world body designed to secure peace. It would have a general assembly of thirty-five to forty-five nations that would meet periodically in different world cities to debate and draft recommendations. An executive committee of ten members would be formed and would include the key four states already designated by Roosevelt as policemen. This body would possess the power and authorization to deal immediately with any threat to peace. In essence, here lay the general blueprint for the postwar United Nations although the notion of four policemen required additional modification, and the inclusion of France among the four (later five) dominant powers remained to be debated. By the time of the Yalta Conference in February 1945, the broad outlines of the United Nations were in place, and in May 1945 the UN held its founding meeting in San Francisco.

While Roosevelt remained convinced throughout the conflict that the forces of the Axis must be destroyed, he also felt a sense of uneasiness over the allies with whom America had joined its efforts. A postwar world pledge to freedom and economic interdependence constituted a threat to the prewar policies of the British Empire that were based upon imperial trade preferences and upon colonialism. As early as the 1941 drafting of conditions for Lend-Lease, Roosevelt had extracted a pledge for freer trade in the postwar world.[4] Throughout the war Roosevelt tried to nudge Churchill from his colonialist stand, going so far as to advise the British prime minister on how to handle the problems of India.

Roosevelt's distaste for the leader of the Free French Force, Gen. Charles de Gaulle, also, in part, derived from a dislike of being allied too closely with an advocate of colonialism. Through much of the war, Roosevelt supported a plan whereby French possessions in the third world would be placed under a postwar "trusteeship" as a first stage to independence. Yet despite concerns about the attitudes of Britain and France, Roosevelt's main problem throughout the conflict concerned his relationship with the Soviet Union. Cast together by fate as comrades in arms, the United States and the Soviet Union held widely divergent views as to what would constitute stability in a postwar world. Excluded from normal diplomatic intercourse ever since the Communist Revolution of 1917, the Soviet Union retained its suspicions as to American and British objectives even after the three states found themselves allied against a more dangerous threat: Germany.

To argue that Roosevelt misunderstood the likelihood of Soviet expansion once Germany was defeated is to overlook the documentary materials from the wartime period. In 1943 the former U.S. ambassador to Moscow and to Paris, William Bullet, sent a series of top-secret messages to Roosevelt, cautioning that Russia was an expansionist power.[5] A postwar Europe controlled by Moscow, Bullet warned, would be as dangerous as one controlled by Berlin. Roosevelt's awareness of this threat expressed itself in many forms, the most obvious being his continuing interest in Churchill's idea for an invasion of the Balkans prior to an invasion in France. In part, this plan was designed to create a wedge of British and American troops between the retreating German forces and the advancing Russians, ensuring that Western forces would liberate Eastern Europe. At the Big Three Conference at Tehran in late 1943, Roosevelt advocated the Balkan invasion plan on his own initiative. When his close friend and adviser, Harry Hopkins, sent a note to the U.S. navy chief, Adm. Ernest King, asking who was behind this suggestion of a Balkan invasion, King quickly responded, "As far as I know, it is his own idea."[6] The following year Roosevelt took personal charge of efforts to promote the defection of Bulgaria from the Axis as a means of opening a pro-Western beachhead in the Balkans.[7] And yet such efforts always fell short of success. Eventually, Roosevelt agreed with Stalin that such a Balkan thrust would be a diversion to the main goal of Germany's rapid defeat. Only Churchill held out for the Balkan invasion plan almost until the end.

The reasons for Roosevelt's inability to take decisive measures during the war against what he feared were Soviet expansionist aims arose from real constraints that bound U.S. war policy. FDR believed that the American people would not tolerate major casualties without demanding significant changes in America's domestic and foreign policy. Wishing to continue as much of his New Deal program as possible and fearful that expanded American casualties might produce a postwar isolationist spirit that would doom plans for a United Nations, Roosevelt realized the Russia had to be kept in the war at all costs. The absence of the 300 divisions the Soviets were contributing would both prolong the conflict—perhaps beyond the tolerance of the American people—and require total mobilization in the United States. Even after the tide of war had turned on the eastern front following the early 1943 German defeat at Stalingrad, FDR's fears persisted. Now his concern became the possibility of a separate Soviet-German peace, a fear intensified by reports of secret Soviet negotiations in 1943. Thus, Roosevelt's wish to be firm with the Soviet Union regarding any postwar aspirations toward expansion was tempered by the priority of retaining Soviet divisions in the war.

A second constraint upon Roosevelt's dealings with the Russians was his conviction that the American public would neither support nor maintain a postwar settlement that revealed the war had been fought for selfish aims. As an active politician in the intrawar years and as an unsuccessful candidate for vice-president in 1920, Roosevelt was well aware of public revulsion produced by evidence that World War I had merely advanced the profits and territorial desires of the victorious European states. America's refusal to join the League of Nations in 1920 tolled the death bell for President Wilson's efforts to create a stable international order in which America would take its rightful place. If World War II were revealed to be merely a replay of such selfish motives, American public opinion might reject Roosevelt's plans as well for postwar stability. As a result, Roosevelt refused to give clear and public sanction to any territorial demands among his allies until the final peace conferences were convened. When the Soviet Union suggested that some prior understandings ought to be reached, Roosevelt tried as best as he could to have it both ways.

At the Tehran Conference, when confronted by Stalin's demand that the Baltic states of Latvia, Lithuania, and Estonia ought to be incorporated in postwar Russia, Roosevelt temporized. Telling Stalin that from the American perspective the holding of a referendum would be advisable, FDR also stated that America would not go to war over such an issue. American public opinion, he informed Stalin, did not understand the historic ties between these states and the Soviet Union. "They should be informed and some propaganda work should be done," Stalin retorted.[8] And yet this is precisely what Roosevelt could not do without raising the specter of selfish war aims that might seriously affect all plans for postwar stability. While Roosevelt would admit in private to select groups that postwar spheres of influence were beyond the power of America to prevent, he resolutely opposed such spheres in public. Such inconsistency, while understandable given Roosevelt's domestic fears, left a legacy of ambiguity that would embitter postwar relations between Moscow and Washington.

A third determinant of Roosevelt's interactions with the Soviet Union derived from his belief that Russia was an immature newcomer in the global diplomatic game who could eventually be won over to more Western goals. Indeed, the assumption that Russia would take its place as a solid and reliable member of the postwar world was a crucial one if such notions as the four policemen or the United Nations were to bear fruit. For Roosevelt

Soviet intransigence toward the West arose in equal measure from basic unfamiliarity with the democratic way of life and from a deep hostility and suspicion toward the capitalist West. Both traits had their roots in the historic development of the Soviet Union since its 1917 revolution, and both could be ameliorated by patient and tolerant negotiations. In a revealing cable to Churchill, Roosevelt spelled out in detail the assumptions that constrained his dealings with Stalin. "I think we are all in agreement . . . as to the necessity of having the USSR as a fully accepted and equal member of any association of the Great Powers formed for the purpose of preventing international war. It should be possible to accomplish this by adjusting our differences through compromise by all the parties concerned." At the bottom of the cable, in Roosevelt's own handwriting, there is the following addition. "And this ought to tide things over for a few years until the child learns how to toddle."[9]

This message gives a clear expression of Roosevelt's belief that the Soviets' "difficulties" were both temporary and changeable. Once Moscow realized America and Britain were not a threat to legitimate Soviet aspirations, Moscow would reorient its policy and become a full-fledged partner in preserving the postwar peace. To prove America's goodwill, Roosevelt went out of his way during the war to show his trust in Stalin. For example, at the Tehran Conference, despite the evident possibility of electronic bugging, Roosevelt took up residence within the Soviet embassy. In 1944 Roosevelt presented Stalin with documents showing the breaking of highly secret Soviet codes, documents received from German sources. In this fashion it was hoped that an atmosphere of trust would replace existing suspicions between East and West. While such an approach may seem naive to the more cynical observer of the eighties, it must be remembered that no alternate way of harmonizing East-West relations was then apparent. Germany's defeat and the creation of a postwar system capable of retaining the fruits of the hard-won victory depended upon full and continued Soviet participation.

The basic principles and constraints guiding Roosevelt's participation in war planning expressed themselves in various ways: letters to foreign heads of state, discussions with the Joint and Combined Chiefs of Staff, and private conversations with domestic political allies. With the structure of the postwar world uncertain, the most important forums in which Roosevelt's ideas played a major role were undoubtedly the diverse Allied conferences convened to exchange proposals designed both to hasten termination of the conflict and to resolve disputes as to the preferred postwar reconstruction. From the fall of 1941 onward, Roosevelt and Churchill met frequently, although most of these discussions focused upon military matters. And yet the military decisions themselves created conditions that soon required at least some resolution of disputed political issues. The postponement of the second front, for example, in conjunction with the decision to abandon the possible invasion of Europe through the Balkans meant that the Soviet Union would be left in sole occupation of Eastern Europe. Such an expectation required the drafting of some minimum guidelines as to how each nation would conduct itself in this area prior to final resolution at the anticipated peace conference. These types of political debates took place largely at the infrequent meetings of the Big Three: Roosevelt, Churchill, and Stalin.

The first Big Three Conference occurred in Iran's capital, Tehran, in November 1943. By this time the final demise of Hitler's Germany could be confidently predicted although the exact timing of its defeat remained a matter of speculation. The German drive on the eastern front had been blunted, and Soviet troops were on the offensive although still confined to Soviet territory. North Africa had been cleared of Axis troops, Italy had left the war, and the plans for opening the second front the following year in northern France were well advanced. Clearly, it was time for the top political leaders to meet and to reach at least tentative decisions on outstanding problems concerning the likely shape of the postwar world. All such decisions, naturally, would require final confirmation at the peace table.

The first major issue for discussion concerned the boundaries of postwar Poland. This problem had been complicated by the inability of the three Allies to agree upon the membership of the postwar Polish government. At the start of the war, the remnants of the prewar Polish regime had fled to London, forming a "government-in-exile" usually referred to as the London government. While this group of Polish politicians was somewhat anti-Soviet in policy and clearly conservative in political outlook, the Soviet Union had extended it recognition following the German invasion of Russia in June 1941. In the spring of 1943, however, Moscow had withdrawn recognition following discovery of the Katyn Massacre. This event, one of the most brutal of the entire war, involved the execution of thousands of Polish officers whose bodies were discovered by German troops on Soviet soil in April 1943. Naturally, the Germans claimed the Soviets had been responsible. When the Polish government-in-exile, without prior consultation with its allies, requested an international investigation to determine exactly who had committed the crime, the Soviet Union broke diplomatic relations. While Moscow did not in turn recognize an alternative government in exile, the Western Allies knew that a number of pro-Soviet Polish exiles did indeed reside in Moscow. Thus, Poland's political future was unclear at the very moment discussions between the Big Three attempted to determine Poland's postwar frontiers.[10]

The territorial issue concerned the common border between Poland and the Soviet Union. Drawn not by logic but as a result of a short, fierce Polish-Soviet war in 1920–21, the frontier sliced through diverse nationalities, leaving millions of White Russians and Ukranians within prewar Poland and lesser amounts of Poles within the Soviet Union. After signing a nonaggression pact with Germany in 1939 and following the nazi invasion of Poland in September of that year, Soviet troops occupied these disputed territories. At Tehran Stalin demanded they be returned to Moscow at the war's completion.

Fortunately for the West, there was an independent basis for meeting the Soviet claim. In the aftermath of World War I, a British Cabinet minister, Lord Curzon, attempted to determine a rational frontier between the feuding states that would place most Poles in Poland and most Soviet minorities in their own nation. The frontier, known as the Curzon Line, formed the basis of discussion at Tehran. In fact, Roosevelt and British foreign minister Anthony Eden had approved the use of the Curzon Line with slight modifications at an earlier meeting in Washington.[11] While no actual agreement was reached at Tehran—all territorial issues were postponed until the peace conference—Stalin was given to understand that the West would not oppose such territorial transfers. In compensation for the shift of Polish lands to the USSR, Roosevelt suggested that Poland might receive former German lands to its west. When pressed by Stalin to reach a clear territorial understanding, Roosevelt pleaded for time given the proximity of the upcoming American presidential election in which the domestic Polish-American vote could be crucial. Churchill, in turn, promised to persuade the Polish government-in-exile of the wisdom of accepting a modified Curzon Line with compensation to the west.[12]

Polish territorial changes were not the sole question involving frontiers debated at Tehran. Stalin quickly raised the issue of whether America would support the postwar annexation of the three Baltic states, Lithuania, Latvia, and Estonia, by the USSR. These states, too, had been mentioned in the German-Soviet nonaggression pact of 1939, and in the summer of 1940, under severe pressure, all three had "requested" incorporation within the Soviet Union. When pressed by Stalin about America's position regarding the future of these states, Roosevelt lighthandedly noted that America would not go to war with the USSR on this issue, suggesting that perhaps Stalin might hold referendums to assuage American popular opinion.[13]

The discussion of Japan's future at Tehran combined both military and territorial questions. Bound to a Europe-first strategy in the prosecution of the war, Roosevelt desired to involve the Soviet Union in the Pacific conflict as soon as possible. The month before the Tehran meeting, Stalin had promised that Soviet troops would eventually attack Japan. At Tehran Roosevelt wished confirmation of this pledge and discussion of what territorial rearrangements in the Pacific Stalin would demand. In anticipation of Soviet requests, Roosevelt had met with Chinese president Chiang Kai-shek, extracting an agreement that all of the Pacific island of Sakhalin plus the Kuril Islands north of Japan might be given to the Soviet Union after the war's end. Chiang also appeared amenable to Soviet usage of the Chinese ice-free port of Dairen. In return, Chiang demanded that Stalin support his right to rule China as against the strong challenge of the Chinese Communists. These possible concessions were discussed with Stalin at Tehran although no firm territorial commitments were made. Stalin informed his military to prepare an attack upon Japanese forces within three to four months after the war against Germany ended—a necessary respite due to the gigantic distances across which Soviet troops would have to move.[14]

The final key agreement reached at Tehran concerned the route for the future western invasion of the continent. Finally, plans for an invasion through the Balkans were laid to rest, with the Big Three agreeing upon an attack in northern France scheduled for the following spring. Stalin promised to launch an offensive on the eastern front to coincide with the Allies' thrust. The political result of this decision was that Soviet troops alone would liberate Eastern Europe.

By the fall of 1944, the war had entered its concluding phase with the Western Allies having reentered the continent on the beaches of Normandy and Soviet troops having advanced on a broad front in Eastern Europe. In August and September, Romania and Bulgaria capitulated to the Red Army, and Hungary appeared open to the relentless Soviet drive. Farther south in Eastern Europe, British troops landed in Greece in early October. With a German surrender close at hand, once again the need to discuss outstanding political issues made itself felt among the Big Three. Roosevelt, unfortunately, was unable to attend a major conference abroad due to the impending American election, and so the next main political conference was arranged between Churchill and Stalin with Moscow picked as the meeting ground. Anxious to keep informed of what transpired, Roosevelt requested that the American ambassador in Moscow, W. Averell Harriman, attend the important discussions. There was not a single important issue, Roosevelt advised Stalin, in which the United States did not have an interest.[15]

To Churchill and his foreign secretary, Anthony Eden, the prime purpose of the October 1944 Moscow Conference was to arrive at some common consensus as to postwar spheres of influence in Eastern Europe.

An initial effort at reaching some agreement with Stalin on this matter had failed the preceding summer due to American objections. Now, with Soviet troops in occupation just north of Greece and British troops arriving in Athens, an accord needed to be struck. The resulting "bargain" is related in Churchill's own memoirs. "The moment was apt for business, so I said, 'Let us settle about our affairs in the Balkans. Your armies are in Rumania and Bulgaria. We have interests, missions and agents there. Don't let us get at cross-purposes in small ways. So far as Britain and Russia are concerned, how would it do for you to have ninety per cent predominance in Rumania, for us to have ninety per cent of the say in Greece, and go fifty-fifty about Yugoslavia?' "[16] By the time the meeting had ended, Bulgaria and Hungary had also been added to the list, ensuring Soviet dominance in both countries.

The meaning of this understanding became clear in the following days of the Moscow Conference as Anthony Eden and his Soviet counterpart, Vyacheslav Molotov, debated how the Balkan states would be reintegrated into the postwar family of nations. In Bulgaria, Romania, and Hungary, Allied Control Commissions would form on a pattern similar to that enacted in Italy in 1943. Although American and British delegates would be assigned to these commissions, Eden promised that, since Russian influence would dominate, the Western representatives would not take their seats at the Allied Control Commission meetings until after the defeat of Germany. Even in the postwar period, these states would be administered by the Soviet High Command to the exclusion of the Western Allies. While Churchill's promise to give predominance in the Balkans, except for Greece, to Russia was dutifully reported to Washington by Ambassador Harriman, its precise meaning as set by Eden and Molotov at their secret meetings remained unknown to the Americans. Not until January 1945 did Washington discover exactly how badly war aims had been compromised. Still, Roosevelt and his advisers were not naive, and some inkling of what transpired must have been felt in the American capital. The British gain in all this soon became apparent. Facing stiff resistance as they attempted to restore the Greek king to his throne in the face of concerted armed opposition from the communist-led Greek underground, British forces took heart from the total absence of Soviet support for their fellow Greek Marxists. Having promised Britain predominance in Greece, Stalin kept to his word.[17]

In February 1945, with the American elections finished and the final days of the war at hand, the last of the Big Three conferences between Stalin, Roosevelt, and Churchill took place in the Soviet city of Yalta. For six days the heads of state debated and discussed the nature of the postwar world and the programs and demands they would put forward at the postwar peace conferences. While a great number of topics were negotiated, four in particular led to decisions that were to affect strongly the years ahead. On each the three allies showed some willingness to compromise, although their positions on each one showed varying degrees of commitment.

Among the major issues, none seemed more intractable than the future of Poland. Following the discussions of Poland's postwar frontiers at Tehran, Churchill had attempted in vain to persuade the Polish government-in-exile to compromise on this issue with the Soviets. On July 22, 1944, Soviet troops crossed the Curzon Line during an offensive against German troops. More important, the Soviets quickly installed a quasi-independent Polish government in the Polish town of Lublin and gave it more and more of the daily tasks of governance. In early January 1945, on the very eve of the Yalta meeting, Moscow extended official diplomatic recognition to its Lublin ally. Thus, by the time of the Yalta discussions, two problems were evident: the territorial frontiers of the postwar Polish state and the membership of its future government.

At Yalta Churchill's pleas that Britain had sacrificed men and treasure for the sovereignty of Poland were met by Stalin's demand that postwar Poland must have a foreign policy friendly to the USSR. The territorial issue was resolved essentially along the lines of the previous Tehran agreement although, in deference to Roosevelt, final territorial awards would await the inevitable peace conference. In exchange for ceding territory to the Soviets in the east, Poland would receive compensation from German lands to the west. The political question of which government should rule in Poland—the London government-in-exile or the Lublin government— was a bit more difficult. Roosevelt insisted that his country could not recognize the Lublin government as constituted, a position seconded by Churchill who estimated that this government did not represent even one-third of the Polish people. Stalin, in his turn, insisted that there was little or no difference between the Lublin government and the de Gaulle government in France: neither had yet received the clear approval of its countrymen. With such opposing positions, only a compromise could bring a semblance of harmony among the discussants.[18]

By the end of the conference, it was agreed that the Lublin government would reorganize along broader, democratic lines, accepting other democratic leaders from both within and without Poland proper. Supervision and assistance in this reorganization process would be extended by a special committee of three, composed of the British and American ambassadors to Moscow and the Soviet foreign minister. The reorganized Polish government would remain provisional, having as its primary goal the holding of free elections that, in turn, would produce a government responsive to Polish wishes. Once the Lublin government had reorganized to accept other democratic leaders, but prior to the holding of elections, the Western Allies would extend recognition. Elections, Stalin mentioned in a casual manner, could probably be held within six months. The final, postelection Polish government, in turn, would negotiate the exact Polish borders with its two neighbors.[19]

While the agreements on Poland appeared to be a compromise that promised the emergence of a postwar free Poland, Roosevelt remained apprehensive. With Soviet troops in occupation, however, few alternatives suggested themselves. As Roosevelt commented to his chief of staff, Adm. William Leahy, "It is the best I can do for Poland at this time."[20]

At Yalta the future of the United Nations weighed heavily upon Franklin Roosevelt. His early ideas as to how this body ought to be structured had evolved considerably since the suggestion of the four policemen, but the central role of a postwar international assembly remained a persistent theme in American diplomacy. With a functioning international organization, problems unresolved by war's end would find a forum capable of reconciling divergent views. The USSR's membership in such a body would be a big step toward the full integration of the Soviet Union in the postwar international efforts to maintain the peace. And by the time of Yalta, several important meetings between the Allies had all but resolved conflicting opinions as to how the United Nations ought to be formed. Thus, Roosevelt was somewhat taken aback when he discovered that the Soviets now had two new suggestions for the future United Nations.

The Soviet Union, Stalin opined, should be granted seats in the future General Assembly of the United Nations equal to the individual republics that formed the USSR. In effect, this would increase the Soviet representation from one to sixteen seats, a significant expansion since the anticipated membership in the General Assembly was less than forty. With some bargaining the Soviet leader agreed to reduce Soviet demands to three seats, promising to support an equal number of seats for the United States if Roosevelt so wished.

The second Soviet suggestion, however, initially appeared even more threatening. While earlier discussions of the future Security Council had agreed that the Big Three ought to possess a veto that would block any action deemed contrary to their individual interests, the precise nature of such veto rights remained unclear. Stalin wished the veto to apply not just to matters of substance but to matters of procedure as well. In effect, a procedural veto would allow any one of the Big Three to prevent the

Security Council from even discussing an issue found objectionable. This, in turn, would preclude the United Nations from acting as an international forum designed to bring the pressure of public opinion to bear upon a recalcitrant state. Roosevelt and Churchill thought the veto should be restricted to matters of substance, that is, to resolutions that would be offered *after* a given problem had received full debate. In this manner world opinion would quickly discover which state was acting in its own selfish interests. On this issue as well, Stalin was amenable to compromise. It was resolved that the vote of seven of the eleven members of the Security Council would be sufficient to place an item on the agenda. Objection by the Big Three alone would not suffice.[21]

The third important topic of discussion—the entry of the Soviet Union into the war in the Pacific—was resolved in private sessions between American and Soviet discussants. American military planning at the time of Yalta still foresaw a lengthy struggle against the Japanese even after the war with Germany terminated, with the actual invasion of Japan not scheduled until late in 1946. Even with Soviet participation, the war was expected to last at least eighteen more months. It must be remembered that the United States had yet to test an atomic bomb and that planning for the Pacific campaigns followed conventional rules. The Soviet role was not to include the actual invasion of Japan—that task would be left for America—but rather the destruction of Japanese units in Manchuria and Korea. American intelligence estimated that Japan held nearly half a million well-trained and seasoned troops in this area, troops that might continue resistance even after the home islands were invaded. Their destruction would be the task of the Red Army.

On February 10 Stalin agreed in writing that Soviet troops would enter the conflict two to three months after the defeat of Germany. But there would be a price. In return, America would use its good offices and its special relations with Chiang Kai-shek to persuade the Chinese to acknowledge certain Soviet interests in the Far East. The status quo (read puppet status) of Outer Mongolia would be acknowledged, the Manchurian city of Dairen would be internationalized, and the USSR would be allowed to lease Port Arthur as a warm water naval base. A joint Chinese-Soviet company would be formed to run the main railroads that crossed Manchuria. In return the Soviet Union would sign a pact of friendship with the Chiang government, an accord that would recognize Chiang Kai-shek as the ruler of postwar China and undercut efforts by the Chinese Communists to gain power. Besides claims to Chinese territory, the Soviet Union would also benefit by the cession of certain Japanese lands at the war's conclusion. The entire island of Sakhalin would be given to Moscow as would the Kuril island chain north of Japan. Such transfers of territory, naturally, would occur at the postwar peace conference in a legal and proper manner.[22]

The final important discussion at Yalta concerned the way in which the various Eastern European states would return to the peaceful family of nations. Prior to Yalta influential advisers within the American State Department had suggested formation of a Big Three Council that would undertake supervision of such transitions to peace and democracy in Eastern Europe. Roosevelt, ever wary of delegating authority to a committee, blocked this proposal but did retain a keen interest in how this process might take place. Eastern Europe by now was, aside from Greece, under Soviet occupation, and the political future of these states would reveal much about Soviet postwar intentions. Thus, Roosevelt supported a joint resolution that pledged Big Three assistance in the restoration of democratic governance throughout the area. While no permanent committee was instituted to supervise this transition, provisions were made for immediate consultation if problems arose.

In this fashion America demonstrated its continuing concern without being tied to a particular forum of deliberation. The final resolution, entitled "The Declaration of Liberated Europe," stated the following:

To foster the conditions in which the liberated peoples may exercise their rights, the three governments will jointly assist the people in any European liberated state or former Axis satellite state in Europe when in their judgment conditions require (a) to establish conditions of internal peace; (b) to carry out emergency measures for the relief of distressed peoples; (c) to form interim governmental authorities broadly representative of all democratic elements in the population and pledged to the earliest possible establishment through free elections of governments responsive to the will of the people; and (d) to facilitate where necessary the holding of such elections.[23]

If problems arose, the Big Three "will immediately consult together on all the measures necessary."[24] Thus, with the "Declaration of Liberated Europe," the United States and Great Britain served notice that events transpiring within the Soviet-occupied parts of Europe would remain under close scrutiny. Violations of pledges for a swift return to democracy in the region could be met by demands for consultation and three-power intervention within the Eastern European state in question.

On the whole, the Yalta Conference reflected both the realities of the war in early 1945 and the spirit of compromise that, it was hoped, would allow postwar harmony among wartime allies. The signs augured well for the future, with each of the Big Three taking account of the important interests of the others but none totally abdicating its own global concerns.

Only the future would demonstrate whether Roosevelt's strategy of treating the Soviets with respect while integrating them into the postwar political structures of peace might bear fruit. But unfortunately, Roosevelt himself would not see whether his plans to bring about a world at peace would succeed. Only two months after the Yalta Conference, Roosevelt died, bequeathing his hopes and fears to his inexperienced vice-president, Harry Truman.

3

The Birth of
Containment

The period immediately following the Yalta Conference was one of ambiguity and uncertainty in East-West relations. As the Allies continued their successful drive toward Berlin, political disputes supposedly settled at the recent Big Three meeting caused growing concern. In Poland the Soviet-recognized Lublin government refused to accept new members recommended by the Polish government-in-exile. In Romania Soviet political interference in the affairs of the provisional Bucharest government produced a change in regimes contrary to the desires of Britain and America and in sharp contradiction to the common "Declaration of Liberated Europe." Still, such disputes might well be but the final phase of lingering doubts between the Soviet Union and the West, Roosevelt being willing to gloss over such irritations in the interest of long-range postwar harmony. In his last message to Churchill, Roosevelt cautioned that existing disagreements would probably resolve themselves. "I would minimize the general Soviet problem as much as possible, because these problems, in one form or another, seem to arise every day, and most of them straighten out, as in the case of the Berne meeting." And yet almost as a postscript, Roosevelt, too, revealed his own growing anxieties about future East-West relations. "We must be firm however, and our course thus far is correct."[1] That same day Franklin Roosevelt died. The future of Allied relations would now depend, in part, upon the new American leader, Harry S. Truman.

Harry Truman was a self-made man whose interest in military affairs long preceded his political rise to power. Born into a deeply religious Missouri family in 1884, Truman had applied to both Annapolis and West Point, being turned down by both. In World War I he had served as an artillery commander with the expeditionary forces in France. This was the last time he traveled outside his native land. Elected as a senator during the early days of the New Deal, Truman had devoted his career to domestic political problems, involving himself only marginally in foreign affairs issues. His election as vice-president in 1944 did little to increase his participation in international matters, and upon assuming the presidency after Roosevelt's death, Truman found himself dependent upon his predecessor's advisers for his initial insights into the problems of the moment.

It was Roosevelt's chief of staff, Adm. William Leahy, who prepared the first briefing papers for Truman, and it was Roosevelt's ambassador to Moscow, W. Averell Harriman, who provided regular advice as to how the Soviets ought to be handled. Acting Secretary of State Joseph Grew organized a policy review for the new president, going so far as to call home for consultation the political and military representatives serving in the Allied Control Commissions in Bulgaria and Romania for firsthand explanations of their difficulties with their Soviet counterparts.[2]

The advent of Truman to America's highest office coincided with a deep reexamination among Roosevelt's advisers as to their earlier assumptions and hopes regarding postwar Soviet behavior. Harriman, in particular, had shown growing concern in the post-Yalta days about Soviet intransigence and suggested that America ought to stiffen its approach to Moscow while the means of effecting compromise still remained. With America controlling Lend-Lease, postwar assistance, and having the "Declaration of Liberated Europe," now was the time to insist that Moscow relent in its drive to gain control over the Eastern European states such as Poland and Romania. Indications that the USSR planned to establish satellite regimes in Eastern Europe constituted, in Harriman's mind, a potential postwar threat to the security of the United States and a denial of earlier pledges of postwar East-West cooperation. Acting Secretary Grew's opinion of Soviet policy was even more pointed and pessimistic. In a note written the month after Roosevelt's death, Grew asserted: "Future war with Soviet Russia is as certain as anything in this world can be. It may come within a very few years."[3]

While Harry Truman was most willing to seek advice from those who had planned America's approach to the Soviet Union in the Roosevelt days, he was not merely a puppet, willing to move as his advisers suggested. The significance of admonitions to adopt a firmer policy toward Moscow arose from the near consensus about growing Soviet intransigence. The reports from American representatives in the Balkans gave fresh insight into actual Soviet activities directed against the West, while discussions with the American representative to Poland illustrated the dimensions of the continuing dispute regarding the reorganization of the Lublin government. Increasingly, Truman began to see each individual Soviet activity as part of a larger plan, a plan clearly at odds with Roosevelt's assumptions as to the future course of Soviet behavior. As Truman soon concluded, "Our attitude toward Soviet Russia in connection with the Polish issue should be integrated with the many other issues in Central Europe, particularly the Soviet blackout in the Balkan States and the status of Central Europe."[4]

In later April, ten days after becoming president, Truman had his first opportunity to discuss problems with a Soviet leader. On April 22 Soviet foreign minister Molotov arrived in Washington. And while the initial meeting went well, Molotov's apparent unwillingness to hasten negotiations on the reorganization of the Lublin government produced an unprecedented outburst from the new American leader. The tone of Truman's statement to Molotov was so sharp that the Soviet leader retorted he had never been talked to that way in his life, an interesting admission from a close associate of Stalin. Truman's reply was more of the same. "Carry out your agreements and you won't get talked to like that."[5] Clearly, the new president brought a change in style, if not in substance, that augured ill for any Soviet hopes of business as usual in the post-Roosevelt period.

As the policy reviews continued and as continuing information on Soviet behavior poured into the White House, Truman's growing skepticism about the likelihood of close postwar relations with Moscow increased. While many factors undoubtedly contributed to his anxiety, four issues in particular best illustrate the evidence of Soviet refusals to play the diplomatic game consistent with the acknowledged rules of give and take.

Perhaps the clearest indication of Soviet aggressive interests in postwar Eastern Europe arose in connection with the Allied Control Commissions established to guide Bulgaria, Romania, and Hungary back into the peaceful family of nations. Each of the Big Three possessed a military mission and political advisers in these countries, and thus, for the first time, U.S., British, and Soviet representatives worked together on a day-to-day basis, providing detailed information on how well Soviet promises of restoration of democracy might be carried out in practice. And the results were most disappointing. The official history of the American military mission in Bulgaria best sum up the common experience. "It is hard to think of anything that either the Russians or the Bulgarians failed to do to change the friendly or at least neutral attitude with which the Americans arrived. Constant espionage, so clumsily conducted as to be entertainingly obvious, open and covert hostility, wire tapping, sabotage, actual violence and the threat of violence, evasion, procrastination, delay, incompetence and insolence soon changed the initial attitude of the Americans to amusement, contempt and a certain mild dislike."[6] Similar reports of betrayal and antagonism filled the wires connecting the War and State departments to the Romanian and Hungarian capitals. These reports were brought directly to Truman during the May policy review when leaders of America's Balkan delegations returned to Washington. [7]

The negative impression gained by the Truman administration over the treatment of American representatives in the Balkans was further exacerbated by postwar Soviet policy in Iran. Under a 1941 agreement, British and Soviet troops had occupied Iranian territory so as to provide an assured route for Western military supplies to the beleaguered Red Army. Joint withdrawal was to occur six months after the termination of the European conflict. In December 1945 a revolution erupted in the three Iranian provinces bordering the Soviet Union, and a provisional government demanded autonomy from the regular Iranian regime. More distressing to the West, the uprising was led by the Iranian Communist party, and Soviet troops still on occupation duty refused to allow government forces to put down the rebellion.

Early spring 1946 brought rumors of impending Soviet troop reinforcements and concerns that if the rebellious provinces declared independence, Soviet forces might be "invited" to remain on permanent occupation. Convinced that only a firm stance might bring results, the Truman administration supported an appeal by the Iranian government to the United Nations. In April, under UN pressure and having been promised an oil concession by Iran, the Soviets made plans to withdraw. And while this crisis ended peacefully, it gave further support to the growing American conclusion that only a firm position could blunt a relentless Soviet expansionist drive. [8]

The problems in Iran had their counterpart in the adjacent nation of Turkey. A wary friend of the Allies during the war, Turkey's importance to the West derived from its strategic location astride the exit from the Black Sea. Only through the Turkish-controlled straits could the Soviet Black Sea Fleet leave its home waters, and through supervision of such egresses, Britain and America could limit potential threats to their interests in the eastern Mediterranean. But the end of the European war brought a new challenge. In the spring of 1945, Moscow denounced its 1925 friendship pact with Turkey and demanded significant changes in the common Soviet-Turkish frontiers. Such demands were accompanied by requests for Soviet naval bases in the straits, a revision of the existing rules governing the flow of ships in and out of the Black Sea, and a Soviet port on the Aegean Sea. When these demands were forwarded to Washington, Truman prepared to assist the Turks. As he informed his advisers, "We might as well find out whether the Russians were bent on world conquest now as in five or ten years."[9] Moscow was informed that America believed Turkey ought to have primary responsibility for the straits. To make sure the message was understood, Truman reinforced American naval units stationed in the eastern Mediterranean, dispatching the most powerful aircraft carrier in the fleet. The issue of Turkey appeared to place the entire Soviet threat in a new perspective for Truman, a perspective hardly in line with Roosevelt's assumptions of postwar harmony and compromise. As Truman wrote to his secretary of state, James Byrnes, in early 1946: "There isn't a doubt in my mind that Russia intends an invasion of Turkey and the seizure of the Black Sea straits to the Mediterranean. Unless Russia is faced with an iron fist and strong language another war is in the making. Only one language do they understand—'how many divisions have you?' "[10]

Truman's reference to Soviet preference for divisions over diplomacy was not accidental and reflected growing American concern over the slow demobilization of Soviet forces. The precise size of the postwar Soviet army remains to this day an issue of debate. The majority of American journalists and observers in the late forties estimated Soviet troop strength at between 4 and 5 million, excluding half a million security troops. It was believed that about 30 full-strength Soviet divisions in Eastern Europe faced 10 poorly coordinated British-French-American occupation divisions in the West. The continuation of the Soviet draft that called three-quarters of a million to the colors each year, releasing a similar number to the reserves, provided a strong mobilization basis for any future conflict.[11] Whether analysts of the time were correct is of little consequence. What was important was the *perception* of Soviet strengths, for it was in terms of these figures that America assessed the Soviet threat. Having demobilized to under 1.5 million in the army, navy, and air force by 1948, Washington could only conclude that the paths of compromise and diplomacy were not the main means the Soviets would use to advance their objectives.

While the tensions between the USSR and the Western Powers were increasing, the resolution of still outstanding political issues mandated that efforts continue to remove the consequences of the war. In mid-July Truman traveled to the Berlin suburb of Potsdam for a Big Three meeting with Churchill and Stalin. High on his list of priorities was the eventual peace conference or conferences that would determine the borders and forms of government for many European states. Realizing that the future of Germany might constitute the biggest point of dispute, Truman suggested that peace treaties for Germany's smaller allies should first be drafted. For this purpose Truman proposed that the foreign ministers of America, Britain, China, France, and the Soviet Union should meet to draw up such agreements, which, in turn, would be submitted to a larger peace conference for ratification. Soviet demands that the provisional governments already in existence in Bulgaria, Hungary, and Romania be recognized in their present form were rejected by Truman who insisted they must first reorganize to become more representative.[12]

As with the preceding Big Three conferences, Potsdam, too, considered the still unresolved Polish issue. On the eve of the meeting, the Soviet-recognized Lublin government finally reorganized as promised, although fourteen of the twenty-one cabinet positions were allocated to former Lublin members. Acknowledging that this change was in accordance with the demands of Yalta, the British and American governments recognized the new Polish government on July 5, 1945. At Potsdam it was reconfirmed that this government would hold free elections as soon as possible.

More difficult than the form of government was determination of Poland's postwar western frontier, an issue that had been left vague at the Yalta Conference. By the time of Potsdam, the newly formed Polish army had received occupation rights from the USSR to portions of former German territory up to the western Neisse River. Unhappy about this development that had transpired without consultation, America and Britain grudgingly accepted this presence of Polish troops on a provisional basis. The conference agreed that "pending the final determination of Poland's western frontier, the former German territories . . . shall be under the administration of the Polish state."[13] Final status of the borders would be judged at the future peace conference with Germany.

By the time of Potsdam, the basic rules and regulations governing the occupation of Germany were completed and required only slight modification and approval. It was agreed that Germany would be divided into four occupation zones based upon the 1937 frontier and that the Big Three plus France should provide troops for occupation. Each zone would be administered by one power, with the military commanders of each meeting regularly to determine common policy. The zonal division was not intended to be permanent; its status would change once the peace conference with Germany reached its conclusion. In the meantime, no common political organ to govern Germany would be created aside from the regular meetings of the Allied commanders, although local German government would be encouraged. Economically, Germany would be treated as a single unit with policy to be made together by the four occupying powers and then enforced by each in its separate zone of responsibility. Berlin, as the key city of Germany, was itself divided into four zones, one for each occupying power despite its location deep within the Soviet zone. The activities of the powers while awaiting the peace conference were directed at disarming and denazification. Emphasis was to be placed upon returning Germany to a more agrarian way of life with the powerful prewar monopolies and cartels to be dissolved.[14]

The most difficult problem confronted at Potsdam concerned the issue of German reparations for the enormous war damage inflicted upon other European states. This issue had been debated at Yalta with no decision reached as to the price tag one ought to set upon the damages, although a special committee had formed using $20 billion as a figure for debate. The issue involved more than the precise sum to be required since Britain and America were convinced that reparations following World War I had contributed to the Great Depression. The complex solution achieved at Potsdam again neglected to set the exact figure for reparations but determined that surplus equipment would be the main form of its extraction. Each of the four powers could dismantle and remove such surplus equipment as was located in its own occupation zone. In addition, the Soviet Union, as the largest claimant to compensation, could receive 15 percent of capital equipment deemed surplus in the Western zones of occupation in exchange for an equal value of food and other raw materials plus an additional 10 percent without compensation. Within six months each power was to report to a common commission the value of goods removed, and by then it was hoped that a common figure of reparations would be established.[15]

The ability of the Potsdam Conference to reach some important decisions reflected the still generally friendly relations between East and West and the importance of maintaining such ties as long as the war against Japan continued. But by the time of the next scheduled meeting, the issue of Japan was no longer pressing, and the tensions of the growing Cold War were evident. Convening in London in September 1945, the foreign ministers of America, Britain, the Soviet Union, China, and France quickly deadlocked on the question of how the smaller enemy states ought to be handled. Soviet foreign minister Molotov suggested that the existing armistice agreements with the Balkan allies of Germany ought to serve as the foundations of future peace treaties, a suggestion the American secretary of state quickly blocked.[16] At Potsdam Truman had refused to recognize the existing regimes in Bulgaria and Romania pending reorganization and democratization, a position America still held. With a deadlock reached, the Soviets pulled a surprise maneuver, alleging the entire London Conference was illegal due to the presence of China and France, who had not been at war with the Balkan states in question. For the first time, a major East-West conference ended without sufficient agreement to draft even a final communiqué. Wartime cooperation was coming to an end.

In December 1945 the American secretary of state and the British foreign minister traveled to Moscow for another attempt to draft peace treaties with the smaller Axis states as mandated at Potsdam. And now some progress was made. While America still refused to recognize the unrepresentative governments in the Balkans, Stalin promised that both Romania and Bulgaria would "be advised" by the Soviet Union to broaden their respective cabinets. The Soviets also showed a willingness to support a United Nations commission on atomic energy and agreed to participate in a common commission governing the occupation of Japan. But by now the cumulative efforts of Soviet behavior in Eastern Europe and Turkey, plus the freewheeling style of Secretary of State Byrnes, had produced a skeptical frame of mind in Washington. Upon his return from Moscow, Byrnes received a presidential dressing-down in the best manner of Truman's reproach to Molotov some nine months earlier. "I do not think we should play compromise any longer. We should refuse to recognize Rumania and Bulgaria until they comply with our requirements; we should let our position on Iran be known in no uncertain terms . . . and we should maintain complete control of Japan and the Pacific. I'm tired of babying the Soviets."[17]

By now the assumptions and hopes of the preceding Roosevelt administration regarding postwar Soviet behavior were in tatters, and the prospects of a common agreement on Germany's future, or even for a final peace conference, were dim indeed. Clearly, a fresh set of guidelines on how to relate to postwar Moscow were in urgent demand, guidelines that might make sense of the growing Soviet intransigence and insensibility to basic Western interests. The very next month George Kennan, the American chargé in Moscow, began transmitting his eight thousand–word "Long Telegram" that would form the basis for America's new doctrine of containment.

George Kennan, the individual most responsible for America's postwar policy of containment, was, in 1946, a career diplomat serving as America's chargé d'affaires in the Moscow embassy. Educated at Princeton in the twenties, Kennan entered a special training program in the State Department designed to produce future Soviet experts and was assigned to diplomatic positions in Berlin, Latvia, and Estonia. From 1933 to 1937 and again from 1944 to 1946, Kennan served in Moscow, becoming familiar with the Soviet political system. Upon leaving Moscow in 1946, Kennan became the State Department's representative to the National War College and was subsequently named the first head of the State Department's Policy Planning Committee in 1946 by Secretary of State George Marshall. His notions of containment can be gleaned from such diverse sources as the famous "Long Telegram" of February 1947, his lectures at the War College, his "Mr. X" article in *Foreign Affairs* published in July 1947, and his other writings. These writings presented a comprehensive and thoughtful challenge to the basic assumptions concerning Soviet behavior that had guided the Roosevelt administration.[18]

To Kennan Soviet foreign policy was not founded upon an objective analysis of the actual world situation. Rather, at its base Soviet behavior derived from a traditional Russian sense of inferiority and anxiety that arose in the historic experience of a peaceful agrarian people dwelling in an exposed plain open to raids by hostile nomads. This insecurity was compounded by past Russian contacts with advanced Western societies and the realization that their particular Russian form of tyrannical rule could not stand comparison with governing techniques of the West. As a result, Russian-Soviet governments, past and present, had restricted all ties with the West, shielding their peoples from awareness of advanced forms of more benign rule.

Marxism, the chosen ideology of the contemporary Soviet regime, was but one creed in a succession of beliefs that stressed the uniqueness of Russia and the hatred for alternate forms of rule; this creed provided expression for the traditional Russian insecurity and justification for its dictatorial methods of rule. Marxism functioned not as a set of ground rules suggesting preferred policy options but rather as a cloak of rationalization and expression for policies selected on other grounds. Soviet insecurity and official repression were so pervasive that the Soviet government was incapable of functioning as a traditional Western state within the postwar family of nations. The evil nature of the West and the supposed threat to the Soviet government were mainstays of the regime's efforts to remain in power. Thus, at least in the short run, there was little that could be done to modify Soviet behavior since objective factors were of minimal importance. Kennan, a master with a pen, best summarized his disheartening conclusion in the "Long Telegram" itself.

In summary, we have here a political force committed fanatically to the belief that with the U.S. there can be no permanent modus vivendi, that it is desirable and necessary that the internal harmony of our society be disrupted, our traditional way of life be destroyed, the international authority of our state be broken, if Soviet power is to be secure. . . . It is seemingly inaccessible to considerations of reality in its basic reactions. For it, the vast fund of objective fact about human society is not, as with us, the measure against which outlook is constantly being tested and reformed, but a grab bag from which individual items are selected arbitrarily and tendentiously to bolster an outlook already preconceived. This is admittedly not a pleasant picture. Problem of how to cope with this force is undoubtedly greatest task our diplomacy has ever faced and probably the greatest it will ever have to face.[19]

Most basic to Kennan's notion of containment was the search for a modified balance of power as the preferred means of restricting Soviet expansionism. Such a balance of power should not be achieved by an attempt to remake the world in the American image. Rather, Washington ought to strive for a world of diversity, a world in which states remained true to their own traditions and customs. To Kennan there were five global regions whose combined industrial potential, social organization, and tradition of discipline might allow a major threat to peace: America, Great Britain, Germany and Central Europe, the Soviet Union, and Japan. It would be acceptable if any one of these regions was hostile to the United States. The American objective would be to ensure that a second such region did not adopt an anti-American posture. It was contrary to America's traditions, Kennan noted, to interfere in the internal affairs of other states to remake them in its image. And it was equally unnecessary. The other main world regions need not become like America; they need only not become like the USSR. Indeed, Kennan even suggested that America could perhaps find good relations with communist states outside the reach of the USSR, a suggestion that would bear fruit in 1948 when Yugoslavia was expelled from the Soviet bloc.[20]

The main threat that the war-weary Soviet Union posed to the world was not military but political. The devastation produced by the war had undermined the self-confidence and optimism of the West, leaving the states of Central and Western Europe especially susceptible to communist subversion. The old order in Europe was in shambles, and a new generation of leaders was just emerging. This period of transition and economic uncertainty provided unique opportunities for communist expansion, opportunities that America had to try to curtail. Thus, America had to focus its unparalleled economic prosperity and potential on ensuring the rebirth of strong, viable European and world states, states confident of their own traditions and able to resist the foreign creed of communism.

If guaranteeing the continued heterogeneity of the main global regions was step one in Kennan's plan for providing a postwar peaceful world, undermining the Soviet hold over their own satellites was step two. Soviet dominance over and access to the raw materials and riches of Eastern Europe, was, to Kennan, tenuous and contrary to centuries of independent and proud Eastern European traditions. Eventually, these traditions would reassert themselves to Soviet disadvantage. In this process the time needed for the states in question to affirm their own values and ideals was important. This process, however, could be furthered by a careful American policy designed to rebuild the devastated countries of Europe outside the Soviet bloc. The resulting differences in wealth and the stabilization of the Western European way of life would promote the disintegration of Soviet control in the East as the satellite states began to compare themselves with neighbors. As further inducement, America had to be willing to support separatist movements within the Soviet orb. In time the independent traditions of Eastern Europe would reassert themselves.[21]

While the West proceeded to promote diversity throughout the world, including within the Soviet bloc itself, it should, Kennan argued, interact with the Soviet Union in a strictly businesslike fashion. America had to be willing to restrict Soviet expansion by applying counterpressure at selected points. Such counterpressure ought to be primarily political and economic since the Soviet threat manifested itself mainly in these areas. Military counterpressure, however, was not excluded, and Kennan would subsequently support American military aid to Greece and Turkey as well as American plans for possible military intervention in Italy in 1948. Through time, if counterpressure were skillfully applied and given the continued economic dominance of America, the Soviets would find their interests frustrated. This, in turn, might well prompt a Soviet reconsideration of their basic techniques of international behavior, leading to a more objective assessment of global conditions. In short, hope for a potentially peaceful postwar world would await a Soviet reconsideration of its own interests and posture, a reconsideration made necessary by a determined and enlightened American resistance to Soviet expansion.

In the interim America ought to interact with Moscow in a cool but correct manner. In an essay written in the winter of 1946, Kennan provided a list of dos and don'ts quite different from those guiding the behavior of Franklin Roosevelt. "Don't act chummy with them." "Don't assume a community of aims with them which does not really exist." "Make no requests of the Russians unless we are prepared to make them feel our displeasure in a practical way in case the request is not granted." "Do not encourage high-level exchanges of views with the Russians unless the initiative comes at least 50% from their side."[22] In retrospect, it is difficult to think of anything more foreign to Roosevelt's principles of interaction with Moscow.

It is one thing to enunciate the fundamental principles of a strategic doctrine but quite another to apply them to diverse and often unclear situations. This was especially the case with respect to Kennan's analysis given the constraints of America's political process and the existing assumptions and concerns of the Truman White House. Nevertheless, America's policy in the last half of the forties generally followed the objectives and premises Kennan had authored.

American policy toward Germany was a prime example of the growing influence of the containment doctrine. As agreed at the 1945 Potsdam Conference, each of the four powers possessed an occupation zone in Germany from which each might extract reparations. The Soviets, however, had the additional advantage of receiving 25 percent of the surplus capital existing in the Western three zones in exchange for a smaller amount of agricultural products. Within six months of the Potsdam Conference, all recipients were to forward figures on reparations received to a central accounting board. When the time allotted had passed without a full accounting—a result of both French and Soviet intransigence—the American military commander, Gen. Lucius D. Clay, announced that no further Soviet reparations could be taken from the American zone. While the failure of the accounting process bore a major responsibility for Clay's decision, the growing need for American monetary assistance to support the meager German standard of living at a time when the Soviets were removing industrial equipment also played a part. In July 1946 the United States suggested that the Western zones be linked to provide a common economic solution to the continuing problems of daily life for the local population. With British agreement the American and British zones were linked in December, forming a new entity called Bizonia. [23]

According to the guidelines of containment, Germany and Central Europe formed one of the five areas of potential economic and military might whose future allegiance ought to be denied the Soviet bloc. More important, the economic reconstruction of Europe outside the satellite states depended upon the reintegration of an economically healthy Germany into the common European community. In September 1946 Secretary of State Byrnes announced America was abandoning its past policy of maintaining a deindustrialized Germany and henceforth would support economic and political reconstruction. The following March an economic council of fifty-two German representatives convened in Bizonia to discuss economic revitalization. It would fall to this committee to draft proposals for subsequent Marshall Plan aid designed to rebuild Germany's economic life and to produce the so-called economic miracle of the early fifties. That same year, 1947, provincial representative assemblies were elected in the three Western zones in preparation for future political autonomy or independence for a West Germany. The following year a constitutional assembly convened in the Western zones to draft the "Basic Law" for the German Republic. In 1949 the Basic Law was approved by the already-existing provincial parliaments, and the American, British, and French military commanders were replaced with civilian high commissioners. [24]

Since the decision to form a unified West Germany had been prompted, in part, by the need for economic reconstruction, it was natural that further economic integration accompanied these political developments. In June 1948 the Western Powers announced the beginning of currency reform in their three zones. The three western zones of Berlin were specifically excluded from the reform. The Soviets, however, quickly responded by announcing a currency reform of their own to *include* all four sections of Berlin. For the West to accept such an act without resistance would have been tantamount to recognizing de facto Soviet control over the entire city. Thus, the Western Powers reversed their initial decision and ordered their currency reform to include their own three zones of Berlin. On June 24 the Soviets closed all land routes entering Berlin although air access was maintained. Thus began the Berlin Blockade, an event that once again emphasized the division of postwar Europe between East and West. Not until the spring of 1949 were Soviet restrictions withdrawn in testimony to the effectiveness of the allied airlift that had kept the city supplied.[25]

The Marshall Plan, America's successful effort to rebuild the devastated economies of postwar Western and Central Europe, can best be understood as fulfilling points one and two of Kennan's containment doctrine: maintaining a diverse political system in the four key industrial areas outside the Soviet Union and providing incentive and example for the Eastern European states to weaken their ties with Moscow. Its genesis can be traced to the harsh European winter of 1946–47 and the resulting extreme economic hardships confronting the European states. By 1947 the split between the wartime allies was obvious with little hope of any common East-West plan for economic reconstruction. Early that year President Truman had appointed the former American army chief of staff, Gen. George Marshall, as the new secretary of state. In March 1947 Marshall flew to Moscow for a meeting with his Soviet counterpart concerning the increasingly strained relations between states once allies. Upon his return Marshall tasked his new policy-planning committee, led by George Kennan, to draft a policy for European reconstruction. Three months later Marshall proposed a bold, new plan for providing reconstruction assistance to Europe. Perhaps the most unconventional twist to Marshall's suggestion was that the European states themselves had to develop plans and programs for aid utilization, with such plans having to be submitted to Washington for approval. The Marshall Plan was to be a client-centered economic program.

Several weeks after Marshall's announcement, the foreign ministers of Britain, France, and the Soviet Union assembled in Paris to draft a common response. At first glance it appeared the Soviets would take full advantage of the offered assistance; Foreign Minister Molotov arrived in the French capital with nearly ninety economic advisers. In less than a week, however, Molotov and his assistants withdrew, charging the American plan was designed to undermine the sovereignty of the European powers. Thus, the blame for Soviet nonparticipation fell squarely upon Moscow.[26]

While most fortunate from the Western perspective, the Soviet refusal to accept Marshall Plan aid was far from fortuitous. In March 1947 Will Clayton, assistant secretary of state for economic affairs and an architect of the Marshall Plan, expressed his fear of increased Soviet penetration of Western Europe. With an anticipated decline in British influence, either

America or the Soviet Union would fill the political and economic vacuum. If the Soviets stepped into the breach in Western Europe, Clayton cautioned, a global war could be predicted within the next decade. Thus, America needed to expand its influence in the threatened area but in such a manner that the resulting division of Europe would not appear the fault of Washington. Both Under Secretary of State Dean Acheson and George Kennan agreed. As the latter affirmed, "If anyone was to divide the European continent, it should be the Russians with their response, not we with our offer."[27]

The exclusion of the Soviet Union from the offer of American economic assistance for the rebuilding of Europe was accomplished by the conditions of aid included in the final Marshall Plan proposals. Consistent with American notions of rational and efficient usage of any scare resource, plan administrators requested that extensive information on the state of the respective recipients' economic life be forthcoming as well as plans for national development. Such information, however, was well known to be considered a state secret in the Soviet Union. In addition, aid was tied to the promotion of a multilateral trading bloc with stipulations that funds requested for national development be harmonized with the goal of pan-European recovery. To promote such recovery, recipients ought to move toward currency convertibility as soon as possible. This latter goal once again constituted a barrier to Soviet participation since the Russian ruble was a "soft" currency whose value was not set by free competition in the international marketplace. While the other European countries, too, would have problems making their currencies fully convertible, there was no fixed state policy acting as a permanent bar to such efforts. Thus, the USSR and its Eastern European allies found themselves unable to participate in the new economic venture without serious modification of their own economic policies. The results were what Kennan and others had anticipated: Marshall Plan aid would be restricted to nations outside the Soviet bloc but with a clear Soviet refusal being the apparent reason for nonparticipation.[28]

In mid-July sixteen European states met to consider how best to respond to the offers of American aid, drafting plans and proposals for Washington's consideration. In April 1948 the American Congress approved just under $7 billion as the first installment of an eventual $13 billion assistance program that ran until 1952. By that time industrial production in the Marshall Plan states had risen to 135 percent of the prewar level, and agriculture had risen to 110 percent. Trade had expanded dramatically among participants, and the initial signs of what would become the Common Market were visible in the European Steel and Coal Agreement. With economic recovery came increased European self-confidence and a growing political unity expressed in such institutions as the North Atlantic Treaty Organization (NATO), which was started in 1949. Eastern Europe, by contrast, remained an economic backwater, barely profiting from the advances to its west and increasingly cognizant that the Soviet model of industrial and agricultural development was vastly inferior to that employed in the West. The evident cracks within the Soviet Eastern European Empire that became especially evident in the late sixties and seventies are traceable to this period when the two halves of Europe diverged so dramatically with respect to the abilities of the respective economies to fulfill the basic demands of the consuming population.[29]

While the economic assistance provided Germany and the Marshall Plan countries exemplified basic tenets of Kennan's containment doctrine, they were not its sole expression. Kennan had warned that Soviet expansion must be met by counterpressure skillfully applied at selected points. This notion fit well with Harry Truman's growing predilection to "get tough" with Moscow and led to an emphasis upon military means not wholly consistent with Kennan's initial suggestions. Its clearest expression came with the Truman Doctrine in 1947.

In the spring of 1947, the British ambassador informed a startled State Department that financial constraints made continuation of British assistance to the royalist government of Greece impossible. Since the Greek government at that very moment was enraged in life-and-death struggle with the communist-led EAM-ELAS, withdrawal of assistance threatened to expand Soviet control in Eastern Europe. This result, in turn, would both destabilize the eastern Mediterranean and further demoralize the Western European states that might conclude communism was indeed the wave of the future. To further complicate matters, information suggested that the financial situation in Turkey was equally bleak and that Soviet pressure for revision of Turkey's frontiers was continuing. A series of emergency meetings in the State Department and White House led to a quick decision to substitute American assistance for that no longer available from Britain. To sell the new aid package to Congress, Truman was advised that only by "scaring Hell out of the American people" could he be assured of congressional approval.[30]

Nineteen days after the British notification, Truman appeared before Congress to request significant military and economic assistance to stave off communist victories in the eastern Mediterranean. While the aid was designed to help Greece and Turkey, Truman expressed his concern in much more sweeping and universal terms. "I believe that it must be the policy of the United States to support free peoples who are resisting attempted subjugation by armed minorities or by outside pressures." He requested $400 million in military and economic aid, and Congress approved this two months later. Within two years the EAM-ELAS was decisively defeated, and the threat to Turkey had receded.[31]

In the near run, the application of pressure at selected points in Greece and Turkey appeared a clear success. Yet to some, including Kennan himself, the Truman Doctrine contained a justification for unlimited American military and economic involvement with little regard for actual limitations upon America's resources. American military advisers were dispatched to both Greece and Turkey, and a commitment of American combat troops was discussed. A precedent had been set for further and deeper American involvement in other threatened portions of the world, a precedent that might one day prompt America to commit itself beyond its abilities.

4

Emergence of the National Security Establishment

In the initial years of the postwar period, President Truman and his advisers utilized the existing structures of government in their efforts to draft security plans aimed at ensuring America's defense. But by 1947 it had become apparent that institutions designed for a more peaceful period were inadequate to the task. Several specific problems pointed the way to a major reform in the manner and means by which security affairs were heretofore conducted.

Hearings in the immediate postwar days as to the reasons behind America's inability to accurately predict the disastrous Japanese attack upon Pearl Harbor concluded that existing American intelligence procedures were inadequate to the challenges of both the twentieth century and the new global power status America had attained. The preferred solution appeared to be a central intelligence body that would interpret data received from other members of the intelligence community and make predictions as to the likely behavior pattern of America's main friends and foes. It was the lack of such a body, many concluded, that had prevented intelligence officers from predicting the Japanese assault despite the fact that bits and pieces of information suggesting such an event had indeed existed in separate intelligence agencies prior to December 7, 1941.

And yet the need for coordination within intelligence agencies was only one legacy of the war remaining to be remedied. A second, certainly of equal importance, was the situation of the Joint Chiefs of Staff. Created as an ad hoc body during the war so as to provide some unity in the advice forwarded to the president and as a means of counterbalancing a similar institution prominent within the British military, the Joint Chiefs still lacked formal authorization. Additionally, since the atomic age had drastically increased the significance of the army air corps, important voices both within and without the military called for a major reorganization that would both grant the air force independent status and more clearly define the purposes and weapons of each branch of the service.[1]

Finally, the need to coordinate America's security policies had placed unbearable strains upon existing institutions. By 1947 the various means of security planning had emerged in full view; they ranged from economic assistance through diplomatic initiative to application of military force. What was urgently required was some forum in which the most efficient combination of such measures might be selected and adapted to a rapidly changing world. While the regular meetings of the president's cabinet suggested itself, the normal and extensive functions of cabinet members in their own right mitigated against the continued use of this body to resolve new problems arising from America's augmented role and responsibility in the postwar era. Some new forum specifically designed to permit discussion of alternate security policies was urgently required. The solution to this problem, and to those mentioned above, was contained in a key piece of legislation passed in the summer of 1947, the National Security Act. While some provisions of this act were later to prove ineffective and were subsequently dropped, the primary result was the creation of the security establishment that still functions in America today.

Central to the new institution was the National Security Council whose purpose was to advise the president "with respect to the integration of domestic, foreign, and military policies relating to the national security" as well as "to assess and appraise the objectives, commitments and risks of the United States in relation to our actual and potential military power." Here then was the body adequate for both initiation of policy options and deliberation of which options appeared best in light of the problems to be solved. Membership was fixed to include the president, the secretaries of state, defense, army, navy, and air force as well as the chairman of the just created National Security Resources Board. Other executive officers who the president might invite to meetings were enumerated. Two years later, in an additional reform to be mentioned shortly, the status of the three service secretaries (army, navy, and air force) was diminished, and in 1949 their names were removed from council membership. The National Security Resources Board also passed into oblivion. By the eighties the statutory membership of the National Security Council included the president, vice-president, and the secretaries of state and defense. The assistant to the president for national security affairs had become the senior staff officer of the council while the heads of the Joint Chiefs of Staff, Central Intelligence Agency, and Arms Control and Disarmament Agency functioned as advisers.[2]

In its original form, the National Security Council was designed to function much as the British War Cabinet that had so impressed Roosevelt. It might also act to restrain any impetuous outbursts or activities of the fiery president from Missouri. And yet, as time would show, the National Security Council, far from acting as a restraint upon the chief executive, was molded by each president into the type of council most consistent with his own decision-making style. By the seventies and the advent of a strong national security adviser in the person of Henry Kissinger, the council had assumed a shape and function quite at odds with the founders' intentions.

President Truman himself appeared most satisfied with this new institution although he maintained his own individualistic control of security matters by meeting only twelve times with the council prior to the outbreak of the Korean War. With the eruption of fighting, Truman mandated that henceforth all options concerning major issues in national security had to be routed to him through the council, and his increased personal attendance augmented the council's significance. The small staff of the council, assistants designated to help members fulfill their tasks, was supervised by two executive secretaries.[3]

Under Truman's successor, Dwight Eisenhower, the importance of the National Security Council grew even greater, and weekly meetings became the rule. The council focused primarily upon long-range policy-making, leaving issues of immediate importance to other bureaucratic channels of discussion or to the personal discussions of President Eisenhower and his close confidant, Secretary of State John Foster Dulles. A special assistant for national security affairs was appointed with his main function being to supervise the development of policy option papers that would deal with the key issues facing the administration. A Planning Board was established under the council, consisting of assistant secretaries in the various cabinet bureaucracies who would bring together opinion and options for subsequent council discussion. Thus, by the end of the Eisenhower administration, the general pattern of functioning for the National Security Council had been broadly established. Each president would use the council insofar as his own style of decision making was amenable to group discussions and was not constrained by special relations between the White House and some given cabinet minister in whom a president had special trust and confidence. With presidents such as Kennedy, an individual who relished the give-and-take of near open verbal combat, decision making in crisis situations occurred outside the formal constraints of the National Security Council and within broader, ad hoc bodies involving officials whom Kennedy respected and who might be affected by a subsequent decision.

The role of the national security adviser as well evolved consistent with the administrative style of the different presidents. By the time of Richard Nixon, the strength of National Security Adviser Henry Kissinger was so great that his office alone soon eclipsed the council he purportedly led. By the seventies the professional staff of the council that reported to the national security adviser numbered over fifty, and key decisions were frequently made in private consultations between Kissinger and Nixon or through the medium of the Kissinger-run Washington Special Action Group that was not technically subordinated to council regulations. Yet despite its evolution and change, the National Security Council has become a central institution in the discussion and decision of key security issues in most presidential administrations. [4]

The creation of the Central Intelligence Agency in 1947 represented a significant break with respect to the handling of intelligence in the first 175 years of the existence of the republic. America's normal pattern had been to establish intelligence centers, aside from normal military intelligence units, only on the eve of impending conflict and to disband them soon afterward. This seemed most suitable for a nation predicated upon a pluralistic political system with an abiding fear of big government that might threaten civilian rights. In the twenties then Secretary of State Henry Stimson, upon discovering a cryptographic unit still active a decade after the war, closed it with the statement, "Gentlemen do not read other gentlemen's mail." True to pattern, Franklin Roosevelt waited until just prior to America's entry into World War II to request New York lawyer William Donovan to draft plans for a comprehensive intelligence center. In July 1941 the Office of the Coordinator of Information made its appearance, being replaced by the Office of Strategic Services in June 1942. [5]

According to the 1975 Rockefeller Report requested by Gerald Ford, the Office of Strategic Services (OSS) possessed three main operating staffs. The Secret Intelligence Division engaged in overseas collection of information and included espionage. The X-2 Division handled counterespionage, protecting the security of America's agents while ensuring that foreign spies would not infiltrate America's intelligence organizations. Research and Analysis produced reports and analytical assessments useful for governmental and military policymakers. Other functions of the OSS included propaganda and paramilitary activities. By the end of the war, approximately thirteen thousand men and women worked for this organization. [6]

With the war's termination, the traditional pattern of rapid dissolution threatened to repeat itself. Operatives active in the Research and Analysis Division were assigned positions in the State Department while those familiar with espionage who wished to remain on government service went to the War Department. And yet even before the war ended, it became clear that postwar business as usual would be impossible given the greatly augmented status of the United States in world affairs. Donovan himself, in the fall of 1944, sent a special proposal to Roosevelt suggesting creation of a regular peacetime intelligence organization that would "procure intelligence both by overt and covert methods, and . . . at the same time provide intelligence guidance, determine national intelligence objectives and correlate the intelligence materials collected by all Government agencies." He felt that such an organization ought to be allowed to "conduct subversive operations abroad."[7]

As might have been expected, Donovan's proposal quickly engendered opposition from existing bureaucratic groups. The army and navy opposed the peacetime centralization of functions that their small intelligence units normally performed. The State Department suggested the formation of an interdepartmental committee from existing personnel. The Federal Bureau of Investigation (FBI) wished to have worldwide postwar responsibility for civilian intelligence, leaving military intelligence to the respective services. The result of such objections in the face of a clear need for some centralization of intelligence functions was a compromise. In January 1946 President Truman created the Central Intelligence Group (CIG). Presided over by Truman's White House chief of staff, Adm. William Leahy (who soon gave the responsibility to Rear Adm. Sidney Souers), the purpose of the CIG was to coordinate existing intelligence units and to perform those functions that could only be done centrally. Staff for the new agency came from the departments of state, war, and navy. Plans to expand the functions of the CIG, however, continued to surface within the Truman administration. The final result was the creation of the Central Intelligence Agency as part of the National Security Act of 1947.[8]

By its original mandate, the CIA was subordinated to the National Security Council and was directed to coordinate, not supervise, the activities of other agencies. It was to advise the NSC on intelligence issues, make recommendations as to coordination of intelligence activities and collection, and correlate, evaluate, and disseminate intelligence information. It was also to "perform such other functions and duties related to intelligence . . . as the National Security Council may from time to time direct."[9] It was to be this apparently innocuous clause that would give justification for the subsequent drastic expansion of CIA functions and personnel.

The CIA possessed four basic components. The Office of Reports and Estimates, initially formed within the CIG and transferred to the CIA in 1947, was responsible for all finished intelligence production. The duties of this office have been considerably modified in the four decades of the CIA's existence. The Office of Special Operations took its cue from prior OSS activities in the preceding war. It was responsible for espionage and counterespionage. The Office of Operations was charged with overt and domestic collection of foreign intelligence. The Office of Collection and Dissemination established priorities of information collection and organized the raw intelligence as well as the dissemination of the finished products to individuals who needed such materials as an aid to decision making. In September 1948 a new section was added. The Office of Policy Coordination directed covert and paramilitary operations that the National Security Council might mandate. [10]

While the CIA was the first centralized intelligence agency created after the war, it was not the last. Under a subsequent presidential order, the National Security Agency (NSA) emerged in 1952. Its function was to provide centralized coordination, direction, and control of all governmental signals intelligence (SIGINT) and communications security activities (COMSEC). SIGINT involved the interception, processing, analysis, and dissemination of information gained from foreign electrical communications. This included tapping foreign communications worldwide. COMSEC, in turn, protected American communications from similar activities by foreign agents. [11]

In 1961 the Defense Intelligence Agency (DIA) made its appearance. In part an effort to ensure that the president and other key policymakers had alternate sources of information, the DIA derived its personnel largely from military intelligence units. Its responsibilities included review and coordination of all Defense Department intelligence resources, with its head to report to the secretary of defense through the Joint Chiefs of Staff. It was hoped that by the creation of such a centralized military intelligence agency, the obvious rivalry between service intelligence units would be diminished. Intelligence gathering and evaluation in the military might become more professional and less combative. While such hopes have yet to be entirely realized, the DIA soon emerged as a competent competitor of the CIA in furnishing alternate estimates of likely enemy behavior, an important gain for policy officials requiring insight into all possible policy options. [12]

In addition to improving the structure of intelligence and the means by which the president received advice about preferred policy options, the National Security Act of 1947 focused upon regularizing America's military and defense bureaucracy. The Joint Chiefs of Staff, created in the Roosevelt administration, still lacked a formal charter defining membership and responsibilities. The executive departments of the armed forces revolved around two separate centers, the secretaries of war and navy, at a time when coordination of military planning was urgently required. These problems and more were addressed in the 1947 act, with a comprehensive National Military Establishment (NME) emerging as a suggested solution.

The National Military Establishment, renamed the Department of Defense in 1949, consisted of two relatively distinct, if interrelated, tiers. Its head was to be a secretary of defense who would coordinate issues and problems likely to arise from the second tier, the individual armed services themselves. The secretary of defense was designated as the main cabinet officer with responsibility for the entire defense establishment. As such, he had four primary duties: to establish the general policies and programs for the National Military Establishment; to exercise general direction over the military departments of the army, navy, and air force; to minimize duplication in procurement, supply, and transportation among the three services; and to supervise and coordinate preparation of budget estimates for the different branches of the military. Initially, these responsibilities seemed to exceed the secretary of defense's capability since the 1947 act provided inadequate staff for the functions assigned. By the fifties, however, increasing staff came under the secretary's control. A second problem was the power granted to the three service secretaries: navy, army, and air force. In 1949 the three service secretaries lost their status as cabinet officials and their independent right of access to the president, thus elevating the secretary of defense to a unique position as director of defense efforts.[13]

Besides the secretary of defense, the 1947 National Security Act gave formal authorization of the Joint Chiefs of Staff, maintaining in essence their existing organization. The Joint Chiefs were to consist of the chiefs of staff of the army, navy, and air force, joined by the commander in chief to the president if the chief executive wished to appoint such an individual. Two years later, in 1949, this latter position was changed to allow a chairman of the Joint Chiefs independent of whether such an individual served as well in the White House. In 1952 membership was broadened to include the commandant of the Marine Corps who might attend meetings to discuss matters in which his service branch had an interest. In 1978 the marine commandant was granted a regular position.[14]

From the beginning the Joint Chiefs were designated as the "principle military advisers to the President and the Secretary of Defense." At first, they retained their position in the chain of command whereby orders were sent from the president to troops in the field. By the late fifties, however, the Joint Chiefs had been removed from the command loop, and orders proceeded from the president to the secretary of defense to the commanders of the various worldwide commands. Thus, planning for the diverse strategic and tactical contingencies and offering advice to the president and the secretary of defense became the primary mission of the Joint Chiefs. To help fulfill these tasks, a joint staff was authorized providing a reserve of experienced officers able to analyze the alternate options for planning and acquisitions of weapons that the separate services might suggest.[15]

The second tier of the newly established National Military Establishment consisted of the three separate services, the air force being granted equal status along with the traditional branches of navy and army. Each service was headed by a cabinet-level secretary who was responsible for the affairs of his military branch and possessed direct access to the commander in chief. In 1953 the service secretaries were placed in the chain of command from the president to the worldwide commands, but in 1958 they lost this responsibility. In 1949 the service secretaries lost their cabinet rank and became military departments.[16]

The reorganization of the military occurred during a period of intense debate as to the likely future of both warfare and preferred strategic planning. Defining America's postwar strategy, in turn, would have major impact upon funding levels for each service. Thus, from the start an intense rivalry emerged, with the newly created air force asserting its capability for delivering nuclear weapons most efficiently to far-flung corners of the world. This competition for funds and capabilities was addressed in a presidential order issued the same day as the signing of the National Security Act of 1947. Under its provisions the mission of the army was confined to being "organized, trained and equipped primarily for prompt and sustained combat incident to operations on land." The navy was to prepare for "prompt and sustained combat incident to operations at sea," while the air force focused training and procurement to permit "prompt and sustained . . . air operations."[17] Clearly, this order, which, in essence, simply proclaimed that the army fought on land, the navy on sea, and the air force in the air, was inadequate to soothe competition for scarce funds and service prestige.

The following March a further agreement between the services was reached at a meeting at Key West. It was agreed that the navy would retain its own air forces and would be responsible for determining how such assets would be used on behalf of naval air missions. Such authority, however, could not be used to justify creation of a naval strategic air capability. Strategic bombing was allocated to the air force. Thus, an important issue of rivalry was solved, with air force preeminence in strategic matters recognized despite the fact that with their then current planes many potential targets of strategic bombing lay outside air force ranges and within range of naval aircraft carriers. The army, in turn, dropped its long-standing objection to the Marine Corps—an objection that had aimed at restricting marine units to less than division size. In compensation, the Marine Corps was not to exceed four divisions nor to have a field unit headquarters above the corps level. While these compromises left numerous problems unre-solved, they began the process whereby each branch slowly began to recognize the legitimacy of some outside claims. It would fall to the Joint Chiefs and the secretary of defense to ensure that each service functioned within its proper domain in the overall objective of providing a national defense.[18]

5

Strategic Planning under Truman

The collapse of Japanese resistance following the explosion of two atomic bombs initiated a period of peace in which American thoughts were little concerned with future war. Much like two decades before, the American public assumed that the magnitude of the recent military efforts ensured a world in which peace and diplomacy would become the mainstays of security. While such beliefs certainly were not as dominant among those governmental officials charged with actual strategic planning, other equally important factors significantly hindered a clear assessment of the likely future.[1]

The new role America had gained as the dominant global power necessitated a detailed analysis of what global events might constitute danger to America's expanded interests. Equally important, the mood of the American people and their congressional representatives remained unclear as to whether the burden of global leadership would be maintained, the alternative being a relapse into a "return to normalcy" characteristic of the period following the last war. Such a retreat from responsibility would naturally mandate important changes in what America saw as its basic interests and how they ought to be protected. To add to the confusion, the primary threat in the postwar world was far from evident. While many suspected growing Soviet intransigence would stand as the main barrier to a future peaceful world, the notion that strategic doctrine ought to target the USSR as a prime enemy was inconsistent both with Franklin Roosevelt's legacy and with his main diplomatic efforts that had created a network of international institutions such as the United Nations and the World Bank in which Soviet and American representatives expected to work in harmony. To compound the problems, the revolutionary development of the atomic bomb left conventional planning principles in question, raising suggestions of the future irrelevance of large ground armies in an era when planes loaded with unparalleled destructive power streaked over opposing ground forces to obliterate targets in the center of the enemy homeland. During the half decade separating the Japanese surrender of 1945 from the North Korean invasion of 1950, Americans had to decide what interests they held most dear and what means would be provided for their defense. In many ways, it was the very debate about means that, in the long run, determined the goals and interests to be defended. And as emphasis slowly shifted to atomic power and air delivery, America's global concerns increased.

As one might expect, the initial assumptions about security in the postwar world reflected the lessons of the recent past. In the fall of 1944, Army Chief of Staff George Marshall issued a circular calling for postwar enactment of Universal Military Training as the best way of providing a strong defense. The details of his plan were drafted by Gen. John Palmer who was a veteran of the post–World War I debate over military reform. To Palmer there appeared two distinct approaches to military readiness. The German and Japanese examples relied upon a trained and professional military class whose very existence was incompatible with democratic principles. The alternate option was the creation of a citizen reserve army that would mobilize whenever the nation was in danger. Universal Military Training would teach basic war skills to the vast majority of the male population, with the draftees subsequently being released for a required term of duty in the reserves and National Guard. Talent and ability would facilitate the creation of a trained reserve officers corps avoiding the emergence of a professional military caste while providing a large force capable of mobilization in time of danger. To Marshall and Palmer, the war just ending clearly proved the advantage of democratic principles of military preparedness over the discredited warrior castes of the defeated enemy.[2]

The advent of Harry Truman to the presidency gave further support to plans for Universal Military Training with the president informing Congress in October 1945 that all young men ought to serve a one-year military term prior to their twentieth birthday. Those found unfit for duty would be assigned other tasks. After their year the men would be released to the reserves where their obligation would continue for six more years.[3]

Had Truman appeared before Congress earlier in his term, before the atomic devastation of Japanese cities, perhaps his plea would have been heeded. But with the dawn of a new era in which America's defense appeared assured with a cheaper and more effective weapon, Congress hesitated to appropriate funds needed for a "common" defense. It did, however, extend the existing draft until 1947 and authorized the expansion of the peacetime National Guard. Twenty-seven divisions and 21 regimental combat teams were to form the postwar guard, although funding was appropriated for only a fraction of this amount. When the regular draft ended in March 1947, the flow of experienced soldiers into the guard diminished to a trickle. Only in June 1948 was the conventional draft reinstated in the face of a growing Soviet threat, a draft that required twenty-one months' service instead of the desired one year. Youths seventeen to eighteen-and-a-half were exempted if they enlisted directly into the reserves for five or more years. Thus, the guard/reserve components received renewed life although the quantity and quality of training remained low. By the end of 1948, the guard possessed over 300,000 members, increasing thereafter to become nearly three times as large in 1950 as it had been on the eve of the 1947 draft expiration. In that year, 1950, there were also 175,000 officers and men in the organized Army Reserve and nearly 400,000 in the inactive reserve.[4]

While the number, if not perhaps the quality, of the guard/reserve forces by 1950 showed great improvement, the same could not be said of the standing army. As the war against Germany and Japan had reached its final phase, the War Department had developed an intricate point system that might allow demobilization according to individual length of service and toughness of duty. But with the surrender of Japan, the War Department felt compelled to release all servicemen with two or more years of duty. By June 1947, with demobilization completed, the 12 million men and women on active duty at the war's end had shrunk to 1.5 million in all services, half of whom were on occupation duty in Europe or Asia. The following spring, as the West recoiled from the communist coup in Czechoslovakia, the combined manpower of the army and marines was under 650,000. Even the reinstatement of the draft in the summer of 1948 did little to improve force levels with only 300,000 being drafted in the years prior to the Korean War. By 1950 the army had a combat strength of 10 divisions and 9 regimental combat teams. The majority of these divisions, however, had been subject to economic restraints with respect to both equipment and personnel, the usual infantry regiment having 2 instead of 3 battalions. No division had its full wartime complement of weapons. Clearly, a strategic plan based upon a quick response by a well-trained and equipped ground force would find its execution nearly impossible.[5]

The inability of the president and the Congress to reach common accord on the importance of a vast citizen army increased the importance of the newfound atomic weapons. Yet here too uncertainties and disagreements wreaked havoc upon efforts to design a comprehensive strategic plan. Incredible as it may seem today, in the first several years following the destruction of Hiroshima and Nagasaki, no one knew how many atomic weapons were in the American arsenal. In early 1947 the head of the Atomic Energy Commission discovered to his horror that only 1 assembled bomb existed, and it was a rather inefficient type of weapon at that. By July 1947 about 13 bombs existed in unassembled form, requiring nearly forty men two days for assembly. The loading equipment required to mount the weapon on bombers was absent.[6]

The problem of hardware was matched by uncertainty at the highest levels as to whether the bomb should ever be used again and under what circumstances military authorities might authorize nuclear missions. Truman himself considered the weapon as "uncivilized," believing it would be used again only under the most drastic of conditions. Sole authority to use the bomb lay in the president's hands, and provisions for the delegation of such authority were not drafted until the later forties. Even if the bomb had occupied the center position of U.S. strategy beginning at the war's end, the absence of detailed information on potential Soviet targets would have severely limited its effective employment. Soviet territory was far more extensive than German-occupied Europe, and maps and charts of this vast domain were simply not available. It was, in part, to remedy this vast absence of knowledge about the new enemy that American intelligence officials sometimes "overlooked" the past nazi activities of German and Eastern European citizens who purported to possess information about the USSR. Thus, the first phase of strategic planning with reference to nuclear weapons began with heavy handicaps and proceeded by trial and error.[7]

The first nuclear-based plan of which we are aware emerged from the Joint Chiefs of Staff planners in the summer of 1946 under the code name *Pincher.* In order to specify the time frames in which preparedness would be required, Pincher posited the outbreak of war with the Soviet Union between the summers of 1946 and 1947. Such time frames in military planning do not necessarily mean the planners themselves anticipate an actual conflict. They simply mean that the defense must make use of assets and conditions as they exist or will exist within the given temporal constraints in preparations for action. Thus, any plan to procure a new weapon outside of the selected time lines must be disregarded for purposes of the plan itself. Pincher, in addition, assumed America would possess three months' warning of the impending attack, an important assumption in any plan since the amount of time available determines the degree of mobilization possible and the maximum number of men and weapons that will be on hand.[8]

The most interesting aspect of Pincher was the low degree of importance assigned to the atomic bomb. At the start of hostilities, Pincher posited American and Allied forces would evacuate Europe and Asia, withdrawing to unspecified "tenable" areas. The United Kingdom would be defended to the last man since this would be an essential mobilization base for eventual reentry onto the continent. Perhaps Japan would fulfill the same function in the East. The assumption running through Pincher was that the superior Red Army would conquer Europe as well as much of the Middle East before the communist offensive was stalemated. In the Middle East, the Soviets and their allies would be blocked north of modern day Israel, with the subsequent counteroffensive being launched using Turkey as a mobilization area. Conventional techniques of war fighting were to be employed, including naval blockade and heavy ground engagements. The atomic attack upon the USSR would concentrate on 20 cities. The number of bombs to be dropped was not specified since the military planners were unaware of how many such weapons were on hand. It was later discovered that a number of the Soviet cities targeted lay outside the range of America's longest-range bombers of the period.[9]

In August 1947, with the time frame of Pincher having elapsed, a replacement plan was drafted under the name of *Broiler.* By now a number of postwar atomic tests had increased military confidence in the potential of atomic destruction, and Broiler offered a greatly enhanced estimate of the bomb's importance in rapidly stemming a Soviet advance. American and Allied forces would still need to retreat rapidly from the continents of Europe and Asia, but the nuclear assault upon the USSR would begin early in the conflict. It was now assumed that within the first six months of the war, atomic power would stabilize the battlefield, leading to a rapid allied counteroffensive. With this goal in mind, the appended targeting plan of Broiler focused upon Soviet industrial sites and centers of war production as well as certain important political objectives and research institutes. By contrast, Pincher had focused its attack upon urban targets. Broiler, for the first time, gave importance to the psychological impact a major nuclear assault would have upon the Soviet people's will to fight. It assumed "an increased element of hopelessness and shock" would be produced by numerous atomic explosions.[10] Two months later the military recommended that fulfillment of Broiler's objectives could best be met by use of 400 atomic devices aimed at 100 separate targets.[11]

The newly discovered importance of the bomb and the willingness to employ great numbers as part of a comprehensive strategic plan gave rise to pressures to increase America's nuclear arsenal. In 1948 new sources of uranium became available through an agreement with Great Britain and the use of vast resources in the Belgium Congo. A new fabrication technique facilitated production of more bombs with more killing power in shorter periods of time while the expansion of America's B-29 fleet in 1948 from 33 to over 120 provided the means for deeper penetration against

Soviet targets. As a result, the targeting objectives appended to the frequently updated strategic plans included more and more bombs against more and more targets. By the fall of 1948, *Fleetwood* posited that America's nuclear potential might allow the Red Army to be held at the Rhine River, obviating the need for instant withdrawal from the continent. The American counteroffensive would be accompanied by a massive nuclear assault that would destroy 70 Soviet cities and use 133 bombs in the early stages of the war. An adjunct plan to Fleetwood suggested that if the war failed to end in two years 200 more bombs would be used, obliterating 40 percent of Soviet industry and producing 7 million deaths. *Offtackle*, drafted in October 1949, called for dropping 220 bombs on 104 urban targets.[12]

While the growing number of bombs—by the summer of 1953 about 1,000 lay in U.S. arsenals—naturally produced pressure for the expansion of their use, so too did the dramatic increase in the number of identified profitable Soviet targets. Between 1949 and 1953, American intelligence conducted extensive interviews with returning German, Austrian, and Japanese prisoners of war in a project code-named *Wringer*. Over 300,000 were interviewed in Germany alone, resulting in an extensive list of likely targets in cities and rural areas where the prisoners had been detained or through which they had traveled on their way from and to freedom. It was to be this combination of nuclear potential and profitable targets that would form the basis, in 1953, for the new Eisenhower administration's reliance upon a strategy of massive retaliation as the cheapest and most effective means of forestalling a communist attack.[13]

The numerous proposals, from Pincher through Fleetwood and beyond, that flowed from military planners constituted what might best be termed *strategic military plans*. Such proposals attempted to identify and marshal existing military forces so as to compel a future enemy to bow to demands American leaders would subsequently put forth. But as the last phrase clearly indicates, strategic planning in its most basic form is a political process, a process in which the central political objectives are defined and the military means required to gain their acceptance are enumerated. Throughout most of the postwar period, the most important source of such strategic planning has been the National Security Council created in 1947. And it is to its deliberations and decisions one must turn to trace the changing interpretations as to the relative importance of nuclear power in gaining American political objectives as well as the shifting nature of the objectives themselves.

The first comprehensive analysis of the postwar communist threat and the means required to meet it was contained in National Security Council (NSC)–7, drafted in March 1948. It emphasized that the continuing goal of

"Soviet-dominated world communism" was nothing less than "the domination of the world." Consistent with Kennan's doctrine of containment, especially with the notion of a finite number of industrial bases capable of enhancing a nation's war potential, NSC-7 argued that such industrial areas must be denied the Soviet Union. "There are in Europe and Asia areas of great potential power which, if added to the existing strength of the Soviet world would enable the latter to become so superior in manpower, resources and territory that the prospects for the survival of the United States as a free nation would be slight."[14] Arguing that the Soviet Union had scored great gains in the preceding few years in expanding its influence and satellite control, NSC-7 concluded that America could no longer remain on the defensive. It must take the lead in organizing a worldwide counteroffensive and increase American military preparedness. The primary emphasis, however, remained with the expansion of American conventional forces with stress being placed upon the need for some form of compulsory military service consistent with Truman's desire for Universal Military Training. America's arms industry ought to be reconstituted, and programs such as the Marshall Plan designed to rebuild Europe should be implemented. With respect to the atomic bomb, uncertainty continued to prevail as to its potential uses. While it was recommended that America should "maintain overwhelming superiority in atomic weapons," it was noted that a future international agreement on the control of nuclear weapons would cause this proposal to be reconsidered.[15]

By the fall of 1948, major changes in both the perception of the global Soviet threat and the relative importance of conventional military defenses versus reliance upon the atomic bomb produced a revision of strategy. By now plans for Universal Military Training had foundered before Congress at a time when the Berlin crisis revealed a Soviet willingness to engage in direct confrontation with the West. Arms negotiations aimed at international control of atomic energy were dead, and the new sources of uranium and better methods of constructing bombs were producing a much expanded American inventory. As a result, NSC-30, drafted in September 1948, placed greater emphasis upon the nuclear weapon as the backbone of military planning. It pointed out that "in the event of hostilities, the National Military Establishment must be ready to utilize promptly and effectively all appropriate means available, including atomic weapons . . . and must plan accordingly." For the first time, the bomb was described as "the present major counterbalance to the ever-present threat of Soviet military power."[16]

If NSC-30 appeared to resolve the dilemma as to which weapons America would rely upon in the event of future war, NSC-20, being discussed at approximately the same time, determined the political goals its use ought to obtain. In its final form as approved by President Truman in November 1948, NSC-20/4 remained America's basic strategic plan until it was replaced by NSC-68 in 1950.

NSC-20 began with a lengthy account of America's containment policy as practiced in peacetime. Its basic objectives were to reduce the power and influence of the Soviet Union to the point where it could no longer mount a threat to world peace and to bring about a fundamental change in Soviet international behavior. The document, however, recognized that war between the powers was possible and that America must have a set of cogent political objectives to be secured if hostilities broke out.

The wartime goals and admonitions contained in this lengthy statement were both negative and positive. Among the things America ought not to attempt were the occupation and administration of the entire territory of the USSR. Since it was unlikely the Soviets would agree to unconditional surrender, America should be prepared for a negotiated peace unlike the situation in the preceding war with Germany. Given the likelihood of protracted negotiations at the war's conclusion, American military forces ought to do all possible to avoid needless antagonism of the Soviet people. "There is a strong possibility that if we were to take the utmost care, within the limits of military feasibility, not to antagonize the Soviet people by military policies which would inflict inordinate hardship and cruelty upon them, there would be an extensive disintegration of Soviet power during a war which progressed favorably from our standpoint."[17]

The positive objectives revolved around reducing Soviet influence both in Eastern Europe and in the world at large which was an objective of America's peacetime containment policy as well. Soviet military influence and dominance in areas contiguous to the USSR ought to be destroyed as well as communist control of those sections of the USSR itself that possessed significant industrial capability for future war making. In the event the Soviet Union dissolved into a number of smaller nations, no resulting political entity ought to be allowed to develop a war-making potential. Aside from these objectives, America should undertake no large-scale decommunization. On liberated territories local authorities that might emerge could decide this issue for themselves.[18]

With the completion of NSC-20/4 and in conjunction with NSC-30, America had progressed a long way from the initial postwar confusion as to who the future enemy might be and the best means available to meet the emerging threat. The importance of the bomb had been recognized by 1948, and NSC-7 had emphasized that America must "maintain overwhelming superiority in atomic weapons." This appeared to constitute no immediate problem since the best estimates from American intelligence were that the USSR would not produce an atomic weapon until well into the next decade. Thus, American goals and means appeared in balance for the foreseeable future.

In the fall of 1949, two major events took place that prompted immediate reconsideration of America's military planning. The Chinese Communists completed their conquest of the mainland, and the Soviet Union tested its first atomic bomb. And if these were not enough to require a major strategic reappraisal, the end of 1949 saw the fruition of America's efforts to support European efforts at self-defense. The North Atlantic Treaty Organization (NATO) became the key institution by which America and its European allies would harmonize policies and objectives to deny the Soviet Union future conquests on the continent. With such momentous events, it was but natural that the secretary to the National Security Council, Adm. Sidney Souers, called for a new appraisal of preferred security doctrines to replace NSC-20.

Souers was not alone in requesting such a review. Following considerable debate, Truman, in late January 1950, approved development of the hydrogen bomb. Appended to the presidential directive was a letter requesting the secretaries of state and defense to begin an overall reassessment of defense and foreign policy, taking into consideration the impact of the "loss of China," the Soviet nuclear test, and the possibilities for defense inherent in the U.S. decision to proceed with the hydrogen weapon. This letter, in turn, shifted the focus of strategic debate from the National Security Council to a joint State-Defense Department committee that included a representative of the Joint Chiefs of Staff.[20]

From the beginning of discussions, the State Department's Policy Planning Committee dominated the talks primarily due to the firm support for the policy debate extended by Secretary of State Dean Acheson. In contrast, Defense Secretary Louis Johnson was a strong advocate of frugality in federal spending that made him an opponent of any new policy that was likely to require increased fiscal outlay. Within the State Department's Policy Planning Committee, the single most important individual was Paul Nitze who, in January 1950, replaced the prior committee chief, George Kennan. Only at the conclusion of the joint committee's deliberations did the resulting document, later named NSC-68, go to the National Security Council for consideration.[21]

Like Kennan's famous "Long Telegram," NSC-68, too, was a response to the demands and confusions of the moment. But NSC-68 had an even more urgent orientation: evaluating the real threat that the Chinese communist victory and the explosion of the Soviet bomb might hold. Since this threat was more immediate than the challenge Kennan had perceived in 1946, the resulting document was much less philosophical, much more a call for action than its predecessor of four years before. In contrast to

Kennan's early pronouncements, NSC-68 argued that the perception of American weakness was as important in the overall global balance as weakness itself. The loss of China was significant because it suggested the forces of communism were on the ascent.

Nitze was later to recall that he was visited by Alexander Sachs, the man who had introduced Albert Einstein to Franklin Roosevelt prior to America's entry into the last war. Sachs brought along a set of charts detailing the Soviet notion of Correlation of Forces, a list of political, military, and economic categories by which Moscow purportedly measured its relative strength against the United States. The fall of China and the detonation of the Soviet bomb, Sachs argued, would be seen as a basic change in these measurements, favoring the Soviet cause. This, in turn, might well impel the Soviets to adopt a decidedly more aggressive military posture. Curiously, Sachs suggested that a military assault upon South Korea was likely.[22] And yet more important than the specific area that might be under direct threat was the notion that with the victory of the Chinese Reds, the distinction between Soviet and communist expansionism was no longer important. The advancement of either produced a corresponding correlation change contrary to American interests.

The second main difference between NSC-68 and Kennan's containment lay in the former's emphasis upon a worst-case scenario. Likely Soviet activities would henceforth be inferred from their actual capabilities to cause harm, not from their intentions or historic traditions, however imperfectly understood. By now the first intelligence reports in the aftermath of the Soviet nuclear explosion predicted that the USSR *might* have as many as 200 atomic bombs by 1954.[23] Although the Soviet delivery capability was known to be small, a crash program in this area, similar to that which had produced the Soviet atomic bomb years before the West had expected it, might soon leave the United States at the mercy of an atomic attack. Responsible security planners, Nitze believed, could not afford to merely argue as to whether this awesome ability would someday be used against the United States. Plans had to be made to ensure America's defense before the actual threat became real.

The third major difference between NSC-68 and the strategic plans that had preceded it concerned assumptions about America's ability to bear a significantly larger fiscal burden on behalf of a comprehensive defense policy. During the Truman administration's first term, defense spending at presidential demand had been held below $15 billion per year. The normal procedure for calculating the size of the defense budget was for the director of budget to estimate likely revenues for a given fiscal year, subtract costs for domestic programs, and allot the remainder to military and aid requests. Even in Truman's second term, the preferred defense figure hovered at about $13.5 billion. Any larger sum, the administration believed, would set off a spiral of inflation, new wage demands, price hikes, and all the accompanying problems of an economy out of control.

In contrast to this orthodox fiscal approach, several key people of the second Truman administration believed that deficit spending on behalf of important national causes would not doom the economy but rather would act as a stimulus. Leon Keysering, eventually appointed charman of the Council of Economic Advisers, argued that economic growth rates would rise in the face of short-term deficits.[24] Such notions were also compatible with Nitze's own beliefs. Unlike Kennan who had spent his life within the foreign service, Nitze was a Harvard-trained investment banker, well acquainted with the possible economic responses to increased defense outlays. Thus, the drafters of NSC-68 felt less constrained than their predecessors. Their goal was to formulate a defense policy adequate to the new threat with less regard as to whether the final document called for spending within conventional ranges.

The final document, which was declassified only in the second half of the seventies, offered four possible American responses to the twin threats of China and the USSR. The first course consisted of doing business as usual without any special provisions for the new challenge. At present, the document noted, America had a respectable military capability. Yet the best information available indicated America's military prowess was declining with respect to the Soviet Union. America was spending between 6 and 7 percent of its gross national product on the military. If one added the investments made by the private sector in factories and equipment that might be converted to defense production in time of war, the figure rose to 20 percent of the gross national product. Estimated Soviet outlays were about 14 and 40 percent respectively. As America's relative strength fell, the danger of war would increase. At first, there might be probing actions short of all-out war as the Soviet bloc tried to measure the West's willingness and ability to resist. The recent conquest of China showed that at current levels of American military spending, communist aggression was far from deterred.[25]

The second course America might select was even more fraught with danger; it could return to its prewar posture of isolationism. This, Nitze acknowledged, was an attractive alternative to some. But if adopted, the likely result would be a Soviet expansion into Europe and Asia, an expansion that might gain success without military confrontation. In such an event, the USSR would acquire an economic and military potential second to none, clearly a danger for the United States. As NSC-68 remarked: "There is no way to make ourselves inoffensive to the Kremlin except by complete submission to its will. Therefore isolation would in the end condemn us to capitulate or to fight alone and on the defensive, with drastically limited offensive and retaliatory capabilities in comparison with the Soviet Union."[26]

A third course, diametrically opposed to isolation, would be consideration of preventive war. And yet this option, too, was fatally flawed. Such a policy would contradict two centuries of American tradition. Even if attempted, it would not guarantee success, since Soviet land power would ensure the overrunning of the European continent and a lengthy conflict of attrition.

With the first three options listed and found wanting, NSC-68, in a pattern that was to become increasingly familiar in policy documents, moved on to the fourth and preferred alternative. This would embrace a rapid buildup of America's political, economic, and military strength in the face of an unprecedented Soviet challenge. Armed forces would be sized to allow confident defense of the Western Hemisphere as well as the essential areas of the world needed to ensure reliable mobilization bases in case of conflict. Lines of communication would be secured, an impossible task with the then reduced size of America's military establishment. Foreign aid to allies would be augumented and the possibilities of the just-created NATO alliance used to the fullest. Scarce resources would be diverted from regular civilian consumption to the degree necessary and reallocated through the mechanism of the national budget to strengthen America's defense might. "In an emergency, the United States could devote upwards of 50 percent of its gross national product to these purposes."[27]

Concomitant with expansion of America's military, diplomatic, and economic capabilities, the fourth option recommended a revitalization of psychological programs aimed at undermining Soviet rule and at convincing Americans about the seriousness of the challenge. A comprehensive effort designed to block the Kremlin's pernicious designs of world conquest would probably include the "development of programs designed to build and maintain confidence among other peoples in our strength and resolution, and to wage overt psychological warfare calculated to encourage mass defections from Soviet allegiance and to frustrate the Kremlin design in other ways."[28]

In an already remarkable document, perhaps this final appeal for increased psychological efforts directed at both friend and foe was the most remarkable of all. Unfortunately, the implementing orders for this generalized section of NSC-68 remained highly classified, precluding detailed discussion of programs subsequently undertaken. Open sources, however, allow some insight into the dimensions of the effort. Thus, Radio Free Europe and Radio Liberty were established in southern Germany to permit regular broadcasts into Soviet and Soviet-controlled territory. In

America itself, and probably in friendly countries as well, programs were initiated to bring the threat of communism directly to the citizens. Rumors suggest that the CIA now established a "private" press, unknown to the public, that would publish "correct" books without detection. Courses on communism were promoted in schools, while CIA funding for Americans traveling to conferences in other lands was provided in cases where ideological debates between opponents and proponents of communism were likely. Hand in hand with increased efforts to persuade the world of the communist evil went an expansion of intelligence gathering so as to better identify and understand the Soviet threat.[29]

When the initial draft of the document was completed in the spring of 1950, it was referred for discussion to the National Security Council by President Truman. Nitze and others had consciously failed to include any estimate of the likely costs of such a peacetime defense expansion, and Truman, still wedded to a Spartan defense budget, needed such information. Secretary of State Dean Acheson privately suggested that the price tag for NSC-68 might reach $50 billion, a figure that, all else being equal, undoubtedly would have left the document stillborn. And yet fate, in the guise of the unanticipated North Korean attack on South Korea in late June 1950, provided a basis for accepting NSC-68 despite its gigantic costs. As Acheson himself later recalled, "It is doubtful whether anything like what happened in the next few years could have been done had not the Russians been stupid enough to have instigated the attack against South Korea and opened the 'hate America' campaign."[30]

By the time of the North Korean attack, NSC-68 had been assigned to the National Security Council and from there forwarded to the Pentagon for estimates of costs. Thus, military planners were already hard at work determining the force structures and increased procurements necessary to accomplish the suggested buildup. Given the unanticipated crisis in Korea that was seen by many as a clear sign of renewed Soviet aggressiveness as predicted in NSC-68, the military planners utilized many of the premises of the document in determining what America's responses must be. Thus, NSC-68 and the urgent demand for reassessment of American security interests in the wake of this new communist attack naturally complemented one another.

The cost issue was quickly submerged in the overall frenzy to augment defense capabilities. In July 1950, with American troops already committed to Korea, Truman asked Congress for a $10.5 billion supplement to the existing defense appropriations. The magic figures of past defense spending were at last broken. Of the new funds, $4.5 billion were to be used in support of the Korean effort, while the remainder would be expended on a general expansion of America's defense capabilities. To Truman and many others, the communist offensive in Korea appeared as a possible feint, designed to involve deeply U.S. troops in the recesses of Asia while other attacks were planned in places more vital to Western interests. Thus, the military buildup encompassed all aspects of America's forces. Given the assumption that Moscow had directed the North Korean advance—a not illogical conclusion since it was known that three thousand Soviet advisers were assigned to the North Korean military—reconsideration of the time frame for a possible all-out Soviet attack was in order. In the final draft of NSC-68, the time of maximum danger was advanced from 1954 to 1952. American defense efforts were advanced correspondingly.[31]

There are a number of ways by which the impact of NSC-68 and the Korean War can be measured, the national budget being one of the most explicit. Following the suggestion of military revitalization, the Truman administration drastically increased the revenues collected by the federal government. In fiscal year 1950, $36.5 billion flowed into Washington through the taxing agencies. In 1951 the figure rose to over $47 billion, reaching in excess of $61 billion by fiscal year 1952. Allocation of these funds also revealed the new efforts to enhance defense preparedness. Expenditures for nonsecurity programs declined from almost $22 billion in fiscal 1950 to just over $18 billion in fiscal 1952. Allocations to defense rose from $22 billion in fiscal 1951 to over $50 billion in fiscal 1953. And yet while such figures suggest the overall magnitude of the response, the actual changes in America's force procurements show more clearly the perceived intensity of the threat and the strategy designed to meet it.[32]

In June 1950, on the eve of the North Korean attack, the American armed forces consisted of 10 understrength army divisions, 11 army regimental combat teams, 2 understrength marine divisions, a 671-ship navy, and 48 air wings. A total of 1,461,000 Americans were under arms. The demands of NSC-68, intensified by the assumed threat of near future communist aggression in the wake of the Korean invasion prompted military planners to accentuate America's retaliatory capability and to increase ground forces committed to NATO since the Korean events were perceived as a possible prelude to an all-out invasion in Europe. In December 1950 the final draft of NSC-68 called for major changes in U.S. force levels with a target date for readiness set at July 1952. By that time America was to have 18 army divisions and 12 regimental combat teams.[33] In fact, by the summer of 1952, these levels were achieved. The navy was to reach 1,161 ships; 1,130 were actually deployed by the target date. While there were to be 2.5 marine divisions in place, 3 were deployed by July 1952. The goal of 95 air force wings was met. All told, 3,600,000 Americans were projected as being under arms by mid-1952. In fact, 3,636,000 were in place by the proposed date.[34]

While some of the military expansion mentioned above could be credited solely to the Korean emergency, the actual deployment of these new forces showed how deeply NSC-68 and planning for the Korean War had intertwined. Aware of possible parallels between North Korea/South Korea and East Germany/West Germany and convinced that a new wave of aggressiveness was sweeping the Soviet bloc, America focused its attention upon meeting a Soviet challenge in Europe. In the fall of 1950, America began open advocacy for the rearming of West Germany and the admission of German troops to NATO. In November of the same year, the American Seventh Army was reactivated to form the command structure of the 4 American divisions assigned to European defense the following spring. In 1951 an integrated command for NATO was established with Gen. Dwight Eisenhower being designated the first commander.

Preparedness on the ground both in Asia and in Europe was but one part of the military revitalization. Assets also flowed into America's capability to retaliate at the nuclear level, with the Strategic Air Command (SAC) being the major beneficiary. Established in 1946, SAC, now under Gen. Curtis LeMay, received greatly increased quantities of an improved B-36 bomber and of the new B-47 medium jet bombers. This enhanced emphasis upon America's ability to bring nuclear destruction to the Soviet Union proper was the first stage in a drastic expansion of such capabilities, culminating several years later in the "New Look" doctrine of the Eisenhower administration.[36]

Hand in hand with such efforts to prepare the American military for a possible global conflict went attempts to persuade the American public of the dangers the new era possessed. A major program was mounted to ensure public support for a reallocation of federal funds unprecedented in a period when war had not officially been declared. But the implementing orders governing this campaign remain classified in Washington, and only unconfirmed speculation as well as the personal remembrances of those who lived through this period suggest the size of this effort. There can be no doubt, however, that by the end of the Truman administration in 1952 few Americans had any doubts about who their main enemy was or about the likelihood that the Soviet Union would find military weakness in the postwar world an excuse for expansion. Maintaining America's national security during periods of peace as well as during war would henceforth be the single most important item of national concern.

6

The Shifting Soviet
Threat of the Fifties

The postwar doctrine of containment emphasized the political threat of
Soviet communism with diminished concern for Soviet military power. As
Kennan foresaw, despite a good deal of bluster and bravado, Moscow
pursued a constrained and cautious military policy in the last half of the
forties. Eastern Europe remained to be pacified, and in some newly
acquired areas, such as the western Ukraine, armed resistance plagued
Soviet efforts at pacification into the next decade. By the late forties, a
strong Soviet presence in the newly created satellite states was still necessary due to massive purges aimed at removing the last of the homegrown
Communists. But all this was about to change.

At the conclusion of the war, Soviet forces embraced approximately 12
million men under arms, arranged into some 500 divisions.[1] According to
an often quoted article by party chief Nikita Khruschchev, these forces
were diminished to just under 3 million men at arms by 1948 as the USSR
returned to its more peaceful goal of increasing the national economy.[2]
While there appears to be good cause to accept this Soviet figure, U.S.
intelligence sources in the late forties continued to posit force levels with
much greater numbers, suggesting that Moscow retained between 4 and 5
million soldiers through the decade, arranging them into some 175 divisions. About 30 Soviet divisions were located in Eastern Europe and
consisted of about 500,000 men.[3]

In contrast, American force levels shrank to under 1.5 million by 1947
while units capable of resisting a Soviet advance in Europe consisted of 10
poorly coordinated American, British, and French divisions. Equally
ominous, the ever-present Soviet draft continued to induct three-quarters
of a million Soviet citizens into the military each year, returning an equal

number to the rapidly expanding Soviet reserve forces.[4] Thus, despite some suggestions of immediate postwar Soviet partial demobilization, Western leaders felt compelled to credit the USSR with strength far in excess of that needed for mere internal security.

Soviet postwar military planning emphasized the importance of a future conventional conflict similar to the recent one. As the leader in all important areas of thought, Stalin contributed the essential principles of military preparedness premised largely upon the successful conflict with Germany and took little official account of the new atomic age. The permanent operating factors included the stability of the home front, the morale of the army, the quantity and quality of Soviet divisions, the equipment of the army, and the organizational ability of the army commanders. First enunciated in the fall of 1941 so as to deny the importance of surprise at a time when Soviet troops were being pushed backward by the unanticipated German assault, these principles appeared to confirm Western speculations that a new war would find Soviet troops in a rapid conventional attack on Europe.[5] America, in turn, adapted its own postwar planning to these assumptions, believing that a rapid withdrawal of troops from the continent would be required in the first days of any future East-West conflict. And consistent with this Soviet threat to hold Europe hostage to any American nuclear attack on his own homeland, Stalin, in the late forties, began improving his conventional forces.

From 1949 through 1953, the readiness and the number of Soviet troops assigned to European duties increased. The key attack group consisted of 30 Soviet divisions stationed in the satellite states, possessing full complements of men and equipment and set at high levels of preparedness for battle. The most ominous of these forces were the Group of Soviet Forces, Germany (GSFG) that numbered about 400,000 through most of the fifties. Following the Berlin Blockade and the improvement of the war-damaged Soviet economy, these units were reorganized and reequipped. Mobility and firepower were greatly enhanced due to the creation of motorized infantry sections and the addition of more armored units. By 1952 and 1953, the new and highly respected T-54 tank was replacing the wartime T-34. By now the Soviet general, Vasili Chiukov, held command in East Germany of 10 mechanized, 4 motorized, and 8 Soviet tank divisions. The new jet-driven MIG 15s were beginning to appear with the GSFG, and by the end of 1952, the Soviet Twenty-fourth Air Army in East Germany had an estimated inventory of 1,700 planes, including 500 MIG 15s and over 200 IL-28 jet bombers. The following year the MIG 17 made its appearance.[6]

Other Soviet forces stationed outside the frontiers included the Northern Group in Poland and the Southern Group in the area of Austria-

Hungary-Romania, embracing another 100,000 soldiers with their own tactical air units. And behind them stood an estimated 50 to 60 Soviet divisions located in the western military districts of the USSR itself. According to Soviet figures, the military went from some 2.8 million in 1948 to just under 5.8 million by 1955, almost an exact doubling of men under arms.[7]

The growth of the Soviet army alone was enough to inspire concern in the late Truman and early Eisenhower administrations. But when added to Soviet efforts to reconstitute the prewar Eastern European armies, Soviet policy appeared to confirm the deep apprehensions written into NSC-68 as to the likelihood of a new period of Soviet aggressiveness. For the first few years after the war, Soviet policy had focused upon ending objections to its rule in the satellite region. But beginning in 1949 a major rebuilding and reorganization of the Eastern European forces became the new focal point of Moscow's demands. The armies of the new "Peoples Democracies" were modeled upon Soviet forces, with detailed liaison and control established to ensure total loyalty to communist ideals. Eastern European military leaders were trained in the best Soviet academies, and in Poland Soviet general Konstantin Rokossovsky, hero of the Soviet army, was appointed minister of defense. Large quantities of surplus military equipment were transferred from the Soviet Union, increasing standardization among all Eastern European forces. By 1953 these forces were estimated at 1.5 million men arranged into 65 to 80 divisions. About half of this force was considered well trained and combat ready. In East Germany, an area that would undoubtedly experience fighting if a new conflict erupted, the paramilitary forces of the *Volkspolizei* (Peoples Police) were expanded to 100,000 men in 1953 and arranged in 7 divisions. Three years later the Peoples Police officially becme the nucleus of the National Peoples Army.[8]

The dramatic expansion of Soviet land forces in the first years of the fifties was matched by significant changes in the navy. Traditionally, the Soviet Union had possessed little sea capability aside from a few units designed to guard coastal waters. But in 1950 a separate ministry of the navy was established, indicating the start of a long campaign to one day challenge America's naval superiority. The magnitude of the initial efforts can be seen in comparisons of ship numbers between 1945 and 1953. At the war's end, the Soviet navy was primarily a limited coastal force, possessing but 3 cruisers and between 20 and 30 destroyers. But by 1953, just three years after establishing the new naval ministry, the Soviets possessed 15 cruisers and 60 destroyers as well as about 300 submarines, half of which were oceangoing. The advent to power of Nikita Khrushchev after 1953 caused a shift in naval priorities consistent with the needs of the new nuclear era. By 1964, the time of Khrushchev's "retirement," the Soviet navy included 19 cruisers, over 100 destroyers with numerous destroyer escorts, and 400 patrol boats, many with short-range surface-to-surface missiles. Also, 400 submarines were in the Soviet naval inventory, 40 of which were nuclear powered and carried ballistic missiles. Nearly 800 modern aircraft had joined the naval air arm, 500 of which were bombers.[9]

The fifties witnessed a major expansion of Soviet air units capable of intercepting any attacking force at the very time America was giving increased stress to nuclear retaliation in the event of war. With a moderate level of antiaircraft and interception capability at the close of the war, the Soviet Union began a major buildup, responding, no doubt, to the growing importance of nuclear attack in postwar American strategy. By 1953 the Soviet interceptor force consisted exclusively of new, jet-driven planes and numbered about 2,000 aircraft. Problems remained in the area of night fighting and poor-weather interception, but these, too, were addressed in ongoing force improvements. In 1955 a major reorganization created a distinct antiaircraft service named the PVO-Stranny. It was quickly provided with modern, all-weather interceptors, the MIG-19 and YAK-25. The supersonic MIG-21 soon followed. By the early sixties, the PVO-Stranny possessed 4,000 modern interceptors. And yet this was only one aspect of the new threat to any foreign effort designed to deliver bombs on Soviet targets. Hand in hand with the drastic expansion of in-flight interceptors went efforts to construct an impenetrable ring of surface-to-air missiles (SAMs) around key cities. By the mid-fifties such a shield of SAM-1s was in place around Moscow. By the end of the decade, SAMs were in place throughout the USSR.[10]

While the growth of conventional forces illustrated well the new Soviet drive for military parity with America, it was the Soviet atomic program in conjunction with efforts to develop a long-range Soviet bomber capable of hitting American targets that prompted the greatest anxiety in the West. We now know that German attempts to split the atom in the late thirties were followed with intense interest in the Soviet Union, the initial center of nuclear research being the laboratories of Igor Kurchatov in the Leningrad Physicotechnical Institute. In April 1939 two of Kurchatov's colleagues showed that nuclear fission produced an excess of neutrons that might subsequently be used in a chain reaction. The following year, at Kurchatov's suggestion, the Soviet Academy of Sciences established a Uranium Commission.[11]

By 1942 the political leaders of the Soviet Union began to show interest in this new area, with Stalin and Foreign Minister Molotov holding meetings with key nuclear scientists. Kurchatov was selected as project director in the effort to develop an atomic bomb and suggested that such a device might be ready within ten to twenty years. By the end of 1943, 50 people were working with Kurchatov; by 1944, 100. The following spring Kurchatov's research had progressed to the point that a reactor capable of producing the important element plutonium was under design. In August 1945, in response to renewed requests from Stalin to advance the date when an explosive device might be ready, Kurchatov and his fellow workers set their sights on 1950.[12]

Concomitant with the development of an atomic bomb, the Soviets concentrated great energy upon designing a new vehicle that might deliver the weapon to its target. As early as the thirties, the USSR had made important strides in rocket engineering and in radar, but the purges of that decade had decimated the involved personnel. During the war against Germany, rocket research concentrated upon short-range models useful in conjunction with the advance of ground troops, and the Katyusha rocket became a hallmark of the Soviet army. The appearance of the German V-1 and V-2 rockets in the summer of 1944 rekindled Soviet interest in such systems, and a special Rocket Council under Dmitry Ustinov was created. Stalin showed personal interest in this branch of military research as well, meeting with the scientists working in the new council.[13]

In 1947 the first Soviet long-range rocket modeled upon the German V-2, the R-1, was successfully tested; this was a harbinger of the time when advancement in nuclear weapons technology and rocket developments would combine to create the first realistic threat to American cities. In late August 1949, the Soviets detonated their first atomic bomb. Four years later, in August 1953, they exploded a thermonuclear weapon. A new era was dawning. And yet, in the short run, it was not the threat of long-range rockets tipped with nuclear devices that concerned Washington but rather advances in the Soviet bomber program that might create a more conventional means of destroying the American way of life.[14]

At the time of Stalin's death in March 1953, the USSR possessed a limited-delivery capability for its new atomic weapons, a capability focused primarily upon Western Europe. The Soviet bomber fleet consisted of a piston-drive medium bomber (Tu-4) copied from the American B-29. With no forward bases outside Eastern Europe and with poor refueling ability, the Tu-4 could reach American targets only in one-way flight at slow speeds. A medium-range jet bomber was just entering service in 1953 as a follow-on plane keyed also to European contingencies.[15]

In the next two years, however, the Soviets deployed two new bombers with true intercontinental ranges: the four turbo-jet Bison and the multi-turbo-propeller Bear. On Aviation Day in 1955, the Soviets staged a flyover of their new planes that produced consternation in the West. Numerous Bison turbo-jets flew by in perfect formation, causing American intelligence to reexamine their projected figures as to the likely expansion of the

Soviet bomber threat. Secretary of Defense Neil McElroy later confirmed that revised American estimates predicted the Soviets would have 600 to 700 Bisons by the end of the decade. Thus began the famous episode of the "bomber gap" as well as frantic U.S. efforts to expand its own long-range aviation program. As later evidence would show, the lengthy flyby of Bisons had been a Soviet trick designed to impress the West and was accomplished by flying the same planes in wave after wave above the startled spectators.[16] In fact, Soviet efforts were even then shifting from manned carriers of atomic weapons to the more sophisticated intermediate- and long-range rockets. Regardless of intent or accuracy of reporting, the Soviet deception produced a major response. President Eisenhower, following a request from Congress, greatly expanded American procurement of the new, intercontinental B-52 bombers, setting delivery targets at a full twenty a month. With this new program went increased concerns for civil defense and the ability of America to survive a nuclear war. To further complicate the issue, in 1955 American intelligence sources detected Soviet testing of an 800-mile medium-range ballistic missile. A special committee headed by MIT president James Killian, hastily assembled to analyze these new Soviet developments, glumly reported that by the sixties the Soviet Union would achieve a decisive lead in strategic weapons.[17]

The anticipated bomber gap, the explosion of a Soviet hydrogen bomb, and the initial tests of a medium-range ballistic missile capable of destroying American bases in Europe stimulated increased anxiety in Washington. And yet the menace of Soviet strategic capabilities was only partially recognized. The following year, in 1956, the USSR began deployment of intermediate-range ballistic missiles capable of reaching targets as far away as the British Isles. By the early sixties, the number of such missiles exceeded 700. Even more ominous, intelligence detected the first test of a Soviet intercontinental missile in 1956. The following year a regular testing facility for these new vehicles was identified. In October 1957 the Soviets launched man's first orbiting satellite in an impressive display of missile mastery. Revised American estimates in the wake of the Sputnik success suggested that a crash program might deliver 100 Soviet intercontinental ballistic missiles (ICBMs) to various staging sites by 1960; 500 by 1961.[18]

While the mere launching of Sputnik in 1957 was enough to cause great concern in the West, Khrushchev dramatically expanded such worries by his constant reiteration of Soviet superiority. Even prior to Sputnik, Khrushchev bragged that the Soviet Union possessed the ability to send missiles to any part of the world. In the fall of 1957, as the world began recovering from the surprise of Sputnik, Khrushchev informed American reporters, "I think that it is no secret that there now exists a range of missiles with the aid of which it is possible to fulfill any assignment of operational and strategic importance."[19] And the Soviet press quickly picked up such claims of superiority, alleging that a fundamental shift in the correlation of forces between East and West had occurred. The advent of Soviet intercontinental rocketry, Khrushchev's press asserted, had eclipsed any prior American military advantage, and U.S. forces now stood vulnerable to direct attack. Such claims were accorded a most serious hearing within the United States itself. In January 1959 a *New York Times* article based on discussions with officials who had "intimate knowledge of [U.S.] defense efforts" detailed the following anticipated imbalance between U.S. and Soviet ICBMs: 1960—100–30; 1961—500–70; 1962—1,000–130; 1963—1,500–130.[20]

As luck would have it, an important presidential committee considering America's defense posture was meeting at the very time the Soviets launched their first artificial satellite. Headed by Rowen Gaither, chairman of the Rand Corporation, the group had initially convened to consider prospects for expanded civil defense in the wake of the Soviet nuclear buildup. But the new success in Soviet rocketry quickly produced a change in emphasis to include the entire range of threats to the American system. The committee's final report predicted that America would become a second-class power if it failed to keep pace with Soviet advances. Even if a maximum effort were now mounted, the Soviet lead in intercontinental ballistic missiles could not be matched until the early sixties. Indeed, the Soviets were perceived as rapidly approaching the point where they could successfully cripple America's main deterrent—the Strategic Air Command (SAC)—upon which the burden of Eisenhower's strategy of massive retaliation rested. As the Gaither committee reported, "By 1959, the USSR may be able to launch an attack with ICBMs carrying megaton warheads, against which SAC will be almost completely vulnerable under present programs."[21] Soviet air defenses were also increasing in both number and effectiveness, further imperiling an American defensive strategy predicated upon threats to devastate the USSR in response to Soviet aggression. Two centuries of America's near imperviousness to direct attack appeared at an end, and the danger of a future Soviet assault upon the American homeland henceforth became a terrifying possibility.

The dramatic augmentation of weapons and organization characterizing the Soviet armed forces in the fifties was but one aspect of the enhanced threat as perceived in the West. In this decade the very rules of the game appeared to change as the Soviet/communist influence transcended the Iron Curtain states to menace the entire globe. In the half decade following World War II, the primary areas of communist subversion were restricted to Eastern Europe where, one by one, the heretofore traditional states from Poland to Bulgaria adopted constitutions modeled upon their Soviet master. Each of these states had well-demarcated frontiers, and George Kennan's containment policy fit well into an orderly European world in which America's allies possessed a common resolve to maintain their freedom. By the end of the decade, the formation of NATO and the fruits of the Marshall Plan provided real hope that communist expansion had been forestalled.

The difficulty with the fifties was that the communist threat now imperiled areas far distant from the traditional regions of Russian dominance. The communist victory in China created a new, powerful center of potential subversion, and the entry of Chinese "volunteers" into Korea showed Peking possessed both resolve and capability to challenge American interests. The presence of three thousand Soviet military advisers in North Korea at the time of the invasion of the South and the 1950 signing of the Chinese-Soviet Security Treaty suggested deep collusion between revolutionary communist states bent upon gaining world dominance. And as the decade continued, rebels in Indochina and in other parts of the world appeared as beneficiaries of this new, global communist drive, receiving weapons and diplomatic support. In the fifties there was rapid decolonization, and both China and the USSR claimed to possess the preferred model for newly independent states searching for a means of national development. If such new nations were to become communist, the threat to American security interests would clearly grow. Even a movement toward neutrality among the third world states would imperil raw materials vital to the American economy and defense efforts.

Contemporary historians have frequently chastised the Eisenhower administration for failing to perceive the early signs of Sino-Soviet discord and for neglecting to examine indigenous causes for the wave of socialist ideas that apparently surfaced in the newly decolonized states. And yet such confusion can be viewed not as an example of American ignorance but as a result of careful study of Marxist-Leninist doctrine proudly trumpeted from both Moscow and Peking. Indeed, the perceived threat of world communism rested upon the firm basis of the communist classics, augmented by the confident chiding of spokesmen who glimpsed a unique opportunity to advance their cause amid the confusion and turmoil accompanying the withdrawal of the capitalist West from its colonial domains. To many propagandists in Moscow, the blurring of distinctions between communist states and third world revolutionary movements, as well as the emergence of a worldwide revolutionary movement, was an anticipated development well enshrined in Marxist thought. In part, it was the serious study of such ideas in the West that complicated the task of identifying national and international motives in the new revolutionary situation.

To Marx and his followers, nationalism and the conventional national state of the modern era were but transitory phenomena on the long road to communism. As Marx argued, the notion of nationalism was hardly present in the Middle Ages, and the states of that time united their citizens by appeals to a common religion rather than to a common nationality. Few medieval states coincided with the distribution of any given national group. Only in the eighteenth century did the ideology of nationalism emerge, with the French Revolution being its most noticeable manifestation.

The belated triumph of nationalism over the more medieval traditions of religion and monarchy was, to Marx, far from accidental. Nationalism was the chosen creed of the newly emerging capitalist class, and it functioned to increase trade and profit. Nationalism destroyed the artificial barriers within states that, in the medieval period, had sanctioned regional trade and prevented manufacturing and marketing for the nation as a whole. Nationalism had also provided an alternative to religion, furthering a sense of belonging among the people within the new nation-state. And yet to Marx such developments were but a stage in the eventual conquest of socialism. By promoting capitalism, nationalism assisted the growth of the working class as well. And as the main opponent of capitalism, the working class would reject nationalistic appeals, preferring instead to join forces with fellow workers regardless of what country they inhabited. Thus, for a modern worker, the slogan "workers of the world, unite," would replace the capitalist's reliance upon a common language and a national tradition.

Eventually, the working class would be victorious in its struggle, and the nation-states so evident in the twentieth century would be replaced by a large federation representing the world's proletariat. As a step to such a transformation, Moscow called upon the world's workers to abandon their love of country and to replace it with a love of working-class ideals. In the struggle with the capitalists, workers must join hands, put aside petty, national values, and advance the *common* cause of all. Local communist parties in the new third world states were admonished to proclaim their eternal loyalty to Moscow as the center of the victorious workers' movement.[22] In such a situation, the evident confusion among Western security planners as to where Soviet expansionism left off and local communism began is more understandable. The world increasingly appeared to possess a common revolutionary pattern directed and controlled from Moscow. The dilemma for the fifties was to design deterrence strategies that would prevent the emergence of new communist states regardless of whether they appeared to be the result of open expansion by one of the two existing communist giants or the result of outside subversion in combination with indigenous revolutionary movements pledging allegiance to Moscow or Peking. Clearly, different strategies of containment would be needed, depending upon the relative balance of external and internal communist efforts. Interestingly, the most successful of the deterrence strategies developed were those that treated the USSR and China as traditional nation-states despite their propaganda to the contrary.

At the start of the new decade, the immediate challenge to Western interests emerged from the newly consolidated Chinese communist regime in Peking. In the late fall of 1950, Chinese "volunteers" crossed the Yalu River that formed the border between Manchuria and Korea, directly engaging American forces. This intervention had been preceded by what, in retrospect, was a clear warning that China would feel threatened if United Nations and American forces approached its Manchurian border. After a period in which American troops retreated toward South Korea, the Chinese offensive gave way to armistice talks. These talks were still going on when the Eisenhower administration assumed power. [23]

While the new political leaders in Washington were as convinced as their predecessors that a worldwide communist effort to subvert freedom was in operation, their specific efforts to solve the Korean problem involved somewhat different techniques. China was correctly perceived as the main bulwark of communist expansion in Northeast Asia, and efforts were made to convince Peking that its best interests would be served by terminating the conflict. In short, China was approached not as the center of an amorphous, worldwide conspiracy but as a traditional state with its own complex calculus of benefits and losses. In February 1953 the Eisenhower administration indirectly but unambiguously informed China that further delays in the truce negotiations would enlarge the scale of the war. In short order, Chinese concessions at the talks produced tentative agreement of several key points for a future agreement. When, several months later, Chinese objections to the free exchange of prisoners once again threatened the discussions, Washington let it be known that a resumption of full-scale war on the peninsula might well include American use of nuclear weapons. To show its resolve, America made no effort to disguise the movement of missiles with atomic warheads to the island of Okinawa. Once again, Peking appeared to grasp the message, accepting at the next session the disputed clause on prisoner exchanges. By late July an armistice had been signed. [24]

The breathing space allowed by the termination of the Korean conflict lasted little over a year, with the new threat again being mounted by Peking. In the fall of 1954, Chinese artillery positions on the mainland began a systematic shelling of the Chinese nationalist island of Quemoy. Quemoy, which lay only two miles from the mainland port of Amoy, was garrisoned by 50,000 troops loyal to Chiang Kai-shek, and its loss might function as a sign that communism was on the ascent in Asia.

In the midst of the shelling, the Eisenhower administration completed a treaty with the Chinese Nationalists, pledging to defend the main nationalist stronghold of Taiwan and "such other territories as may be determined by mutual agreement." They hoped that this intended ambiguity concerning Quemoy and other nationalist-held islands would dissuade further communist encroachment. But in January 1955 when the Communists attacked one of the nationalist-held Tachen islands some two hundred miles north of Taiwan in a possible test of American intentions, Eisenhower took stronger action. A resolution was hurried through Congress giving the president authority to commit U.S. troops to the defense of Taiwan and "closely related localities." As the crisis deepened in March 1955, Secretary of State John Foster Dulles informed the press that America was prepared to use tactical nuclear weapons if need be, a pledge reaffirmed by Eisenhower himself the following day. Shortly thereafter, the communist leadership expressed an interest in ending the crisis by negotiations, a suggestion that led to direct American-Chinese talks first at Geneva and later in Warsaw. For the moment, the possibility of conflict had passed.[25]

In the fall of 1958, the troubles surrounding the offshore island of Quemoy as well as the island of Matsu again became headlines. In August the Chinese Communists unleashed a major bombardment, with shellfire being so intense as to constitute an effective blockade of the targeted islands. Equally ominous was the enthusiasm with which the Chinese Communists now demanded return of all nationalist-held territory, a result of the startling success the previous fall of the first artificial satellite launched by the Soviet Union and the belief that the correlation of forces had once again shifted in communism's favor. In late August 1958, Chinese spokesmen called for the surrender of the nationalist garrison on Quemoy, and early the next month Soviet party chief Khrushchev cautioned that an attack on the Chinese Peoples Republic was an attack on the Soviet Union. Rarely in postwar history had the Marxist doctrine proclaiming the unity of communist goals independent of the "national" interests of the respective sovereign states appeared so evident. And yet the American response was selected as if such a unity was a secondary matter.

The American Seventh Fleet in Chinese waters was quickly put on alert and reinforced with two aircraft carriers. Secretary of State Dulles issued a thinly clad statement suggesting that atomic weapons might be employed in any conflict, and the American marines began to move cannons capable of firing nuclear projectiles to Quemoy itself. In October the Communists declared a one-week cease-fire, allowing the resupply of nationalist troops on Quemoy, and the crisis soon passed. By all appearances, treating Peking and, by inference, Moscow as traditional states anxious to avoid destruction and to resolve problems by means other than conflict was effective regardless of ceaseless propaganda proclaiming the transcending importance of the world proletariat and its overriding interests.[26]

In contrast to the two Quemoy crises and the intervention of Chinese troops in Korea, the Eisenhower administration's ability to design effective deterrence strategies where indigenous communist movements were engaged in revolutionary activity was much less apparent. This became painfully obvious early in the decade in a region that would one day put the power and prestige of America to a total test—Indochina.

Indochina, composed of the states of Vietnam, Laos, and Cambodia, presented a challenge in the postwar world that admitted few easy solutions. By the beginning of the fifties, a bloody war was in progress between the French who were attempting to reimpose their prewar colonial rule and an indigenous resistance in which communist and nationalist motives were deeply intertwined. Initially, America had pursued a neutral position in this conflict, but as the Soviet threat in Europe became more intense, the Truman administration had increased its support for its French ally. Clearly, no conventional defense of the European continent was possible without strong French participation, and such participation was impossible given the continuing French commitments in far-off Indochina. In January 1950 the new Chinese communist government in Peking extended recognition to the communist-led Democratic Republic of Vietnam, once again suggesting a tight linkage between world communist movements and ideals. This, in turn, led to enhanced American support for the French cause, and by 1954 America was providing 78 percent of the French military budget. That same year a small number of American technicians were dispatched to Southeast Asia.[27]

In early 1954 the French forces in Vietnam approached a major crisis. With a significant portion of their troops surrounded in the Vietnamese city of Dien Bien Phu, the French chief of staff flew to Washington to request a bombing strike by U.S. planes. While such assistance was supported by the American head of the Joint Chiefs of Staff, Adm. Arthur Radford, it gained little support from other U.S. leaders or from the president. To Eisenhower, deeply concerned with the deteriorating situation in Vietnam, such American intervention would be foolish on both military and political grounds. With no clear opposition government to attack and a decentralized rebel infrastructure, air assaults alone would have limited long-range effects. And yet Eisenhower's political restraints upon possible direct intervention were even more stringent. Only with the approval of Congress, pledges of support from America's more important allies, and a French commitment to major reform in the region would Eisenhower consider armed involvement. When the British refused to consider sending troops to the region before negotiations, and with the fall of Dien Bien Phu, the issue of Vietnam's future moved to the bargaining table at Geneva. Here it was decided that Vietnam would be temporarily divided at the seventeenth parallel, with national elections in two years to decide the country's future. While the American representatives at Geneva were not directly involved in the discussions, they did promise not to act so as to "disturb" the agreements by "threat or the use of force."[28]

Such promises, however, could not conceal the continuing anxiety in Washington as to the likely fate of the region if the Geneva agreements were fulfilled; Eisenhower himself noted that the communist leader, Ho Chi Minh, would probably receive 80 percent of the vote in any national election.[29] With the French now removed from control, the Eisenhower administration quickly took their place, shoring up the new, anticommunist South Vietnamese government with extensive economic and military aid.

A condition of possible American intervention in 1954 had been the active participation of America's allies in any such venture. Now with the French having given way, Secretary of State Dulles carefully crafted an alliance designed to resist a communist threat in the region. The new grouping, entitled the Southeast Asia Treaty Organization (SEATO), soon identified Indochina as an area where the threat of revolutionary change would endanger the security of all SEATO signatories. In 1956 when the South Vietnamese government refused to abide by the Geneva agreements that required national elections, it knew it could count upon at least tacit regional support and continued American military and economic aid. And yet, while this American strategy appeared effective in avoiding the immediate loss of South Vietnam to communism, it provided no effective solution to the inevitable outbreak of a new war. Communist-led forces of resistance began once more to regroup for action.[30]

The difficulty in determining where indigenous nationalistic-radical movements within the decolonizing postwar would began and outside communist influence left off was not limited to Southeast Asia. If one took into account the very survival of the industrial economies of the West, the loss of Indochina would cause minimal hardship. But such was not the case in the Middle East where the British found it increasingly difficult to fulfill their traditional directing and stabilizing role. By the mid-fifties, Middle East oil was estimated at 70 percent of the world's known reserves, supplying nearly 75 percent of the oil actually used in Western Europe. And yet by 1956 this region particularly seemed in uncertain turmoil. Despite a 1954 British-Egyptian agreement that foresaw the evacuation of all British troops from the Suez Canal area by the close of 1956, the Egyptians nationalized the canal that summer, provoking a joint British-French-Israeli attack that failed for lack of American support. That spring Jordan, a traditional ally of Britain, expelled the British head of its armed forces and appeared to move toward an alliance with the radical leadership of Syria.

With such rearranging of traditional relationships in the offing, the

Soviet Union quickly presented itself as an alternative to reliance upon the former colonial powers, drastically expanding its assistance programs to Syria, Turkey, the Sudan, and Yemen. Thus, if the USSR was not the sole cause of the evident instability that threatened the future of fuels vital to the Western democracies, it appeared to be both a supporter of such changes and an obvious beneficiary. For the Eisenhower administration, the question was how to prevent the clear slide toward neutralism and, perhaps, communism in a crucial region of the world. How might one deter radical movements supported by, but not controlled from, Moscow or Peking?[31]

The answer to this dilemma was the Eisenhower Doctrine, which was requested by the president in January 1957 and passed into law two months later. In essence, it possessed three main points. First, the executive branch was authorized to assist any Middle East state in developing its economic potential so as to strengthen national independence. Second, authorization was also given to permit military assistance to any regional state that might request it. And third, the doctrine asserted that America considered the preservation of the independence and integrity of the Middle Eastern states as vital to U.S. national interests. "To this end, if the President determines the necessity thereof, the United States is prepared to use armd forces to assist any nation or group of such nations requesting assistance against armed aggression from any country controlled by international communism."[32]

While this new declaration at first sight appeared to be a dramatic expansion of pledges contained in the earlier Truman Doctrine, its potential application was much less clear. The Truman Doctrine had focused upon two states, Turkey and Greece, both of whom were known to desire American aid. In both the threat—an open rebellion in Greece, external pressure in Turkey—was relatively clear-cut. In the Middle East, however, it was the ambiguity of the threat that formed its most distinctive characteristic. In the fall of 1957, for example, Syria began receiving major shipments of Soviet military assistance, causing concern both in Washington and in some Middle East states. While the American Sixth Fleet was rapidly dispatched to the eastern Mediterranean, there was little hope of any state "requesting" American assistance as required by the new doctrine. And in the sole case where such aid was requested and was subsequently dispatched, the threat was so different than that foreseen that Eisenhower himself was unable to invoke his own doctrine as a justification.

This occasion was the 1958 landing of American marines in Lebanon following the violent overthrow of the pro-Western monarchy in nearby Iraq. Understandably uncertain as to what policy the new Iraqi regime might follow and having been asked to send troops to Beirut due to an internal dispute between the Lebanese president and his parliament, Eisenhower acted quickly. And yet this action could not be justified by reference to the Eisenhower Doctrine since there was no "armed aggression from any country controlled by international communism." Instead, Eisenhower explained to Congress that his goals had been the protection of American civilians in Lebanon and the preservation of Lebanon's territorial integrity. Later the White House cited Article 51 of the United Nations Charter, the article dealing with collective defense, as the basis for its action. By years' end American troops were withdrawn from Lebanon as were British troops dispatched at the same time to Jordan. The newly elected Lebanese government quickly rejected the Eisenhower Doctrine as a source for its protection, and the Arab states sponsored a joint resolution in the United Nations forswearing interference in each other's internal affairs.[33]

By the end of the decade, it was increasingly apparent that the real threats to stability in the emerging third world could only occasionally be met by traditional methods of deterring outside states from direct interference in their neighbors' affairs. But this was not to argue that no threat existed. Whether it be communist or nationalist movements, instability in the third world might wreak havoc among the raw material–poor nations of Europe, producing situations of opportunity for the eventual penetration of Moscow and Peking. What was needed was a more sophisticated approach to maintaining a pro-Western balance among the warring factions, groups, and tribes struggling for power within these new states. It was in this direction that the presidents following Eisenhower quickly moved.

7

Military Planning
under Eisenhower

The successful republican challenge to twenty years of democratic rules in Washington brought with it new ideas about how America ought to structure its defensive forces in the continuing fight against communism. Actually, the Eisenhower administration had a number of positive and negative goals in this area, reflecting the different values among republican politicians as well as the disagreements between the factions within the party itself. To Eisenhower, long an advocate of an active international policy, a key objective was to overrule calls for a more isolationist international stance, calls that were deeply rooted among the more conservative Republicans led by Sen. Robert Taft. Having served as army chief of staff in the early postwar years and as the first supreme allied commander of NATO, Eisenhower wished to maintain America's global presence as the main deterrence to communist expansion.

The American deterrent, however, would have to be purchased and structured at lower levels of expense. Perhaps more than any postwar president, Eisenhower had an abiding concern for the values and beliefs that he felt had made America strong, values such as thrift and frugality. To him military outlays were by their very nature nonproductive, usurping raw materials and skills better used to satisfy the needs of a growing population. If military expenses increased, so would the budget. The dependence of the people upon government spending, in turn, would undermine the traditional sense of self-reliance and individuality. Large budgets would spark inflation, and inflation would shift the investment pattern to the benefit of speculators. Prolonged deficit spending, Eisenhower feared, would eventually produce a backlash among the American people and would lead to renewed demands for isolation. With the important goal of restraining defense spending always in mind, the Eisenhower administration held the defense budget nearly constant during its eight years in office, at roughly $140 billion in 1983 dollars or approximately $45 billion in the currency of the fifties.[1]

To stabilize the budget, the Eisenhower planners maintained that a better balance between means and ends would have to be achieved, a balance that would take account of America's continuing nuclear superiority. In the summer of 1952, as the campaign was intensifying, John Foster Dulles advised Eisenhower that continuation of the Truman approach to containment would require increasing defense outlays year by year as the Soviets probed each line of Western defense. In addition, containment as a doctrine left the initiative to the Communists, restricting America to mere response once a target area was identified. A preferred policy would be reliance upon cheaper but more deadly nuclear responses to any overt communist aggression combined with active measures to promote the "liberation" of those countries already lost to communism. Since communism was increasingly perceived as a monolithic movement directed from Moscow, third world nations ought to be encouraged to rely upon American guarantees of assistance in the ever-present fight against communist subversion.[2]

The combination of reliance upon America's nuclear deterrent and efforts to provide a reasonable degree of protection for the noncommunist world at lower costs formed the basis of what subsequently became known as the "New Look." Its main outlines were provided in a January 1954 address by Dulles who by then had been appointed secretary of state. America would depend upon its ability to apply "massive retaliatory power" to stem the advance of communism. Thus, America's response to a given threat would not necessarily be sized according to the danger but would include the distinct possibility of nuclear engagement. As time would show, in the last stages of the Korean War, during the Quemoy-Matsu bombardment of 1954–55 and again in the bombardment of 1958, the Eisenhower administration gave clear warnings that a conventional assault by Chinese Communists would produce nuclear retaliation. During the 1958 Berlin crisis, Eisenhower also stated that if necessary America would not fight a conventional war in Central Europe. In sharp contrast, however, Eisenhower took pains during the 1958 crisis in Lebanon to avoid the threat of nuclear confrontation, refusing to allow American troops to carry nuclear-capable weapons ashore. This ambiguity, too, was an intrinsic aspect of the New Look. The Soviets and their allies must never be certain in what situations America would or would not employ its supreme deterrent. In this way it was hoped that all levels of potential East-West violence would be excluded, since Moscow might reasonably expect any of its probes would meet the ultimate response. This sense of ambiguity was carefully cultivated in Washington, in part by Secretary of State Dulles's claims that America had often gone "to the brink" of nuclear war in its search for peace and stability.[3]

If Eisenhower and Dulles were kindred spirits with respect to reliance upon the nuclear threat as the cheapest and most effective means for deterring communist expansion, they parted company with respect to the means of achieving the liberation of states already behind the Iron Curtain. In the midst of the 1952 presidential campaign, Eisenhower pointedly objected to Dulles's suggestion that force be employed to liberate Eastern Europe, stressing that peaceful means alone would be used.[4]

Such peaceful means were those used by the rapidly growing Central Intelligence Agency, especially its branches controlling radio stations outside America's border. In the Eisenhower administration, Radio Free Europe and Radio Liberty, both located in southern Germany, greatly expanded their broadcasts to the Eastern bloc. Other forms of psychological warfare were also used to weaken communist influence outside the Soviet frontier.

In the Middle East, the threat of increasing Soviet and communist influence in Iran was met by a CIA-sponsored coup against the radical Iranian prime minister, Mohammed Mossadeq, in 1953. The following year a CIA-trained and backed conservative army overthrew the government of Guatemala after American fears were raised by growing communist influence in the Guatemalan cabinet. Thus, the pledges of liberation were met by application of limited means without danger of provoking an East-West confrontation. When an opportunity actually presented itself to "free" an Eastern European nation from Soviet domination—during the 1956 Hungarian uprising—Eisenhower and Dulles restricted their activities to denunciation and condemnation, employing the more traditional methods of initiating United Nations resolutions instead of military confrontation.[5]

While the general principles of the New Look represented the values and beliefs of the internationalist wing of the Republican party, their refinement into a comprehensive military doctrine involved close coordination between the Eisenhower leadership and American defense planners. In the spring of 1953, three separate task forces were appointed to consider the relative merits of various defense postures, the exercise taking its name *Operation Solarium* from the White House sun room where it was first suggested. By the fall of that year, the alternate approaches to defense planning were submitted for National Security Council consideration, with the approved doctrine being assigned the number 162/2. Three main points were emphasized. First, America would have to maintain a strong military posture, including the ability for massive application of nuclear retaliation through offensive striking power. Second, American and allied forces would have to stand ready to move quickly to counter any aggression by the Soviet bloc and to hold vital mobilization areas abroad as well as lines of communication (LOCs). Third, a domestic industrial base capable of sustaining American forces in combat would have to be maintained and protected against the types of damage that nuclear war might bring. Each of these main points required the procurement of certain types of forces and equipment if the overall goal of national security was to be achieved. In December 1953 a three-year defense program was approved to purchase the men and implements of war needed. Thus, NSC 162/2 soon became to the Eisenhower administration what NSC-68 had been to the last years of Truman's presidency.[6]

The emphasis upon possession of an ever-ready offensive striking power within NSC 162/2 reconfirmed the priority of the air force already established in the Truman administration. By the end of 1953, the Strategic Air Command (SAC) possessed 10 heavy and 25 medium bomber and reconnaissance wings. There were 1,500 bombers in the air force inventory, 1,000 of which were nuclear capable. By then the air force was in the process of converting to B-47 all-jet bombers with a speed of 600 miles per hour. In October 1953 the first of the heavy B-52 bombers were ordered, and by the end of Eisenhower's second term, 600 B-52s were deployed, each capable of carrying 6 hydrogen bombs. Under the three-year defense program, the existing 115-wing air force was to expand to 137 wings, increasing air force personnel by about 30,000. In an administration in which frugality was perceived as a national security value second to none, this increased air force allocation necessarily affected funds available for other branches of the service. The air force was to receive 47 percent of the total defense budget; the navy, 29 percent; and the army, 22 percent. In terms of men and equipment, the initial three-year plan foresaw a shrinkage of naval personnel by about 100,000 and a cut in army divisions from the Korean War high of 20 to 14 by 1957.[7]

The second main objective of NSC 162/2 was to prepare to meet any communist aggression in concert with America's allies, a prescription that applied foremost in Europe where NATO was in the process of expansion. European defense, the new strategic doctrine emphasized, was crucial to America's own vital interests. Given fiscal constraints, this defense was to be achieved by an increased reliance upon nuclear weapons that were continually becoming more adaptable to local battlefield conditions. By 1954 nuclear technology in the area of miniaturization was such that America was able to equip its short-range, tactical rockets with atomic warheads. Since NSC 162/2 asserted that "in event of hostilities, the United States will consider nuclear weapons to be as available as any other munition," the era of miniaturization permitted a major reorganization of American force abroad. Nuclear weapons were integrated into the American units down to the company level, with the greatly increased firepower constituting cause for reductions in the number of troops employed.[8]

By December 1954 the NATO nations felt comfortable enough with this substitution of firepower for manpower to project much lower force levels than had been authorized just two years before. If the force levels adopted at the 1952 Lisbon Conference of NATO ministers called for 96 divisions in Europe, the December 1954 meeting asked for 30. Two years later, in 1956, NATO officially changed its own strategic doctrine in MC 14/2, accepting the tactical use of nuclear means as equal with conventional.[9] By now American divisions on the continent were being converted into smaller, more mobile units, nicknamed "pentomic divisions" due to reliance upon nuclear weapons. By 1960 the American army had shrunk by over three-quarters of a million men and stood at 14 divisions, 3 of which were understaffed. Concomitant with this new emphasis upon nuclear weapons, a group of American strategists began to promote the advantages of a limited nuclear war that, they argued, might be confined to the European theater and be conducted by highly mobile units possessing unparalled destructive power.[10]

The third point of emphasis in NSC 162/2—protection of the domestic industrial mobilization base—was met by expanding defensive systems designed to protect the continental United States and to give warnings of impending attacks. The Continental Defense Command was established in 1954, and the North American Air Defense Command was established three years later. Early warning radars were constructed throughout the country and extended well beyond its borders. A low-frequency analysis and recording sound surveillance system, usually known as SOSUS, was installed along the ocean floor to monitor the emergence of Soviet ships from the European and Asian land masses. An alternate national command center was established to which the president and key members of the defense establishment might retire in case the national capital appeared in danger of destruction, and yearly "alert" exercises were begun in which the president and his cabinet took part. America, in short, prepared for the worst in the hope that the clear resolve demonstrated might dissuade the Soviets from ever testing the nuclear-ready forces.[11]

The strategic goal of achieving maximum defense for the lowest possible cost through reliance upon nuclear deterrence naturally had to take into account improvements in the Soviet capability to inflict increasing damage upon America in a nuclear war. In the fall of 1953, the Soviets detonated a thermonuclear device and the following year deployed the first models of a new intercontinental jet bomber able to drop such weapons on American targets. A top secret national intelligence estimate drafted in May 1955 projected likely Soviet heavy bomber totals by 1959 of approximately 700 of the new jet aircraft. Equally disturbing were American intelligence intercepts of data confirming Soviet testing of intermediate-range ballistic missiles (IRBMs) at the close of 1955. Less than two years later the recently designed U-2 spy plane discovered a facility for launching of intercontinental ballistic missiles (ICBMs) in the Kapustin Yar region of the southern USSR. That fall the Soviets launched man's first artificial satellite, proclaiming that the success of Sputnik inaugurated a new era of Soviet superiority. [12]

The changing correlation of forces and the increasing Soviet nuclear threat prompted the Eisenhower administration to convene a number of special committees in the continuing search for protection at the most reasonable cost. The Killian committee, whose report was issued in 1955, attempted to assess the significance of the Soviet threat in the wake of evidence that showed a growing Soviet long-range bomber capability. The Soviets already possessed a modest potential to inflict great damage upon American targets, and the Killian report stated that this ability would grow until America would be open to devastating and perhaps decisive attacks by decade's end. It would be then, in the late fifties, that Soviet improvements in bomb design would combine with increased procurements of long-range bombers to create a truly startling threat. Only if America won the race in missile technology might the insecurities of the late fifties be somewhat diminished. Given the time needed for the Soviets to ready a massive attack upon America, and assuming a distinct technological and numerical advantage in America's hands, it might remain possible for America to blunt an impending assault by destroying Soviet weapons before launch in a preemptive strike. [13]

Other analysis, however, soon cast doubt even upon America's ability to limit damage in a further nuclear war by striking as the Soviets prepared to attack. A study by the military's Weapons System Evaluation Group noted that existing plans to use America's total nuclear arsenal would indeed destroy well over 100 Soviet cities, causing the demise of Soviet industrial capability and the death of some 60 million citizens. But although such plans included the destruction of over 600 identified air fields, this would leave more than 200 other air fields unscathed, over 200 air fields from which Soviet bombers might be launched. [14]

If the Killian committee focused upon the primacy of the 1955 bomber threat, its successor, the Gaither committee, concentrated upon the missile threat made evident by the launch of the artificial satellite Sputnik in 1957. Its prediction that by 1959 the Soviet Union might have the ability to launch a devastating nuclear attack against America's retaliatory forces, which would undermine the entire strategy of massive retaliation, posed a major new challenge to strategic planners still concerned with maximizing defense at the lowest possible costs.[15] The findings of the committee were the basis of recommendations that America's missile program be drastically advanced beyond programs initiated as a result of the earlier Killian committee report. The new goals suggested an increase of 400 percent in the procurement of American intermediate-range ballistic missiles, from a previously recommended level of 60 to 240, with such weapons to be deployed at European sites from which they might strike the Soviet Union. The program designed to deploy America's first generation of ICBMs was also to be expanded and a general plan for the rapid dispersion of bombers assigned to the Strategic Air Command (SAC) completed.[16] By the end of the decade, America, in fact, had deployed its first Atlas ICBMs on land as well as the first two Polaris submarines equipped with nuclear missiles. The air component of America's nuclear force had also been expanded, with 600 B-52 long-range bombers and 1,400 B-47 medium-range bombers being deployed. Yet even with this significant augmentation of forces, security seemed less assured than when the decade had begun. Equally important, the continuing need to match the Soviets in offensive as well as in defensive weapons threatened to make a mockery of hopes to ensure comprehensive defense at reasonable costs.[17]

The growing Soviet nuclear might did more than challenge the ideals of frugality so central to Eisenhower's planning. As Moscow began to deploy modern nuclear weapons in conjunction with an adequate delivery system, the prospects of blunting a conventional Soviet attack in Europe or elsewhere by nuclear retaliation grew increasingly questionable. The deployment of tactical nuclear weapons to NATO and reliance upon a nuclear response to any Soviet bloc attack appeared a less and less creditable strategy as the decade progressed. World America really use battlefield nuclear weapons in Europe if their use threatened to prompt an all-out nuclear conflict in which American targets as well would be struck? In more blunt terms, would America fire tactical nuclear weapons to defend, let us say, Paris from a Soviet advance if the likely response would be the nuclear destruction of New York? It would be questions such as this that would eventually prompt France to develop its own nuclear capability and to diminish its reliance upon NATO for defense.

A more immediate problem for the Eisenhower administration was the impact upon budgetary constraints if nuclear responses to conventional Soviet attacks were precluded. If such a strategy were adopted, the extensive cuts in conventional army manpower so central to the New Look would have to be reversed, and the army would become a main competitor of the air force in the yearly struggle for budgetary allotments. In 1954 a new version of the Basic Army Field Manual, FM-100, suggested that the experiences in postwar Greece and Korea refuted the notion that strategic air strikes would prove decisive in future combat. The use of massive air strikes would likely be "politically" excluded in limited theaters of combat as they had been in Korea despite MacArthur's demand that sites in Manchuria be bombed.[18] The following year, in 1955, retiring Army Chief of Staff Gen. Matthew Ridgway argued forcefully that America must possess the means to defeat local aggression and to be victorious in small wars independent of whether nuclear weapons were or were not employed. His successor, Gen. Maxwell Taylor, held similar views. And as the size and destructiveness of the Soviet nuclear arsenal grew throughout the decade, so did voices arguing that employment of such weapons early in a conventional conflict would doom the world to extinction.[19]

8

Arms Control, 1945-1960

The problems and promises of arms control were far from unfamiliar to American security planners of the immediate postwar world. International conventions devoted to this very topic had convened before World War I, and session after session of the League of Nations' Disarmament Committee had discussed and debated while Hitler's Germany prepared for the next war. Thus, an ambiguous legacy greeted America's postwar strategies: the persistence of prewar arms control talks was equalled only by their consistent failures.

To confuse the issue further, differing lessons concerning arms control appeared to emerge from analyzing the two main wars of the century. World War I, historians concluded, had resulted from an excess of armament, a clear justification for efforts to reduce such implements of destruction to the lowest minimum required for self-defense. World War II, in sharp contrast, was nearly unanimously blamed upon a lack of sufficient arms among the democracies. If Britain and France had possessed adequate weapons and men under arms, they might have avoided the disastrous appeasement policy of the thirties, crushing Hitler's Germany at first sign of aggressive intent. Which lesson, some now wondered, should apply to arms control attempts after 1945? Should nations acquire a distinct offensive capacity so as to extinguish a threat to peace upon first sign of danger, or should only defensive weapons be permitted?[1] This confusion clouded American arms control strategies for the next several decades and found its symbolic expression in the ambiguous title assigned to the agency eventually mandated to carry on such discussions: the Arms Control and Disarmament Agency.

The ambiguous legacy of prewar arms negotiations was but one complicating factor in identifying where America's true interests lay in the post-1945 world. The advent of nuclear power and the unparalleled devastation of the Japanese cities of Hiroshima and Nagasaki raised profound questions about whether or not this new weapon made war obsolete. Some members of the scientific research team responsible for the bomb insisted that it be used before the war ended so as to show the world the destructive powers of the new age and, hence to lay the foundation for permanent peace. Others suggested that any such actual use as was approved for the Japanese cities would doom any postwar arms discussions since America's potential enemies, having seen the magnitude of atomic power, would insist upon acquiring the bomb themselves. These diverse groups, each arguing for its own position, soon entered into competition for the ear of the new American head of state, Harry Truman.[2]

In September 1945, Secretary of War Henry Stimson, himself the object of attention from numerous groups that held different positions on how the bomb ought to be controlled, forwarded his own opinion to Truman. He suggested that in the interest of avoiding a postwar arms race the Soviet Union ought to become a partner with America, Britain, and Canada in the development and control of nuclear energy. In this way nuclear power might be directed away from its military applications to more peaceful uses. The major remaining question in this approach was to select the forum in which such exchanges of information would take place and where mechanisms of control might be constructed.[3] In November of the same year, Truman, in conjunction with the prime ministers of Britain and Canada, agreed that the newly created United Nations was the answer and proposed that it form a special body for nuclear matters. In December at the Moscow Foreign Ministers' Meeting, Secretary of State James Byrnes reached an agreement that America, Britain, Canada, and the Soviet Union would jointly sponsor a resolution to create a United Nations Atomic Energy Commission (UNAEC).[4]

With the efforts at control of the atom showing progress, the Truman administration turned its attention to drafting the rules and regulations that a future UN committee might follow in an attempt to ensure exclusively peaceful use of nuclear power. Undersecretary of State Dean Acheson chaired the group established to chart American policy, relying heavily upon a board of consultants headed by David Lilienthal. The final recommendations, dubbed the Acheson-Lilienthal Report, appeared in March 1946 and were revolutionary in many respects.

The sole way to preclude the use of atomic energy for destructive purposes, the report asserted, was to create an international authority that would hold a tight monopoly over all nuclear research and development. This authority, whose writ would transcend the rights of all national governments, would be granted exclusive control for all atomic developments from the mining and refining of necessary raw materials to the completion of energy-producing plants and generators. It would manage, control, license, and inspect every stage from extraction of uranium ore onward. Despite the fact that this authority would be located within the United Nations, it would not possess the right to call for sanctions against a potential violator. No national state, Acheson and Lilienthal reasoned, would violate the rules and regulations of the authority unless it was already determined to fight a war, and hence sanctions would be meaningless. Violations would mean the system had failed, and each nation, individually or in concert, would have to select what course it would take against the new aggressor.[5]

The revolutionary nature of the Acheson-Lilienthal Report, especially its call for internationalization of the peaceful uses of atomic power and its willingness to trust the Soviet Union to full partnership despite the growing strains of the Cold War, prompted Truman to select a well-known American figure, a man whom the people might trust, as the public spokesman for this new proposal. Bernard Baruch, a prominent financier who had been an adviser to several presidents and head of the War Industries Board during World War I, was appointed America's representative to present the proposal for an international authority to the United Nations. But Baruch had not achieved his success due to lack of backbone or will. Before accepting this new task, he insisted that certain portions of the Acheson- Lilienthal Report that he found objectionable be modified.

Baruch argued that the right of any security council member of the United Nations to veto any report or suggestion of the UNAEC would have to be removed. Equally, any violator of the international authority's mandate would be met not simply by sanctions but by "prompt and certain" retaliation. Consistent with earlier plans, the international authority would indeed control all aspects of nuclear production from ore extraction to eventual energy production. But the procedure by which this was accomplished would be regularized, beginning with surveys of existing and potential sources of fissionable materials to final construction of energy-producing plants. No time limit would be fixed for each stage, and all members of the appropriate United Nations' committees would need to agree that a stage was finished before proceeding to the next. With no veto allowed, this would mean, in effect, domination by the Western members of the UNAEC at the possible expense of the Soviet Union.[6] Nuclear-generating plants would be built throughout the world in accordance with standards and strategies drafted by the same UN body in which the USSR would control only a minority of votes. Once the United Nations affirmed that all stages of control were in place, and only then, America would end its existing monopoly of atomic weapons. At any stage short of full control, in the face of evidence that suggested violation of authority rules, America would be able to use its unparalleled atomic power to punish the violator. The decision as to potential violations would naturally be taken within the UN but without the Soviet Union being allowed a veto and in the presence of a pro-Western majority of nations. Perhaps by accident or perhaps by intent, the destructiveness of America's nuclear monopoly was demonstrated again by atomic tests in the Pacific the very month debate began in the UN over the Baruch Proposal.[7]

While we remain unaware of the precise nature of Soviet decision making, it is reasonable to surmise that the Baruch Proposal generated initial confusion in Moscow. Here was an internationalist solution to the issue of atomic energy advanced by a country that traditionally retreated into isolationism after each war. Equally strange, capitalist America, for whom private property ranked as a central value worth protecting, was suggesting nationalization and external control over perhaps the most lucrative approach to energy production since the invention of steam power. But despite their likely awe, the Soviets quickly declined to participate in the American scheme. Their alternate plan, dubbed the Gromyko Plan due to its main spokesman, Soviet delegate to the United Nations (and later foreign minister and president of the republic) Andrey Gromyko, called for an international convention devoid of verification or inspection that would prohibit the production, possession, or use of atomic weapons. Once those states having atomic bombs destroyed them, a second convention establishing penalties for violators would be drafted.[8]

The second treaty, dealing with potential violations, would allow the permanent members of the Security Council to retain their veto rights and thus block any penalties that might be invoked. Since only the United States had a functioning atomic bomb at the time, the Gromyko Plan, while universal in language, would impinge only on Washington's war-making power.[9] Needless to say, the Soviet alternative was perceived as inequitable by the Truman administration, which was already deeply worried about postwar Soviet expansion. Thus, a stalemate developed. On December 31, 1946, the Baruch Plan came to the Security Council for a vote, passing with ten yes votes and two abstentions. Since it was Poland and the Soviet Union that abstained, the apparent victory for Baruch actually signaled the death of his plan.[10]

The remainder of the decade witnessed diminished interest in arms control on both sides as the former wartime allies drifted further apart. Truman had felt comfortable in the initial presentation of the Baruch Plan since he believed his arguments for universal military service would produce an American peacetime army capable of waging a successful conventional war. But with the congressional refusal to maintain a large standing army or to consent to universal training so as to produce an effective reserve, American planners realized that nuclear and conventional arms control would have to go hand in hand. The alternative might be to create a world in which America's nuclear superiority would no longer offset the significant imbalance between the Soviet and Western land armies. With the surprise detonation of a Soviet atomic blast in 1949, in combination with the visible rearming of Soviet and Eastern European troops in the early years of the fifties, Washington began to insist that only comprehensive, across-the-board arms restrictions would be fair and equitable. In January 1952, with American support, a single UN Disarmament Commission replaced the UNAEC in a new effort to reach an arms agreement linking nuclear and conventional forces. That spring America and its NATO allies proposed a stage-by-stage process of disarmament that would be verified by international inspectors holding rights of access to the entire national territory of every state. But like the Baruch Proposal, this, too, foundered upon Soviet refusals to allow on-site inspections. Thus, the Truman administration left office without significant progress in a crucial area of security policy.[11]

The year 1953 brought not only new faces and ideas in Washington— the advent of the Eisenhower administration—but also new faces in Moscow as well—the result of Joseph Stalin's death in March of that year. Yet 1953 was also the year in which the Soviet Union exploded its first hydrogen bomb, sparking yet another race for nuclear superiority. In December President Eisenhower did give his "Atoms for Peace" speech in which he suggested that those nations possessing fissionable materials ought to donate a portion to an international atomic energy agency that would use such radioactive materials for research and medical technology. And yet even this modest proposal was rejected by Moscow, although a later reconsideration would eventually create the agency Eisenhower had requested.[12] Intent upon providing the best defense possible at the lowest cost, the Eisenhower planners were even less willing to consider a partial arms control agreement limited to atomic and hydrogen weapons than their predecessors had been. Such a partial agreement would force Washington to expend major new resources upon conventional forces, which was not an inviting prospect to the Republicans. Although President Eisenhower did appoint a special assistant for disarmament, the linkage between conventional and nuclear control remained firm during his first administration.

At the 1955 Geneva summit conference with Soviet leaders, Eisenhower offered a new scheme for ameliorating the uncertainties caused by the arms race—a plan for reciprocal aerial inspections of the United States and the Soviet Union entitled the "Open Skies." It called for the exchange of blueprints and information on the military installations and troop concentrations of both sides. And yet by itself it contained no proposals for arms reduction. Rather, Open Skies attempted to increase the ability of each side to verify that its opponent was not actively preparing for war and constituted what in the seventies would be called a confidence-building measure. In any event, the Soviets rejected the plan as thinly disguised espionage, although party chief Nikita Khrushchev later showed some interest in a more restricted version.[13] The bloody Soviet invasion of Hungary the following fall ended even these tentative efforts for a limited understanding. By now demands for achieving at least some partial understanding in the area of arms control were becoming an important element of the American political debate. By the time of the second Eisenhower administration, the public outcry for partial arms control seemed so strong that some type of agreement became almost inevitable.

In the early fifties, the first reports of possible dangers from radioactive fallout associated with the ongoing testing of nuclear weapons appeared in the American and world press. Strontium 90, an isotope similar to calcium, became a special object of concern since its radioactive properties threatened to produce a permanent source of invisible radiation within a whole generation of children raised in the atomic age. But an incident in 1954 dramatically broadened individual expressions of concern into a growing wave of protest.[14]

In March 1954 the United States conducted a routine nuclear test on the Marshall Islands in the South Pacific. The hydrogen bomb exploded was approximately 600 times the size of that used on Hiroshima, and the radioactive fallout exceeded the distances anticipated. Some eighty miles from the test site, a Japanese fishing vessel, with the unlikely name of the *Lucky Dragon*, received a heavy dose of radioactive particles and, upon returning to home waters, registered one dead with the remainder of the crew sterile. In the resulting worldwide demand for an end to such tests, American chemist Linus Pauling launched a campaign for a total test ban among nuclear powers. The following year Bertrand Russell, the well-known British philosopher and mathematician, as well as Albert Einstein, issued a manifesto appealing for an end to testing.[15] By 1956 the issue of a test ban had found its way into national politics, with the democratic presidential challenger, Adlai Stevenson, coming out on its behalf. In 1957 scientists from around the world, including some from the Soviet Union itself, held the first of their annual conferences at Pugwash, Nova Scotia, to discuss ways of both policing such a ban and persuading their respective governments of its wisdom.[16]

Responding to increasing public attention in the fall of 1957, Eisenhower established a special panel to examine the pros and cons of instituting a complete cessation of nuclear tests. The panel, under the direction of

Hans Bethe, concluded that a ban would be consistent with American security interests and that verification to ensure no cheating by adherents to any agreement was feasible. While this latter point was disputed by some leading U.S. scientists, America's first underground nuclear tests conducted that fall under the code name *Rainer* gave new information about the characteristics of such explosions and means for their detection.[17]

In the spring of 1958, the Supreme Soviet in Moscow approved a decree ending Soviet nuclear testing that would last until a Western power detonated a test weapon. Realizing that this move established a propaganda victory for the Soviets and already convinced that a test ban was at least within the realm of possibility, the Eisenhower administration now called upon the Soviet Union to send scientists and technicians to a conference where the verification of nuclear testing would be discussed. The Soviet leader, Nikita Khrushchev, accepted on May 1, 1958, and the conference, attended by technical experts (not politicians) from America, Britain, France, Canada, and the USSR, opened in Geneva two months later. Four means of detecting nuclear explosions were examined: acoustic waves, radioactive debris, seismic signals that traveled through the earth from the explosion site, and radio signals. By August the conference concluded that existing technology was sufficient to police a test ban. This, however, would require construction of between 160 and 180 land-based detection stations, each manned by 30 to 40 technicians. About 100 of these stations would be located on the earth's continents, with a number naturally lying within the boundaries of America and the USSR. The rest would be positioned on islands. The conference concluded that with such stations in place, above-ground tests of one kiloton or more could be detected (the bomb dropped on Hiroshima, for example, was estimated at twenty kilotons), and explosions above five kilotons could be detected if a weapon were discharged underground. With evident progress being reported, the United States called for a conference of political and technical experts to hammer out an actual test ban treaty, promising to refrain from all testing while such a conference was in session. However, in the interim between the ending of the first technicians' conference in August and the convening of the second conference at the end of October, both the United States and the Soviet Union had engaged in a lengthy series of tests.[18]

When the conference convened in Geneva, the inevitable political disputes threatened to negate the progress achieved at the more technical level. The Soviet Union, while willing to accept detection stations on its own soil, insisted that such facilities be staffed exclusively by each country's own technicians. The West insisted that the staffs be at least 50 percent foreign to prevent cheating. The Soviets also demanded that the three powers assigned to supervise any future test ban treaty—America, Britain, and the USSR—each ought to retain a veto over supervision and publication of results. [19]

While such disputes would undoubtedly have stalled negotiations and would possibly have prevented a successful conclusion, a new technical factor introduced by the United States in early 1959 undercut even the earlier technical agreements that had led to the test ban conference. Having analyzed the data from the August, September, and October 1958 nuclear tests, American technicians reported diminished confidence that the mentioned number of detection stations would be sufficient. While the Soviets saw political machinations behind this startling new American position, in retrospect it appears that good cause existed to demand more stations if full confidence were to be accorded a test ban treaty. [20] Despite these various political and technical hindrances, some progress toward a final agreement was made. Yet by the time of the American elections and the victory of John Kennedy in 1960, the issue of how to preclude the undetected explosion of underground nuclear weapons still remained unresolved. The last meeting of the Geneva Test Ban Conference was held in December 1960.

Although the first fifteen years of arms control negotiations had failed to produce a meaningful agreement, important steps had been taken, and the interest and resolve of both sides had been examined. Perhaps the most positive aspect of the negotiations designed to reach a comprehensive test ban agreement lay in the new willingness of the United States to explore an arms agreement covering just one part of existing arms inventories. In short, the linkage between restrictions on nuclear weapons and corresponding deep cuts in conventional arms had been broken. It would be the Kennedy administration that would capitalize upon this new opportunity for agreement.

9

Strategic Planning
under Kennedy and Johnson

Just as his predecessors had done, President John Kennedy and his national security advisers took power in 1961 amid definite problems and within a rapidly changing world in which the threat from the Soviet Union appeared to be growing. In the late fifties, reports of a dangerous missile gap began to circulate, with estimates leaked to the public suggesting a possible Soviet missile superiority of as high as 6 to 1. The very existence of a Soviet capability to deliver nuclear weapons to American targets, either through manned bombers or by rockets, had caused concern for security planners in the waning days of the Eisenhower administration, and various plans for providing bomb-proof shelters for American retaliatory forces or sending more of America's nuclear deterrent into the invulnerable depths of the sea on submarines were issues of deep debate.[1] Regardless of the dimensions of the alleged missile gap, the problem of vulnerability of America's nuclear defenses required immediate consideration. Equally distressing to the new secretary of defense, Robert McNamara, were existing air force plans to launch nearly the entire stockpile of nuclear weapons against the Soviets and their allies at the first sign of trouble, plans that foresaw a devastating U.S. strike even before war would be declared. Lacking assurances that American forces would survive a sneak Soviet attack and concerned about limiting as much as possible the damage a Soviet assault might cause, air force plans included programs for preemptive nuclear war once conflict appeared inevitable.[2] In an era when nuclear forces appeared to lay open to enemy attack, the distinction between deterrence and preemption had increasingly been blurred. Somehow the difference would have to be reinstated.

A second major problem confronting the Kennedy people was the apparent passing of the global initiative to the Communists during the Eisenhower strategy of massive retaliation and asymmetric response. While the threat of all-out nuclear war might dissuade the Soviets from a frontal assault in Europe, it did little to remedy local challenges to Western influence in the rapidly decolonizing world. The nuclear threat had played no role in the Middle East Crisis of 1957–58, and the Eisenhower Doctrine designed for this situation proved inappropriate once the crisis arose.[3] The Eisenhower administration's weapons had made it nearly impossible for the West to confront ever-present challenges to its own position throughout the world.

To President Kennedy and his advisers, the uncertainties of the new era required maximum flexibility in designing alternate responses to whatever threat communist forces might mount. The conventional forces of the United States would have to be restructured to allow combat duty in various parts of the globe as the need arose and would have to be augmented in size and in conventional firepower. America would have to develop a "flexible" and "smooth" response capable of meeting any challenge at its own level, while retaining "escalation dominance" to ensure that if the level of violence rose American superiority would be even greater as a result.[4] The ideal situation would be, for example, the presence of sufficient conventional NATO troops in Europe to deter any Soviet-Warsaw Pact assault. If such a conventional war did develop, NATO's forces would be sized to permit successful defense while maintaining violence at the conventional level. If the Warsaw Pact–Soviet forces then contemplated escalation from conventional to tactical nuclear forces, NATO's nuclear ability would be such that at this level communist chances of success would diminish even further. Each level of potential escalation would be smoothly linked, one to another, so that the appropriate response could always be given with respect to the level of violence the opponent selected. This smooth response would run from conventional defense all the way to the last stages of war: the firing of America's central nuclear systems from their American bases against communist targets.[5] By carefully integrating all levels of response, it was hoped that the amount of violence accompanying any future conflict would be kept at its lowest possible level since communist forces would have no rational motive to escalate violence once assured of America's and NATO's will to resist and of the West's superiority of forces.

A third requirement of the age, as perceived by the Kennedy administration, was the ability to effect significant political change, positive or negative, throughout the world without the direct application of force. The late fifties and sixties were, as mentioned, a period of rapid decolonization, and the need to keep the newly independent nations free of communist influence was keenly felt in Washington. Visible use of force against unfriendly governments in regions of the globe with long-seated antiwhite feelings could cause a wholesale defection from the Western camp. Thus, expanded covert activity, usually led by members of the CIA in combination with extensive training programs for the military of the emerging nations and a policy of economic assistance aimed at creating stable third world nations, became the order of the day.[6] While the later press would portray members of the CIA as sinister right-wingers, ever looking to undermine popular sovereignty in newly emerging third world nations, the reality of the sixties was quite different. The "best and the brightest" recruited into American intelligence agencies tended to be liberal in persuasion, Ivy League in college background, and confident in their ability to create conditions in countries far from home that would bring the benefits of liberal democracy to third world peoples. Given the revelations of CIA activities in the seventies, it is difficult now to remember that affiliation with the Central Intelligence Agency, even its clandestine, "dirty tricks" department, was considered a position of honor during the Kennedy administration.[7] Effective application of political, social, and economic techniques, integrated through the new approach of systems analysis, promised to preclude violent struggles that historically accompanied a new nation's birth, allowing transition to stable and peaceful societies in the new states. In cases where a determined, violent minority refused to accept the promises of political and economic stability, equally well-crafted techniques of counterinsurgency would provide the answer.

The last, major departure from the preceding administration's policy recommended by the Kennedy people concerned the manner of financing the military budget. With Kennedy's Council of Economic Advisers led by liberal economist Walter Heller, the sixties saw the final triumph of Keynesian economic theory that was at the basis of Paul Nitze's authorship of NSC-68 a decade before. Indeed, it was no coincidence that Nitze himself took a major role in the new administration, accepting the position of assistant secretary of defense in charge of the section for International Security Affairs in the Pentagon, a section frequently referred to as Defense's "Little State Department." Henceforth, weapons procurement and manpower levels would be determined according to the perceived need and not according to some arbitrary budget figure that the president thought was the maximum the economy might sustain.[8] Here then were four of the major objectives as the Kennedy administration occupied their new offices in Washington. As time would show, however, the events and problems of the new decade would have nearly as much influence upon the scientific policies implemented as the perceived shortfalls of the Eisenhower policies of the recent past.

The immediate problem for the new secretary of defense, Robert

McNamara, was to remedy the projected disparity between American and Soviet missiles that had played a major role in the presidential campaign. Air force intelligence figures projected that by 1960 the Soviet Union might have 500 rockets capable of destroying American targets; by 1961, 1,000. Given existing assumptions as to Soviet plans to dominate the world, such weapons, many feared, might target the retaliatory abilities of America's Strategic Air Command (SAC) in an effort to catch long-range bombers on the ground. The Eisenhower administration had increased funding for more secure deployments of American bombers and for procurement of missiles that the Soviets might find more difficult to destroy. But to the Kennedy people, these augmentations in America's nuclear strengths were far too small given the ever-present threat of a disarming Soviet attack. Thus, President Kennedy instructed his defense secretary to undertake a broad reexamination of strategic needs and capabilities preparatory to introducing a supplemental funding bill before Congress.[9] Whereas the Eisenhower administration had requested fiscal authorization for a total of 19 Polaris submarines capable of firing underwater ballistic missiles for fiscal year 1964, Kennedy, upon completion of the study, requested authorization for 29. If Eisenhower wanted 400 land-based ICBMs by fiscal year 1964, Kennedy asked for 800, a figure later expanded to 1,000 by decade's end. Even after photos from the new spy-in-the-sky satellites were analyzed in 1961, disproving once and for all the so-called missile gap, the expanded number of strategic systems was not changed. In fact, the number of Polaris submarines was further increased to 41.[10]

The projected expansion of America's strategic capabilities put a premium upon designing a nuclear strategy that might make the best use of this unparalleled destructive power. And in the first year of the new administration, two differing strategic plans caught Secretary McNamara's attention. A report of the Pentagon's Weapons Systems Evaluation Group (WSEG), entitled "Evaluation of Strategic Offensive Weapons," stressed the advantage of America acquiring a secure deterrent nuclear force so awesome that the Soviet Union would never dare risk nuclear war. This force might best consist of a mixture of bombers capable of carrying nuclear weapons, land-based missiles, and the new submarine missile carriers.[11] Reliance upon such a deterrent would not simply be a replay of the Eisenhower years since America's nuclear might would be complemented by expansion of conventional and tactical-nuclear forces able to restrict a future war to lower levels of violence. In such a world, no rational person, Soviet or American, could find grounds for aggression, knowing the total devastation that awaited them.[12] In addition to this tight chain of reasoning that spoke in favor of using strategic nuclear weapons as a deterrent, such an approach would allow a rational calculation of how many such weapons

America ought to buy. If, for example, 400 megatons of delivered nuclear destruction would destroy Soviet society as an organized entity and if it were assumed the Soviets could destroy a maximum of half of America's nuclear force in a sneak attack, then procurement of 800 missiles and planes, each carrying one megaton of nuclear destruction, would be in order. [13]

The problem with structuring one's forces exclusively for deterrence was that in a crisis it allowed little option between all-out destruction and surrender. If the Soviet Union realized that even a limited nuclear attack upon America would be met by all-out retaliation, there would be no incentive to restrict the size of the attack in the unlikely event that they perceived war as either inevitable or to their advantage. In such a case, the American deterrent posture would ensure the total devastation of both sides and, probably, the entire world. Given this fearful possibility, a number of strategic planners suggested that America ought to adopt a two-stage strategy promoting a less destructive alternative. Consistent with plans for flexible response, America ought to structure its nuclear forces so that the majority would survive even the most destructive sneak attack. America's immediate response would be in the realm of damage limitation; that is, the retaliatory strike would avoid Soviet population centers and target upon those Soviet nuclear weapons that had yet to be fired. [14] Besides the ability to limit damage by negating a potential Soviet second response, America ought to possess another level of nuclear weapons targeted, consistent with a strategy of deterrence, upon Soviet cities. Thus, if a Soviet attack should occur, America would attempt to terminate the war as soon as possible at the lowest level of violence by destroying the Soviet ability to fire more missiles. At the same time, America would threaten to launch a last strike that would disrupt Soviet society to such an extent that its future recovery would be problematic. [15] If America's declared strategy focused upon damage limitation first, perhaps the Soviets, too, would avoid an attack upon American cities in any initial round of a nuclear conflict. In short, a nuclear war under such a strategy would not necessarily be an exercise in mutual destruction.

In May 1962 at a NATO foreign and defense ministers meeting in Athens and in June as the commencement speaker at the University of Michigan, McNamara tentatively announced the new administration's choice among the competing strategies. America, he argued, ought to possess a "controlled response" in the field of nuclear warfare. Nuclear weapons would be configured so as to be able to withstand a first strike by the USSR, with America's response being targeted initially upon Soviet weapons not yet fired. America would continue to hold in reserve another round of weapons designed to destroy Soviet cities if the war was not terminated at an earlier stage. The notion of "no cities" in the first response, damage limitation, and the potential to obliterate Soviet population centers as a last resort had apparently won the day.[16]

While McNamara's speech appeared to make excellent strategic sense, it failed to explain certain problems that lay in the way of any effective damage-limitation approach. For example, such a strategy would require a dramatic buildup of nuclear forces since each year the Soviet Union itself was expanding the number of missiles that would have to be targeted. Plans were also apparent for hardening the protective silos in which the Soviet missiles were stored, making the Soviet weapons even more difficult to destroy.[17] Equally important, the accuracies required to destroy a Soviet missile after a flight of over 4,000 miles were simply not yet available. Odd as it may seem, the accuracy of America's nuclear forces were actually decreasing in the sixties as more and more nuclear bombs were placed upon missiles and fewer were loaded in manned bombers. An airplane, if it could penetrate Soviet airspace, could at least be fairly certain its weapons would land near the target. A missile, launched from some point in the American Midwest, possessed much less certainty. Given the drastic expansion of Soviet air defenses and the cost-effectiveness of missiles, the days when America could rely upon its manned bombers were drawing to a close.

While these objections to a counterforce nuclear strategy were mainly technical, there were objections that even those unfamiliar with nuclear engineering could easily grasp. The expansion in numbers and accuracies required for counterforce targeting would be indistinguishable to Soviet planners from an American attempt to gain a first-strike advantage.[18] By definition, first strike meant a configuration of forces such that in a sneak attack the overwhelming number of the enemy's nuclear retaliatory force would be destroyed. To achieve a reliable damage limitation capability that would accomplish its objective *after* a sneak attack, America would require such numbers of weapons that a first strike would appear possible. In such an event, the Soviets, in turn, would drastically expand their own forces, if only to ensure some residual capability if America should initiate the conflict. This, in turn, would require an increased number of American missiles to complete targeting of the new Soviet acquisitions and so on in what strategists soon labeled the "action-reaction" cycle. The end result would be lower levels of security at much higher levels of defense spending. There would be no winners in such a race.

The significant objections to counterforce or damage limitation slowly produced a change in America's strategic planning as the Kennedy years continued, and by the time Lyndon Johnson was in office, Secretary McNamara was returning to his earlier ideas of targeting for deterrence.

Based upon charts and graphs produced within the Pentagon, McNamara defined *assured destruction,* the new term for a strategy of deterrence, as the ability of American nuclear forces to ride out a first assault by the Soviet Union and still be able to destroy 25 to 30 percent of the Soviet population and about two-thirds of Soviet industrial capacity in a return blow.[19] By the mid-sixties American forces possessed this ability. To most Pentagon planners, it was unthinkable that any government, Soviet included, could seek any gains so important that they would risk war in which their very societies were doomed.

The slowly emerging consensus as to how America's long-range nuclear weapons would be configured and used solved but one problem of the overall strategic doctrine of the Kennedy administration. Central nuclear systems, one must recall, were to be tightly integrated into the entire web of potential violent responses, beginning with conventional forces in the field. Flexible response placed heavy emphasis upon meeting each challenge at the lowest level of violence so as to avoid, if possible, the eventual use of the most destructive nuclear assets. Thus, the correct configuration of forces in the field constituted a major arena of strategic planning for the Pentagon in the sixties. The task was especially difficult given the legacy of the Eisenhower-Dulles period that had seen the rapid expansion of alliances with foreign states and pledges to defend much of the "free world" against any communist aggression. By 1960 there existed nine formal treaties, such as SEATO, that committed America to assist over forty allies and a number of less rigid but still binding "understandings" with many more. The study as to how America's conventional defense might best be structured and controlled was begun in 1962, soon producing impressive results.[20]

All told, defense planners estimated that the Soviet Union and its allies might provoke conflict in some sixteen different regions or theaters of the world. By examining the contributions that America's allies might make, eleven of these theaters would still require U.S. military assistance. Combat in all theaters at once would necessitate a dramatic increase in U.S. forces, approaching nearly 55 army and marine divisions. And yet the ability of the Soviet Union and its main ally, China, to fight in such a large number of regions would require long-term and highly visible enemy mobilization and readiness, just the sort of behavior likely to justify American use of nuclear weapons in an all-out war. If the USSR and its allies wished to maintain a conflict at the conventional phase, testing, so to speak, America's resolve and readiness, it appeared unlikely that more than three separate theaters of battle would be joined: one in which Soviet forces advanced, one in Asia where Chinese troops would hold command, and one more smaller theater of battle where perhaps Cuba would take the lead. Facing three theaters of warfare instead of eleven allowed planners in Washington to significantly abbreviate the initial projections calling for 55 divisions; 28 were now judged sufficient for what became known as a "two-and-a-half-war" defense. This force level, in turn, could be achieved by a combination of 16 active army, 3 active marine, 8 reserve army, and 1 reserve marine division, the figures that became the basis of subsequent conventional force planning.[21]

Reliance upon a combination of active and reserve divisions required other, equally important, changes in how conventional units ought to be positioned and supported. The more units that could be withdrawn from forward deployments throughout the world and repositioned in the continental United States as a strategic reserve, capable of rapid deployment to any world trouble spot, the more likely the chance of victory early in a conflict. Such a strategic reserve, however, would need adequate transportation for both men and supplies, a requirement that appeared capable of being met due to recent innovations in large, long-range transport airplanes. An expanded navy was also called for since supply lines from the American homeland to the deployed strategic reserve would probably be both lengthy and open to sea challenge. The total combination of divisions, air wings for support, cargo vessels and planes for transportation, and an expanded navy for defense, would form an effective conventional response to the most probable conventional challenges anticipated in the decade.[22]

While the plans for creating an adequate conventional force that was able to deploy on short notice anywhere that American interests were challenged became the official goal of the Kennedy and Johnson administrations, unforeseen difficulties eventually intruded upon the planners' schemes. The expansion of the Vietnamese conflict after 1964 and the rapid buildup of U.S. forces there, eventually reaching nearly 500,000 ground troops, undercut plans for a balanced military expansion consistent with earlier assumptions. By 1968 U.S. active ground forces had increased by 60 percent, but 10 of America's 23 divisions were deployed in Vietnam—not in a strategic reserve awaiting rapid deployment to a crisis area.[23] The fiscal constraints of providing for Saigon's defense also impinged upon availability of dollars for needed transportation and naval protection. In short, the well-thought-out and comprehensive strategic plans of the early Kennedy administration had given way to the needs of the moment as large numbers of U.S. troops went to what could only be considered the one-half war of the two-and-a-half-war strategy.

It was not only the expanding Vietnamese war that provided roadblocks to rational configuration of conventional forces for flexible response; America's allies in Europe also took pains to delay its realization. The entire notion of meeting aggression at its own level with force adequate to defend

Europe in the conventional phase impressed many Europeans as an American denial of its past nuclear umbrella. Some wondered if the new strategy was not merely a way to make Europe safe for conventional war, a frightening thought given recollections of the horrible devastation accompanying the conventional war just two decades before. If a Soviet conventional attack were indeed blunted at its own level and if the Soviets threatened to use nuclear weapons, would America then invoke its ultimate atomic deterrent? In short, was flexible response a truly integrated strategy at whose upper limits lay the use of America's central nuclear systems, or was it a means of avoiding the destruction of American civilization by promoting containment of future conflict on European soil?[24]

Perhaps of equal importance, flexible response would require significant increases of European conventional forces at great costs to European taxpayers. For years such forces had been kept small due to the ultimate deterrence that lay in America's pledge to defend Europe by nuclear weapons if necessary. This new strategy would require considerably more European contributions. Not until 1967 were American planners able to convince the NATO allies as to the wisdom of flexible response, the new strategy being enshrined in the understanding MC 14/3 that replaced the earlier MC 14/2 of the Eisenhower administration that was premised upon massive retaliation.[25] By this date France had withdrawn from the military committees of NATO and was developing its own nuclear deterrent as the ultimate protection against a communist attack. By now troop demands from Vietnam plagued U.S. efforts to expand those conventional units programmed for Europe in case of conflict there as the entire American military establishment attempted to meet the new crisis in Southeast Asia for which no solution seemed adequate.

10

Defense Planning
and the Budget

One of the more perplexing problems of the postwar period has been the efficient organization and management of the American defense establishment. With no peacetime precedents for running a defense program requiring a substantial portion of the federal budget, the various secretaries of defense were forced to experiment with diverse techniques for bringing planning and expenditures into order. Thus, it was small wonder that the approach followed by the Kennedy administration was in sharp contrast to that of the previous administration.

The modern National Defense Establishment, later renamed the Department of Defense (DOD), owed its birth to the National Security Act of 1947. The three principle military services were given status as defense departments, each headed by a secretary with cabinet rank, entitled to participate in overall governmental policy deliberations. At the apex of the defense establishment sat the new secretary of defense who was to lend harmony and organization in general defense matters. Two years later, in 1949, amendments to the National Security Act downgraded the three service departments, removing their secretaries from the cabinet. Yet although an intent of this reform was to augment the authority of the secretary of defense, the absence of a comprehensive staff within his office allowed most planning to continue in the separate service departments.[1] Throughout the fifties the secretary of defense's staff was restricted to areas traditionally of civilian concern: finance, science and technology, and personnel, with matters of military strategy and force requirements being left to the services themselves.[2] With limited power in crucial areas of defense planning, the secretary of defense functioned by and large as a mediator, attempting to promote harmonious relations between the service planners who contributed the main items into the yearly defense budget.

In the words of a well-known U.S. expert of civil-military relations, Samuel P. Huntington, there are three basic means by which a superior can control his subordinates. "A hierarchical superior can control his subordinates by determining the goals which the subordinate is to pursue, controlling the resources available to the subordinate, or doing both."[3] Corresponding to these alternatives, two broad schools of preferred defense management emerged in the fifties. One, which might be called the traditionalist school, argued that the president and Congress were charged with ensuring appropriate funding for the military and that the task of the secretary of defense was to see that the services lived within these fiscal constraints. Disputes as to how the pie ought to be divided should remain with the services themselves since their membership possessed the experience and wisdom in military affairs unlikely to be found in a civilian staff. The secretary of defense ought to act as an impartial referee in any intraservice disputes as to how monies ought to be spent. A second approach to the problem, which might be dubbed the activist school, argued that military strategy, preferred force levels and procurement, and budget allocations were so tightly interrelated that decisions in all three areas should be concentrated at a common point. The most reasonable candidate for this job would be the secretary of defense disposing of an expanded and well-trained staff. The traditionalist school was to find its clearest expression during the Eisenhower administration; the activist school, under Kennedy.[4]

During the Eisenhower administration, there were three main determinants of defense planning and budgeting. First, a strict ceiling was placed upon the funds available in any given fiscal year. Eisenhower was firmly committed by ideology and temperament to the proposition that fiscal irresponsibility and profligate spending at the federal level were threats to America's security that were second to none. As he affirmed during the 1952 presidential campaign, "A bankrupt America is more the Soviet goal than an America conquered on the field of battle."[5] One of his first actions after entering the White House was to slash defense spending by 20 percent and to call for further cuts in subsequent budgets. The resulting pattern was for the president to give regular guidance to the secretary of defense as to the preferred budget for the coming year. Funds available were derived from expected governmental revenues minus fixed governmental obligations such as interest on the debt and veterans' benefits, subtraction of needed domestic programs and foreign aid, and a remainder that would be available for defense. The defense "needs" of the nation were not calculated in any alternate, abstract fashion, and the secretary of defense, in the final instance, determined what percentages of the already fixed allocations would go to each service.[6]

The second characteristic of defense planning/spending in the fifties was what might be called "strategic monism." As the cheapest way to purchase adequate defense, the New Look emphasized a nuclear response to communist aggression. Thus, a premium was placed upon the nuclear programs being developed by each service if each were to remain competitive in the yearly battle for scarce funding. Each service advanced plans for its own nuclear weapons, taking little or no account of whether its particular weapon was superior to that of a rival service and criticizing all others. Each service sought allies for its program both within and without the defense establishment, often going to individual congressmen for assistance. Each, in turn, neglected conventional forces since the New Look placed a lower value upon such force procurements.[7]

Oddly, strategic monism went hand in hand with what at first glance appeared to be its opposite: separateness of force planning by each service. As Gen. Maxwell Taylor, army chief of staff in the second half of the fifties, subsequently wrote: "The three services develop their forces more or less in isolation from each other, so that a force category such as strategic retaliatory force, which consists of contributions of both the navy and air force, is never viewed in the aggregate. Similarly, it is impossible to tell exactly how much continental air defense is being obtained from the defense budget since this is another category to which several services contribute."[8] When, for example, the navy briefed the secretary of defense as to the number of new Polaris submarines that ought to be acquired, no reference was made to the nuclear capabilities or plans of the air force in which the majority of nuclear weapons were to be found. Airlift, which was the responsibility of the air force, and sealift, the responsibility of the navy, were poorly coordinated with plans for reinforcing NATO's conventional forces in case of conflict. As a result, the army lacked a clear statement as to how many men could be carried and within what time frames troops might be dispatched to assist our allies.[9]

Robert McNamara, who became secretary of defense when Kennedy took office in 1961, had a background different than his predecessors in the Department of Defense. During World War II he had become part of a new generation of analysts who applied economic and operational concepts to concrete problems, seeking the best combination of factors to ensure the most rational solution. He had helped figure the optimum combination of men and equipment for the Eighth Air Force stationed during the war in Britain and later determined the preferred flight paths for American bombers traveling from India via China to attack Japan. In 1961 McNamara was forty-four years old and had recently been made president of Ford Motors.[10]

McNamara set one main condition for his appointment as secretary of defense: that he be allowed to select his own subordinates. As a result, the men who followed him into the Defense Department were young, bright individuals who were confident that the newest techniques of organizational and systems analysis could lend structure and coherence to the formulation of rational and effective defense planning. As the head of McNamara's Office of Systems Analysis later wrote, the goal behind the new managerial techniques "was to develop explicit criteria openly and thoroughly debated by all interested parties, that could be used by the Secretary of Defense, the President, and the Congress as measures of the need for and adequacy of defense programs."[11] Clearly, men of this persuasion would best be termed *activists* with respect to centralizing defense decisions within the civilian offices of the secretary of defense.

To grasp the revolutionary nature of this new process of systems analysis when applied to defense planning and budgeting, it is best to proceed by way of hypothetical example. Assume that a growing threat in the early sixties is the expansion of Soviet submarine programs with the most important augmentation being concentrated in the Soviet Northern Fleet that sends its ships into the ocean around the Scandinavian Peninsula. Assume also that a request has been sent from the Department of the Air Force that asks for increased funding in next year's budget to purchase patrol planes capable of seeking out and sinking such Soviet submarines. While it is obvious that some protection against the new threat is required, it is not yet clear that purchasing more planes is the most rational and least expensive solution. If the goal is to destroy such submarines as they approach the American coast, purchasing patrol planes that operate from the shore is fine. But upon reflection it appears that an equally positive goal might be to prevent such submarines from ever entering ocean waters in northern Europe. This goal can be met more efficiently by purchasing nuclear mines that can be placed on the ocean floor in European waters. Once one has agreed upon the goal, the most effective mix of defensive systems can be purchased, regardless of whether procurement for the task cuts across service lines, as would be the case here.

The ideal number of planes and mines procured would be reached when one dollar more of either weapon increased the kill probability for Soviet submarines by an equal amount. Yet even now reexamination of both the mix and the goal is in order. If a preferred goal is to prevent Soviet submarine-launched nuclear weapons from striking the United States, should not thought be given to purchasing some antiballistic missiles for continental defense? Yet perhaps the true goal is to prevent civilian casualties through such antiballistic missile procurements. Would it not be cheaper and more effective to spend some portions of the expanded defense request for civil defense preparedness and civil defense shelters? When this *process* of debate/integration is completed, you have identified a particular mission (goal) required for national security here and now. You have also identified the various force structures and components able to meet this threat, and most important, you have selected the most cost-effective combination of such forces despite the fact that such combinations frequently cut across service lines. As McNamara's Pentagon comptroller succinctly described the process, "Systems analysis at the national level . . . involves a continuous cycle of defining military objectives, designing alternate systems to achieve these objectives, evaluating these alternatives in terms of their objectives and costs, questioning the objectives and other assumptions underlying the analyses, opening new alternatives and establishing new military objectives, and so on indefinitely."[12]

There were three overall assumptions and practices of the McNamara Pentagon. First, the secretary of defense would provide strong and direct leadership over both the respective services and national security planning and budgeting. Fortunately for McNamara, a reform of the Defense Department in the last years of the Eisenhower administration provided the secretary of defense with the authorization to determine force structures of the various military commands, supervise all research and engineering within the DOD, and transfer, abolish, or consolidate combatant functions. Second, pure fiscal restraint was no longer appropriate as the means to a rational national defense. To McNamara defense was far too important a subject to be determined by what was left over in the national budget once domestic priorities had been covered. Rather, McNamara and his advisers would determine what defense needs were necessitated by the changing threat in conjunction with American commitments and goals. His prime task then would be to procure what was needed as economically as possible. As the new defense secretary later recorded, "When I took office in January, 1961, President Kennedy instructed me to: (1) develop the force structure necessary to meet our military requirements without regard to arbitrary budget ceilings, (2) procure and operate this force at the lowest possible cost."[13]

The third assumption/practice following the augmentation of civilian authority and the construction of defense planning on a nonfiscal basis was reducing service autonomy in setting goals and force requirements, and in reducing interservice rivalries for scarce defense dollars. This was accomplished, in part, by centralizing decision making within the Office of the Secretary of Defense (OSD). A systems analysis office was established with its director eventually holding the rank of an assistant secretary. Starting with six members in 1961, the office expanded to fifty by 1964 and to two hundred by 1968.[14] Equally important in reducing interservice rivalry was the end of strategic monism in service planning. The new defense concept of flexible response meant that the failure of the army, for example, to gain permission to develop a new atomic weapon no longer resulted in a corresponding cut in army allocations. Certain tasks were assigned to all services, and a nuclear response to a given threat was only one possible alternative that the secretary of defense might support. Interestingly, the efficiency of a systems approach to defense planning soon became so apparent that the services themselves established such offices.[15]

The yearly process for determining the preferred force procurements to meet identified security goals was achieved, at least in theory, by separating the planning and budgetary processes. They would be reintegrated later through application of the Planned Program Budgeting System (PPBS). A five-year defense plan (FYDP) was established in 1961, with the anticipated costs estimated for the five-year period and with projections of forces to be procured lasting eight years.[16] At the broadest level of aggregation, ten major military programs were identified, including such categories as strategic forces, general purpose forces, intelligence and communications, and airlift and sealift. Each major program was further divided into "program elements" that constituted the basic building blocks. Each program element was a force or an activity. Thus, the B-52 bombers together with their support units and facilities formed a program element. So would an infantry division in combination with all support needed to ensure meeting its objective. The program elements combined both costs and benefits; the cost of the bombers, for example, included the planes themselves, maintenance, pilot-training costs, runway repairs, etc.[17]

In finished form the FYDP remained open to modification as the threat changed or as more cost-effective means of defense were discovered. In the spring of each year, the major programs and the identified force levels were discussed in what became an annual force review cycle. In the fall the respective services forwarded their individual budgets to OSD, pricing components of the FYDP according to the most recent cost tables. While the actual accounts of the McNamara Pentagon suggest that things did not always run so smoothly, a definite process or cycle was established that ended in an integrated defense budgetary recommendation derived from the best estimates on the most rational combination of program elements. As a general guide to how force procurements, programs, and elements related to actual national security needs, the latter always in flux as the Soviets also varied their force procurements, the Draft Presidential Memoranda (DPM) were introduced.[18] Originating in OSD, the DPM assessed the functional programs, America's overall strategy of defense, the best mix of forces available, and the likely effects of alternate force combinations. By 1968 sixteen DPMs had been issued, some relating to region defense programs such as Asian Strategy and Force Structures and some to functional programs such as General Purpose Forces.[19]

Almost from its inception, the extensive use of systems analysis provoked criticism both inside and outside the government. A major objection was that this approach placed a premium upon quantifying all aspects of defense planning with little regard for important qualitative factors such as values, experience, and historic precedent. But such an objection appears basically unjustified, as an important example of systems analysis in practice indicates. This example does suggest that the loci of decision making in the Kennedy and Johnson administrations was increasingly concentrated in civilian hands, giving rise to growing disdain for the entire process among military professionals.

A major problem for the Kennedy planners was to determine the number of nuclear-capable missiles and bombers needed to confront the perceived Soviet threat of the sixties. No possible answer to this question could be offered based upon quantification alone; rather, clear policy direction that took account of qualitative values and experience was vitally needed. The top officials, including the president himself, eventually established a declared policy of deterrence as America's fundamental strategic concept. This was to be achieved by the possession of an assured second-strike capability that could destroy about one-quarter of the Soviet population and over 50 percent of Soviet industrial power in a retaliatory strike. Once this decision was reached, systems analysis could be applied to determine the best combination of destructive resources at the lowest cost able to guarantee such devastation. The goals, including the percentages of destruction needed, were not arrived at quantitatively; they represented political judgments.[20]

To solve the problem of the best force mix, the Pentagon had to research a number of related problems. The number, types, and locations of enemy targets had to be established. The number and explosive power of required American weapons was enumerated. Then the nature, size, and mix of the U.S. force best able to accomplish the mission was determined. For example, since bombers with gravity bombs were still more accurate than America's submarine-launched ballistic missiles (SLBMs), a number of these weapons were required for hardened Soviet targets that demanded a direct hit. Factored into the equation of how much force was needed was an awareness of the worst possible case: What percentage of American nuclear assets would remain if the Soviets accomplished a surprise attack. By 1966, after five years of examination and reexamination, the best answer was available and could be displayed in tabular form, as in Table 1.

Table 1. Soviet Population and Industry Destroyed
(assumes population of 247 million)

One Megaton Equivalent Delivered Warhead	Total Population Killed		Percent of Industrial Capability Destroyed
	Millions	Percent	
100	37	15	59
200	52	21	72
400	74	30	76
800	96	39	77
1,200	109	44	77
1,600	116	47	77

Source: Enthoven and Smith, *Shaping the Defense Program*, 207.

This table clearly demonstrated two things. At 400 delivered one megaton equivalent warheads, the stated policy objectives would be accomplished, since 20 to 25 percent of the population would be killed and 50 percent of industry destroyed. These are the figures that the administration, in an explicit value judgment, assumed would deter the Soviets from attacking the United States. But the table lent additional quantitative support to the decision arrived at by qualitative judgment; it showed that a doubling of the destructive forces from 400 to 800 delivered megatons only increased population death by 9 percent and industrial destruction by 1 percent. Thus, the most cost-effective strategy coincided with the politically selected guideline of 400 megatons. Based upon such calculations and examining the capabilities of American weapons and the various targets that had to be destroyed, the Pentagon procured a mixed nuclear fleet of 1,000 land-based Minuteman intercontinental ballistic missiles, 41 Polaris submarines with SLBMs, and 500 bombers. Various analyzed scenarios, war games, and the changing nature of Soviet weapons procurement indicated that such a force, even in a worst-case situation, would be able to deliver the needed firepower to Soviet targets. This, in turn, suggested that the requirements for implementing the declared strategy of deterrence, or mutually assured destruction (MAD) as it became known later, had been met.[21]

It would appear that the main shortfall of the new systems approach lay in the continued political battles for weapon procurements that left little opportunity for sufficient quantification. Government, after all, has traditionally been the scene of intense political and bureaucratic rivalry, the disputes frequently having little to do with defense per se. As one examiner of the Pentagon's approach to systems analysis reported: "Analysis . . . had been relevant in only a small proportion of the discussions. Half the time a decision had been foreclosed by higher political involvement: a call from the White House, interest expressed by key congressmen or committees. In an additional thirty percent of the cases, the careers of immediate supervisors were involved. Analysis could not influence the recommendations; it could only serve as an irritant. But . . . in something like twenty percent of the issues, analysis was unfettered and contributed to much improved overall results."[22]

It appears that the problem of political involvement was one issue that the McNamara Pentagon could simply not overcome. Yet equally important were the political guidelines that determined the entire process of selecting the correct mix of forces required to do a given job. Deterrence and the chosen mix of bombers and missiles to accomplish it were, fortunately, not challenged in the sixties. The political guidelines that determined the broad parameters of selecting the correct mix of conventional forces to defeat the North Vietnamese sadly were. But, especially in this case, one could argue that the political assumptions as to what levels of punishment would dissuade North Vietnam were at fault, not the combinations of destruction selected to accomplish the political objective.

11

Arms Control
in the Sixties

The new decade and the new Kennedy administration ushered in a favorable period for negotiations of a first arms control accord with the Soviet Union. In part, this was due to the unparalleled expansion of America's nuclear forces in combination with the early discovery that the suggested missile gap actually concealed growing Soviet nuclear inferiority. Then, too, President Kennedy's personality and ruling style prompted a deeper sense of the possible among his strategic planners, a feeling that would possibly curtail the seemingly never-ending competition between the superpowers for the largest nuclear arsenal.[1] And yet credit for a decade that was more open to arms discussions must also be given to the Eisenhower administration. During the fifties the linkage between nuclear and conventional arms had been broken, with America showing great interest in an accord that would only limit the more expensive nuclear weapons as a step to full and general disarmament or arms control. With the lengthy negotiations at Geneva between technicians and political experts as to conditions of a nuclear test ban already far advanced, it was easier for the Kennedy people to resume negotiations than to initiate them from scratch.

Eisenhower had also appointed several key domestic advisers who regularly studied the prospects for renewed discussions. In 1955 a special assistant to the president for arms control was created, followed by a special White House assistant for science and technology two years later, concluding in 1958 with the designation of a high-level interagency group to coordinate arms control suggestions arising from various offices within the Washington bureaucracy. Kennedy's establishment of the Arms Control and Disarmament Agency in 1961, headed by a director with the status of an undersecretary of state who reported directly to the president, simply continued a precedent set in the previous decade.[2]

In the first two years of the new administration, ideas for an arms control agreement were discussed primarily through the appropriate UN subcommittee on which representatives of both superpowers sat. The challenge of how to regularize the status of Berlin absorbed much energy and effort during Kennedy's first year in power, and only the creation of the infamous Berlin Wall in the fall of 1961 permitted a shift of attention elsewhere. By now past Soviet claims of nuclear superiority following the successful launch of Sputnik four years earlier had been proven false, thanks in part to the American technological breakthrough in high-resolution aerial photography. The Soviet dispatch of intermedium and medium-range ballistic missiles to Cuba in the fall of 1962 was a last, dangerous gamble to "fix" the growing imbalance of nuclear forces between Moscow and Washington. By the end of 1962, America had deployed nearly 300 intercontinental ballistic missiles (ICBMs) and 155 submarine-launched ballistic missiles (SLBMs). By contrast, the USSR had no more than 75 of the former and none of the latter. Time was propitious for serious arms discussions, especially given Soviet leader Nikita Khrushchev's plans to redirect scarce Soviet resources away from defense and into economic modernization.[3]

Throughout the fifties the main sticking point for any agreement with the Soviets had been the issue of on-site inspection. Fortunately, new American abilities to monitor large Soviet nuclear tests with spy-in-the-sky satellites came of age early in the Kennedy administration. Nevertheless, on-site inspection continued to be of significant importance both as a sign of Soviet seriousness and because a complete ban on nuclear testing could not be verified without it. In 1959 a treaty allowing such inspection went into effect, suggesting a new Soviet flexibility. The Treaty on Antarctica, which was signed by twelve nations including America, Britain, France, and the USSR, allowed each side the right of inspection of the others' facilities to ensure that the neutrality of the area would be maintained.[4] Consistent with this new approach, Khrushchev, in December 1962, informed Kennedy that he would permit the installation of a small number of "black boxes" on Soviet soil and allow several on-site inspections each year as part of a comprehensive nuclear test ban agreement. And while this offer appeared to show continuing Soviet interest in an agreement, disputes about the number of boxes and the number of inspections still precluded the successful completion of negotiations that had begun in the preceding decade.[5]

In an effort to break the long-standing barrier, in April 1963 Kennedy, in conjunction with a similar letter being sent from London, asked that

Western emissaries be received in Moscow at an early convenience; Under secretary of State Averell Harriman, former ambassador to the Soviet Union under Roosevelt, was selected to lead the American delegation. On July 9, two days before Harriman left for Moscow, a high-level committee including the president and his top advisers met to provide final instructions. The preferred objective of any treaty would be a comprehensive prohibition of all nuclear testing in all environments. Yet if a Soviet objection to required on-site inspection made such an accord impossible, Harriman was authorized to fall back to an alternate plan. This would ban testing in all environments that America felt it could adequately monitor without rights for on-site verification and would constitute a "partial" test ban agreement. When Khrushchev showed himself even more recalcitrant than before with respect to verification, the partial agreement became the order of the day.[6] The first major arms understanding with the USSR—the Limited Test Ban Treaty—was signed by American, British, and Soviet representatives on July 25, 1963. A new chapter in the history of arms control had begun.

Under the treaty the signatories pledged to forgo nuclear explosions in the atmosphere, outer space, underwater, or in any other environment "if such explosion causes radioactive debris to be present outside the territorial limits of the state under whose jurisdiction or control such explosion is conducted."[7] The treaty remained open for any other nation to sign if it wished and was to be of unlimited duration. Any signatory, however, could withdraw in case of "extraordinary events" that might threaten its national security after delivering three months' notice of such intent.

Since the Limited Test Ban Treaty was the first of its kind and would set a precedent for future negotiations, Kennedy took steps to ensure its ratification in the U.S. Senate. He took personal control over the ratification campaign, encouraging the creation of the Citizens Committee for a Nuclear Test Ban that he advised about preferred strategy. Kennedy also carefully reviewed testimony that would be crucial to passage, including that of key military leaders such as Gen. Maxwell Taylor. According to the latter, four criteria conditioned the Joint Chiefs' acceptance of the treaty: (1) America should not accept limitations on its own testing if it might lead to a Soviet advantage; (2) Clandestine Soviet testing would not seriously affect America's nuclear programs; (3) America could withdraw from the treaty without undue delay; and (4) If points one and two were not fully met, the treaty would convey compensatory advantages elsewhere. Four safeguards were also identified by Taylor as conditions for the Joint Chiefs' support. America would conduct a comprehensive, aggressive, and regular program of permitted underground nuclear explosions. It would maintain modern facilities and programs of nuclear research. Facilities and preparations for resuming atmospheric testing would be maintained in case of Soviet violations. And America's ability to monitor possible Soviet violations would be constantly improved.[8]

With assistance from a well-orchestrated protreaty campaign and aided by supportive testimony from the military, the treaty passed Senate consideration 80 to 19. Although initially approved only by America, Britain, and the USSR, by the end of the seventies over 100 nations had signed and ratified the agreement.[9] A three-way treaty had become a global agreement on arms control. Unfortunately, China, France, and India, each of whom had exploded a nuclear device/bomb by that time, still remained outside its confines.

As the first major postwar arms control agreement, the Limited Test Ban Treaty has been exposed to detailed examination in an effort to determine whether or not such accords fulfill the promise expected by their proponents. The results have been mixed. A prime reason for this treaty was worldwide interest in diminishing the growing radiation threat resulting from atmospheric tests of the fifties. Since 1963 the United States, Britain, and the USSR have avoided such a testing mode although tests by France and China have taken place. As a result, radioactivity has remained at a negligible level, not assuming the threatening proportions once predicted. On the other hand, those who felt a Limited Test Ban Treaty would diminish nuclear explosions overall have been disappointed. Of the 638 American nuclear tests between 1945 and 1980, 354, or 54 percent, occurred after the agreement was signed. Fifty-six percent of the Soviet nuclear tests also took place after the summer of 1963.[10]

Many supporters of the treaty felt its signing would break open the logjam restricting such accords, producing a flood of similar understandings. In truth, a number of major agreements did follow, including a 1967 ban on nuclear weapons in outer space, a 1968 prohibition on nuclear weapons in Latin America, a 1970 worldwide nonproliferation agreement, and, perhaps the most famous of such accords, the signing of the Strategic Arms Limitation Talks (SALT) I and II in 1972 and 1979 respectively.[11] Perhaps most important for those supporting the Limited Test Ban was the hope that the open nature of the treaty would promote nonproliferation in addition to maintaining a lower level of external radiation. This hope seems to have been met. The fact that over 100 nations, large and small, have signed the treaty allows it to stand as an agreement by these states not to acquire nuclear arms. While the treaty does permit underground testing, that remains the most difficult and sophisticated mode, far beyond the capabilities of the vast majority of countries. Thus, accession to the Limited Test Ban Treaty constitutes an effective pledge by such states not to enter the nuclear arms race. Since 1963 only two additional states, China and India, have exploded nuclear devices; France entered the nuclear club before that date. These three states still remain outside the agreement.

The second major nuclear control agreement of the sixties, the Nonproliferation Treaty, also had its roots in the past. In the immediate postwar period, the United States introduced a resolution before the United Nations that would have created an international monopoly over all nuclear research and development. The failure of this Baruch Proposal produced the opposite effect: The United States, Britain, and the Soviet Union retained national programs of weapons research and testing. In America a national Atomic Energy Commission (AEC) became all-powerful in determining what use the United States would make of nuclear materials. The sharing of information, even with such old allies and partners as Britain and Canada, was restricted. Not until the fifties was the Atomic Energy Act broadened to allow the exchange of information in nuclear questions. This, in turn, was a step toward some type of internationalization since sharing would be a crucial aspect of any new effort at global nuclear control.[12]

In December 1953 President Eisenhower proposed his "Atoms for Peace" program in a speech to the United Nations. It would be best for the world, he argued, if nuclear energy were used for peaceful pursuits. The United States and the Soviet Union, he suggested, ought to divert a portion of their stocks of nuclear material to help others. This, in turn, would diminish the total amount of materials available for destructive purposes.[13] In early 1954 the United States opened direct negotiations with Moscow.

For the Soviet Union, two factors argued for participation in some international scheme of nuclear sharing and/or control. Most important, Moscow, even more than the United States, feared the spread of nuclear weapons to other states since the USSR had more enemies. Equally, it was recognized that America could proceed with its plans for international sharing without Moscow's assent, since the majority of world stocks of uranium were under American or Western control. Thus, a common accord was the sole means by which at least partial internationalization might be achieved with some Soviet participation in policy and decision making within the new organization. In 1956 an agreement was signed to authorize an International Atomic Energy Agency (IAEA). Nuclear materials would be donated to the IAEA for research and common use. The IAEA, in turn, would establish safeguards and an inspection system to ensure that no nuclear assistance granted to a third party found use in a national weapons program. Such safeguards, however, would only apply to recipients of IAEA materials and not to nuclear donors. Thus, the nuclear facilities of the Soviet Union, as well as those of Britain and America, would not be subject to inspection. As the IAEA began to develop safeguards for nuclear transfers, it increasingly became the model institution for those who argued that the 1956 agreement ought to be expanded into a true nonproliferation accord.[14]

The notion of a nonproliferation agreement had been discussed in the United Nations in the early fifties, with a number of smaller states fearful of the growing superpower arms race as prime proponents. In 1961 the General Assembly approved a compromise Irish formula that had received support from both the large and small powers. Under its provisions the nuclear states would promise not to transfer nuclear weapons or the control of nuclear weapons already present on the soil of nonnuclear states to nonnuclear nations. The latter, in turn, would pledge not to manufacture or otherwise acquire such nuclear arms.[15] Shortly thereafter, the new Kennedy administration and the Soviets began serious discussions on the matter.

In the short run, the main stumbling block to agreement between the superpowers was an American plan of the early sixties to create a so-called multilateral force in NATO. Aware that many of America's allies saw the new defense strategy of flexible response as a means of making Europe safe for conventional war and anticipating cries for national inventories of nuclear weapons from NATO states, the Kennedy administration proposed the organization of a NATO nuclear force. This force would be composed of military men or units from numerous NATO states and would possess some nuclear ability as a means of demonstrating America's continued will to link nuclear weapons to the defense of Europe. One of the alternate plans for such a force foresaw the creation of special ships manned by sailors from several nations that would carry nuclear missiles and would be able to deter a conventional Soviet attack by threatening to escalate from the conventional to the theater-nuclear level in response to any Soviet assault.[16] Not until the multilateral force was dropped in 1965 was the way clear for full American and Soviet participation in nonproliferation negotiations. An additional assist was provided by a 1966 Senate resolution that requested the president to do all possible to curtail the spread of nuclear weapons.

By mid-decade a worldwide consensus began to emerge favoring a more balanced approach to nonproliferation. In numerous forums arranged under UN auspices, the smaller, nonnuclear nations affirmed that they wished to place the responsibility for reducing the existing nuclear arsenals upon the states with nuclear weapons in exchange for pledges by nonnuclear nations not to acquire the weapons. In addition, nuclear states would have to guarantee the security of those nations ready to forswear construction of their own nuclear deterrent. And finally, reasonable measures to allow the dissemination of knowledge concerning the peaceful development of nuclear energy must be available to all signatories. In the way of practical measures, a joint resolution sponsored by Switzerland and Romania proposed that nuclear states pledge not to use nuclear weapons against nations that did not possess them. This resolution, in turn, was opposed by the Soviet Union on the grounds that several nonnuclear members of NATO possessed American nuclear weapons on their soil that might be fired against the USSR. The matter was resolved by a common Security Council resolution that promised assistance to any nonnuclear state threatened by nuclear attack. [17]

Benefiting from over a decade of serious debate in which the most important issues had been discussed and rediscussed, the final treaty, ready for signing in mid-1968, took account of the perspectives of both large and small countries. As a concession to the nonnuclear states, the nuclear powers willing to sign promised to negotiate between themselves in good faith for significant reductions in their existing nuclear inventories. The treaty, which was signed July 1, 1968, and became effective in March 1970, contained 97 adherents, although only 47 of these had ratified the treaty by the March 1970 date. Review conferences at five-year intervals were promised to ensure that all signatories were meeting their responsibilities. By the time of the first such conference, 111 nations had signed the Nonproliferation Treaty, and 96 had ratified it. The United States, Britain, and the Soviet Union were the nuclear powers signing and ratifying. France did neither while promising to abide by its provisions. China, while not formally pledging to uphold the treaty, appeared to be following its provisions. India, which exploded a nuclear device in 1974 was a nonsignatory as well. Among the nonnuclear states suspected of having their own clandestine nuclear programs, Argentina, Brazil, Israel, Pakistan, Saudi Arabia, and South Africa were not members of the treaty nations. [18]

The heart of the treaty revolved around four main provisions. First, nuclear nations pledged not to transfer to any recipient whatsoever nuclear weapons or nuclear explosive devices or the control over such weapons. Second, the nonnuclear states promised not to receive nuclear weapons or control over such weapons either directly or indirectly nor to manufacture or otherwise acquire such devices. Third, each nonnuclear state agreed to accept IAEA safeguards as a means of verifying obligations assumed under the treaty. These safeguards would apply to all sources of fissionable materials in all peaceful nuclear activities. Fourth, the nuclear states promised to provide the full benefits of peaceful usage of atomic energy to nonnuclear states without discrimination and under strict control. [19]

In the period since the Nonproliferation Treaty went into effect, membership within the treaty organization has continued to grow, although France, China, and India still remain outside its bounds as do important nonnuclear states mentioned. At the review conferences scheduled every five years, serious debate is still heard regarding the fulfillment of treaty provisions. One of the loudest complaints is voiced against America and the Soviet Union for not undertaking serious efforts, as promised, to reduce their nuclear arsenals. As will be seen, even the major breakthroughs in arms control achieved in the seventies with SALT I and SALT II did little to actually reduce the existing supplies of such weapons; rather, their numbers and characteristics were regularized. The signatories of the Nonproliferation Treaty continue to this day to exert pressure upon Soviet and American negotiators for actual decreases in nuclear arms.

12

America's Vietnam Policy

In the late seventies, Senate Majority Leader Mike Mansfield reflected upon America's recent experiences in Vietnam and reached the following conclusion. "With some of us it will never be forgotten because it was one of the most tragic, if not *the* most tragic, episode in American history. It was unnecessary, uncalled for, it wasn't tied to our security or a vital interest. It was just a misadventure in a part of the world which we should have kept our nose out of."[1] While Mansfield's discouragement is understandable, his sense of history was far off the mark. Vietnam, if anything, was a necessary part of America's postwar security planning. Otherwise, how would one explain its importance for every president since Franklin Roosevelt? Tragic to be sure, but untied to America's vital interests? Unlikely. The lengthy history of America's involvement in Southeast Asia can only be understood as an intrinsic part of our postwar policy toward communist expansion, a policy designed to defend what was viewed as essential security interests. On a regular basis, America's policy toward Vietnam was updated, taking account of changing perceptions of the communist threat. Once U.S. forces were committed directly, Washington feared that withdrawal without victory would undermine promises to aid other nations' fights against communism. The final peace treaty of 1973 that made withdrawal possible was achieved only after the new Nixon-Kissinger administration changed America's view of communism's traditional threat, replacing the doctrine of containment with a more flexible approach of cooperation and competition. Unfortunately, by the early seventies, American public opinion found itself unable to continue a commitment that by now seemed senseless. Throughout its entire history, America's pledge to retain a noncommunist Vietnam was part of the planning for national security.

On the eve of America's entry into World War II, planners in Washington recognized the importance of French Indochina, as the area was then called. Important raw materials were imported from the southern Asian region, and the loss of such assets would be a serious blow to the already depressed American economy.[2] When the Japanese Empire occupied this region in 1941, Roosevelt authorized the suspension of oil shipments to Tokyo. Each proposal for a negotiated settlement of outstanding U.S.-Japanese problems from that date forward included demands that Japan evacuate Indochina. Refusing Washington's proposals, Japan remained in occupation of Southeast Asia until the conflict ended in 1945. Thus, the future of Indochina became an issue for postwar planners.

During World War II Franklin Roosevelt frequently expressed interest in ending the French colonial empire in Asia, placing existing colonies under a form of international trusteeship upon the war's end. Such a status, probably administered through the to-be-created United Nations, would prepare the colonies for eventual independence. But by the time of the February 1945 Yalta Conference, a shift in Roosevelt's thinking had become apparent. Increasingly concerned by the prospect of Soviet expansionism in postwar Europe—a theme stressed by his close ally, Winston Churchill—Roosevelt gave thought to how France might function as a stronghold of democracy on the postwar continent. Yalta was the conference at which France was granted a veto in the United Nations and a zone of occupation in postwar Germany. To strip France of its colonial domain without its consent would undermine the enhanced prestige that granting France the veto and the occupation zone was designed to further. At Yalta Roosevelt suggested that France must voluntarily nominate Indochina for trustee status, a suggestion that precluded any action whatsoever since the French refusal to jettison its empire was well known.[3]

In the fall of 1945, with the war over and with Roosevelt dead, France returned to Vietnam only to find a rival government already administering power. Ho Chi Minh, a local underground leader loosely allied with the United States during the war, had proclaimed the Democratic Republic of Vietnam in part of the former Indochina colony. Oddly enough, given America's subsequent views of Ho, American army officers stood on the reviewing stand when Ho made his proclamation, and a Vietnamese band played the "Star-Spangled Banner." While Washington had known that Ho and much of the leadership of his underground Vietminh were Communists, this had not precluded support. Washington gave equal support to Tito in Yugoslavia despite knowing about his communist affiliations.[4] In wartime the key task was to defeat the main enemy, and all that contributed to that goal was considered eligible for possible support. But with the return of the French, Ho's efforts to perpetuate his rule were met with firm resistance from Paris. From 1945 through 1954, France and the Vietminh waged a no-holds-barred struggle.

Harry Truman inherited an ambiguous and incomplete plan for dealing with postwar Indochina. Initially, he followed the outlines of Roosevelt's plan that took no action to block reconstitution of France's Asian empire but provided no assistance either. But as time progressed, Roosevelt's idea that a strong France was crucial to European stability began to assume dominance. With the outbreak of the Cold War and the initiation of the Marshall Plan to rebuild Europe, Washington became more and more involved in promoting French domestic stability. Within the State Department, a split soon developed between those desks concerned with Asian affairs who remained anticolonial in their outlook and advice and those desks dealing with Europe who stressed the role of a strong France. Resolved to provide assistance to France, the Truman administration made it clear that such aid must not be used in France's Vietnam War. Until the end of the decade, American policy retained this ambiguous trait. The United States would provide assistance to France, economic and military, despite its continuation of a colonial war provided that no assistance was transferred to the Asian colonial theater.[5]

The event that changed the Truman administration's approach to the Vietnamese problem was the victory of communist forces in China in the fall of 1949. With attention now shifted from potential Soviet expansion in Europe to actual communist victories in Asia, Washington began a reconsideration of Vietnam's importance to U.S. security. Having by now adopted the outlines of George Kennan's containment policy, it was but a small step to apply it to the borders of Red China. When in January 1950 Peking as well as Moscow extended diplomatic recognition to Ho's Democratic Republic, Washington's concerns found confirmation. As the American secretary of state remarked, the extension of recognition ended for all times the argument as to whether Ho was a Communist, or, as some misguided individuals thought, a Nationalist at heart.[6]

In the spring of 1950, Washington gave official support to a French plan to grant quasi-independence to Indochina with the successor states remaining within the French Union. Vietnam, the Kingdom of Laos, and the Kingdom of Cambodia received American diplomatic recognition. In part, such recognition was a reward since Washington had long advised France that only some steps toward independence would blunt communist charges that Vietnam was a white man's colonial war. In part, recognition revealed that America had resolved its ambiguity as to the propriety of French actions in Asia and would stand by its ally. The new American support was reflected in a National Security Council reconsideration of the importance of Vietnam, which was completed the month recognition was extended. NSC-64, dated February 27, called for "all practicable measures . . . to prevent further communist expansion in Southeast Asia." If Indochina fell, the document warned, Thailand and Burma would likely fall too.[7] Here, as early as February 1950, was clear expression of the soon-to-be-famous Domino Theory. The fate of noncommunist Southeast Asia was tied to the containment of communism where the first attempts at communist domination were clearly visible: Vietnam.

The outbreak of the Korean War some four months later gave further credence to the notion that communist expansionism had reached a new, postwar high: China, Vietnam, and now Korea. Resistance in Vietnam was increasingly viewed as part of containing each outburst of communist revolution. In May 1951 NSC 48/5 discussed the prospects of eliminating communist influence in the area of Southeast Asia. The following year NSC 124/2 labeled Indochina "of great strategic importance . . . and as essential to the security of the free world not only in the Far East but in the middle East and Europe as well."[8] Such words bear repeating for Americans who even today think the United States somehow blundered into the Vietnam War—"essential to the security of the free world." Concomitant with the elevated significance of a noncommunist Vietnam, America soon became the main supplier of arms and equipment to the beleaguered Frenchmen and pro-French Vietnamese fighting the Vietminh. During 1951 and 1952, U.S. aid constituted 40 percent of the cost of the war. By 1953 and 1954, America had assumed 80 percent of the war's fiscal burden. By now France was the largest recipient of U.S. assistance in the world.[9]

The Eisenhower administration arrived in power with contradictory pledges; it promised to role back communist advances yet scale back American defense spending. Concurring with its predecessors that Indochina must be kept from communist clutches, U.S. aid was forthcoming on behalf of several ambitious French offensive plans that promised defeat of the Vietminh. The small Military Assistance and Advisory Group (MAAG) established in 1950 to assist in training the pro-French Vietnamese forces was augmented in 1954 with the dispatch of 200 American technicians and mechanics and 22 B-26 medium bombers.[10] But despite the augmented American aid, the French optimism failed to produce results. In the spring of 1954, 18,000 French troops were surrounded in the fortress of Dien Bien Phu, and while the loss of this position would be of slight military significance, it would serve as a clear symbol of France's inability to win the war. In Washington the loss of Dien Bien Phu was perceived as a likely reason for the French to demand the end of a commitment that seemed to have no limits. Thus, when the French chief of staff arrived in the American capital for talks, it appeared likely that a further American pledge of aid would be in order. As suspected, the French now requested direct U.S. intervention, the use of American air strikes to relieve the surrounded fortress.[11]

The French request found differing responses among U.S. military and policy elites. Adm. Arthur Radford, chief of the Joint Chiefs of Staff, gave his support and was asked by President Eisenhower to brief a select group of congressmen on the possible consequences of direct U.S. involvement. As perhaps Eisenhower expected, the congressmen showed great skepticism, concluding that Congress as a whole would not support such involvement short of a combined front being formed by all Western Powers having interests in Southeast Asia. When Winston Churchill, again prime minister of Britain, declined to permit British participation in any warlike actions on behalf of France, the plan for American intervention languished. That same spring the fortress fell, and the future of Vietnam became the topic of an international conference convened in Geneva to arrange a settlement between France and Vietminh.[12]

The Geneva Conference hosting delegates from both main communist powers, China and Russia, as well as leaders from the West reached a compromise agreement to regulate the future of what had once been French Indochina. All hostilities in Vietnam were to cease, and the forces of the opposing sides were to regroup on either side of a temporary demarcation line running along the seventeenth parallel. Increases in outside military personnel, arms, or military bases were forbidden, and neither side was to join an international alliance. The Vietminh government north of the seventeenth parallel and the new, independent Republic of Vietnam south of the line were to harmonize their differences and prepare for elections throughout Vietnam in 1956. All agreements reached at Geneva were to be supervised by a three-power control commission including representatives from Canada, India, and Poland. Not a direct participant in the Vietnam War, the United States declined to sign these final agreements although Washington did pledge not to disturb the situation by force. The new South Vietnamese government, now under the command of Ngo Dinh Diem, immediately condemned the accord.[13]

The withdrawal of French forces from Vietnam and the Geneva agreements did little to change Washington's view as to that country's importance in the global containment of communism. In December 1954 National Security Council resolution 5429/5 identified America's objectives as follows: "Make every possible effort, not openly inconsistent with the U.S. position as to the armistice agreement, to defeat Communist subversion and influence, to maintain and support friendly non-Communist governments in Cambodia and Laos, to maintain a friendly non-Communist South Vietnam and prevent a Communist victory through all-Vietnam elections."[14] The means selected to achieve these ends were twofold. America would support the rule of South Vietnamese ruler Ngo

Dinh Diem, especially as he promised no compromises with the communist north. And harkening back to the advice of congressional leaders that only as part of a broader coalition would America find congressional support for intervention in Southeast Asia, the Eisenhower administration created a broad-based alliance of interested world states. Named the Southeast Asia Treaty Organization (SEATO), the new alliance brought together America, Britain, France, Australia, New Zealand, Pakistan, the Philippines, and Thailand in an effort to block further communist expansion. Since the former states of Indochina—Vietnam, Laos, and Cambodia—were forbidden by the Geneva accords to join an alliance system, they were provided for by a protocol to the SEATO agreement that noted that a threat to these states would constitute a distinct danger to the security of all SEATO members.[15]

American assistance to Diem's Vietnam took two distinct forms. Since Vietnam was no longer a French colony, aid was forthcoming for the demanding task of nation building. It is one of the great ironies of the subsequent Vietnamese war that the liberals who eagerly offered their services in this endeavor would later oppose America's commitment as a whole. In the fifties, with the flourishing of the social sciences in American universities, young American idealists concluded that the laws of political development and nation construction could be taught to attentive students in newly emerging third world states. The eventual result, it was hoped, would be the harmonious development of democratic states throughout the underdeveloped world. Even the American Joint Chiefs of Staff advised that the United States ought not to undertake the training of the Vietnamese army unless a strong civil government could be fashioned in Saigon. By the end of the Eisenhower administration, the South Vietnamese government had become the fifth largest recipient of American foreign assistance. About 1,500 civilian advisers had been dispatched, roads had been rebuilt, new crops planted, schools founded, public health programs expanded, and Vietnamese civil servants trained. An extensive commercial import program assured the Diem government of needed imports to maintain economic stability.[16]

Along with political and economic aid, America was also generous with its military assistance. Between 1955 and 1961, fully 78 percent of all aid to Vietnam was in military categories. With the United States now replacing France as the trainers of the native army, the military assistance group soon exceeded the limits contained in the Geneva accords.[17]

Although the American political and military commitment foresaw a rapid stabilization of the Vietnamese military situation, the growth of civil disturbances and outright insurgency soon undermined early optimistic predictions. Following the failure to hold elections in 1956, the remnants of the old Vietminh forces in the South began to regroup for new activities. In 1959 North Vietnam formally approved the strategy of an uprising in the South, sending arms and advisers across the porous demarcation line. The following year the National Liberation Front was proclaimed, uniting opponents of the Diem government in an umbrella organization dominated by Communists. Statistics on violence well reveal the growing threat to the security of Diem's government and to American efforts to ensure South Vietnam as a stable nation. In 1958 700 South Vietnamese governmental officials were assassinated. By 1960 2,500 had met a similar death.[18] In 1959 the insurgents began shifting tactics, combining the usual limited guerrilla attacks with assaults by medium-sized units fighting in conventional battle formations.[19] While the final days of the Eisenhower administration did not see an immediate threat to the continuation of noncommunist rule in South Vietnam, it was readily apparent that the price of resisting communist expansion was going up. Yet even in the face of growing insurgency, few realized that the objectives of containment might one day require outlays of men and treasure that a democratic nation would find hard to sustain. In 1960 the situation, while serious, still appeared capable of control.

The Kennedy administration entered office facing the continuing dilemma of how Southeast Asia might be denied the Communists within reasonable costs. Ordering a study of the entire issue, President Kennedy's National Security Council in a memorandum dated May 11, 1961, reaffirmed America's objective to prevent communist domination over South Vietnam.[20] The key issue now became how best to achieve this goal—by emphasis upon nation building or through expanded military commitment. That fall Kennedy's military adviser, Gen. Maxwell Taylor, recommended the dispatch of 8,000 American troops. Vietcong activities had shown a distinct increase, and a provincial capital just fifty-five miles from the South Vietnamese capital of Saigon had fallen. Recognizing the danger of a possible collapse yet wary of sending U.S. forces, Kennedy compromised, approving an increase in American assistance and advisers.[21] By the end of 1962, U.S. "advisers" numbered 9,000, with their duties including dropping Vietnamese troops into battle by helicopter. But despite the renewed U.S. determination, the Vietcong remained on the offensive in 1962. By the following year, the reverses of the war were further complicated by open resistance to the increasingly oppressive rule of the Diem government. In November 1963, with U.S. approval if not total support, the Diem government was overthrown by a military clique.[22] Less than a month later, President Kennedy himself was dead, and the problem of Vietnam was passed to his successor. By now America had 17,000 advisers working with the Saigon government.

To President Johnson Vietnam was initially only an irritant that threatened to forestall the major domestic reforms the president planned. If America suffered losses in Southeast Asia, conservative foes of his Great Society reforms would likely join with normal patriotic forces to demand an all-out effort to prosecute a successful war against communism. A withdrawal of America's commitment to Saigon, however, might cast America's promises in doubt, undermining pledges and alliances created in the several decades since the war. In this respect, Vietnam was a test of America's will to resist communist expansion. Having been in Congress for many years, Johnson well remembered the outcry when Truman "lost" China in 1949. Johnson was determined he would not "lose" Vietnam. A National Security Action Memorandum (NSAM) of March 1964 confirmed the central importance of resisting communism in Vietnam as a barrier to its spread throughout the entire region. "Unless we can achieve this objective in South Vietnam, almost all of Southeast Asia will probably fall under Communist dominance."[23]

The "holding" of South Vietnam, however, had by now become a much more expensive proposition than in any preceding administration. The nation-building efforts had gone poorly, civil government was in an uproar, and between August 16 and September 3, 1964, three coups occurred in Saigon. In the countryside, the actual fighting continued to go against the South Vietnamese and their American advisers. That fall U.S. ships in the neutral waters off North Vietnam were allegedly attacked without provocation. In response, President Johnson ordered direct air strikes at military installations in the North.[24] The price of containment in Vietnam rose another level. Guarding against a possible future congressional outcry over such use of American forces, Johnson gained congressional approval for the Tonkin Gulf Resolution that granted the president the right to take "all necessary measures to repel any armed attack against the forces of the United States."[25] With the political and military situation still deteriorating, Johnson and his military advisers discussed future attacks against the North plus the possible dispatch of U.S. combat forces.

If the attack in the Gulf of Tonkin prompted America to seek bombing targets north of the seventeenth parallel, it was the attack upon American advisers at the South Vietnamese city of Pleiku the following February that both made the bombing a regular part of America's new military strategy and led to a major buildup of U.S. combat forces. From 1965 until the end of the Johnson administration in 1968, the number of troops and the number of casualties increased. By 1969 nearly 550,000 U.S. troops were in

Vietnam.[26] The termination of the war, however, continued to defy combined U.S.–South Vietnamese efforts.

The decision to dispatch major contingents of U.S. forces and to predicate the future of the war upon their activities meant that some clear guidelines for their use were urgently needed. Normally, there are three ways by which armed units can cause an enemy to concede defeat: destruction of the enemy armies, occupation of the enemy homeland, or breaking of the enemy will to resist.[27] The first two of these objectives were denied American forces due to the political and military environment in which the war progressed. The ability of the North Vietnamese to use neutral Cambodia and Laos as protected sanctuaries for force regroupings, plus the ability to position forces in China if necessary, made the destruction of enemy forces impossible. Occupation of North Vietnam was also unattainable. Experience in Korea demonstrated the sensitivity of communist China to foreign, anticommunist armies on its frontier. An invasion and occupation of North Vietnam threatened to expand the war to include the one Asian power that America wished to contain: China. Such an event would bring about the very war containment was designed to preclude. Thus, the only acceptable military strategy was to engage enemy forces in the South, preventing a communist victory there while applying measured punishment by air against North Vietnamese military and industrial targets.

Throughout his administration, President Johnson dispatched more and more troops to hold the line in South Vietnam while increasing in a measured, step-by-step manner the destruction rained upon North Vietnam by air. Any rational state, Johnson believed, would have a breaking point. Realizing the firmness of the American commitment to a noncommunist South Vietnam and aware that America's military might could destroy everything of value constructed in North Vietnam since communism first took hold there, a realistic communist leadership would soon end its military efforts.[28] Unfortunately, North Vietnam failed to respond in a rational fashion, at least as *rational* was understood in the West. By 1968 Johnson faced an insoluble dilemma, a dilemma that lay at the very foundation of the postwar containment doctrine. To destroy North Vietnam's ability to make war, an invasion of the North would be necessary. Such action, however, would likely precipitate the very event containment was designed to preclude: a global conflict. By now the costs of merely blocking the communist efforts in South Vietnam without going to their source were too great in both treasure and blood. Several important advisers within the Johnson administration were counseling caution where once they had proclaimed optimism. The American people showed increasing restiveness at the prospect of a never-ending commitment. There was, in fact, no solution to the dilemma within the containment guidelines accepted by the Johnson administration. Only a new strategic view of the world complete with significant changes in U.S.-Chinese, U.S.-Soviet, and Chinese-Soviet relations offered a possible solution. In March 1968 Johnson announced he would not run again for office. It would fall to the Nixon-Kissinger administration to develop a new global strategy within which a sort of victory in Vietnam might be possible.

13

Eastern Europe in the Sixties

The doctrine of containment that formed the basis of America's postwar security planning rested on a number of assumptions that only time could prove true or false. The central thesis was that application of selected counterpressure along the edges of the Soviet Empire would eventually produce a change of policy in Moscow itself as the failed aggressive philosophy of Soviet Marxism was replaced by a more pragmatic, more tolerant foreign policy. Ultimately, it would be left to the Nixon administration to test whether such a change had indeed occurred, a test that would underlie the policy of détente in the seventies. But it was in the sixties that another central tenet of Kennan's containment doctrine seemed open to challenge. Kennan had argued that Soviet domination of Eastern Europe was fragile because each of these ancient cultures possessed a proud tradition that the Soviets would find hard to suppress. The Berlin uprising of 1953 and the Hungarian revolution three years later appeared to give credence to Kennan's conclusion. But in the next decade, a concerted Soviet effort, largely successful, to form a stable military and economic block in Eastern Europe raised the disturbing possibility that Kennan had been incorrect in his original suggestions. If Soviet Marxism could indeed transcend the natural tendencies of the satellite states to regain control of their own destiny, then hopes for the eventual breakup of the Soviet bloc would have less foundation. In any event, a new approach, totally divorced from earlier calls for liberation, would have to be mounted to promote at least some Eastern European independence within the increasingly harmonized Soviet family of nations. By the end of the decade, the West German government, under the control of the Social Democratic party, began a diplomatic offensive toward the East premised upon the assumption that Soviet dominance in the region showed little immediate prospect of waning and ought to be accepted in future policy decisions. This new "realism," dubbed the *Ostpolitik* (Eastern Policy), seemed to invalidate a crucial containment assumption while promising to inaugurate a new era in East-West relations.

The individual most responsible for advancing stability in Eastern Europe was Nikita Khrushchev who consolidated his power in Moscow following Stalin's death in 1953. His aim was to establish a Socialist Commonwealth, as the Soviets liked to call it, among states with a similar socialist system of government. He attempted to reduce the role terror had played in past Soviet–Eastern European relations and to replace it with elements of common interest revolving around the common military and economic threat with which America and her allies confronted the East. The Eastern European armies were increasingly integrated into overall Soviet strategic planning with their ground forces reorganized consistent with Soviet strategic and tactical doctrine, which stressed rapid offensive westward once war had erupted. The status and pay of elites within the Eastern European armies were raised, and the Soviet–Eastern European defense alliance began to play a role as an important diplomatic actor in worldwide negotiations. It would be this alliance, the Warsaw Pact, that called for a nonaggression treaty with NATO, which advanced the idea of creating nuclear-free zones in Europe and which gave diplomatic support to the Soviet position during the Berlin Crisis of 1961. By the end of the decade, the Warsaw Pact was a key institution of both joint planning and regional stability.[1]

The Warsaw Pact, embracing the Soviet-dominated states of Eastern Europe, had emerged in 1955 largely as a response to West Germany's entry into NATO. For the first five years of its existence, the organization played an insignificant role in Soviet military planning, providing merely a convenient legal basis for continued Soviet occupations of East Germany, Poland, Hungary, and Czechoslovakia.[2] Not until 1961 were joint military exercises held among Pact forces, an event that heralded Khrushchev's intent to convert an essentially paper organization into a regional alliance of some power. The 1961 maneuvers, commanded by Soviet marshal Andrei Grechko, stretched from East Germany to the USSR and included ground, air, and naval units from Poland, East Germany, Czechoslovakia, and the USSR, with emphasis being placed upon a military offensive in conditions of nuclear war.[3] In the next twenty years, at least seventy more major exercises were conducted. Taking a lesson from the exercises, a joint military doctrine was drafted that stressed the Soviet preference for surprise, concentration of forces, and a rapid offensive (blitzkrieg) westward. Hand in hand with such doctrinal developments went programs designed to enhance the readiness of Pact forces and to create an organizational structure that would ensure smooth and effective joint planning for the defense of Eastern Europe.[4]

Readiness was improved through modernization of Pact equipment to include some of the most advanced weapons in the Soviet inventory. Thus, the modern T-55 Soviet tank appeared with Pact forces in this decade, as did the new MIG-21 and SU-7 aircraft. Standardization of weapons advanced with East Germany and Poland abandoning their own national programs for combat aircraft in deference to common acquisition of Soviet-built or Soviet-designed planes. Soviet short-range ground-to-ground missiles appeared with Pact troops although it seemed likely that nuclear warheads were kept under Soviet control. And between 1962 and 1967, the standing forces of each Pact member were augmented as follows: Bulgaria, 120,000/154,000; Czechoslovakia, 185,000/225,000; East Germany, 145,000/197,000; Hungary, 115,500/137,000; Poland, 302,000/315,000.[5] Only Romania showed a decline in forces, a result of that nation's effort to advance domestic economic production in concert with a new, resurgent spirit of nationalism. Total Eastern European forces continued to be augmented by the presence of 31 Soviet divisions stationed within the Pact area and maintained at high levels of readiness.

The modernization of Pact forces was supplemented by significant organizational changes designed to convert a once makeshift alliance into a smooth vehicle of regional integration and defense. The governing body of the Pact remained the Political Consultative Committee established in 1955, which consisted of the leaders of each state who met periodically to discuss current problems. In structure this body was similar to the West's North Atlantic Council. The Committee of Defense Ministers, which constituted the highest military consultative organ in the alliance and embraced the respective national defense ministers as members, was responsible for suggesting future reforms in the areas of command and control. The Joint Command of the Warsaw Pact armed forces consisted of designated deputy defense ministers of the Eastern European states who served as subordinates to the Soviet commander in chief of Pact forces. A permanent Joint Command Staff included deputy chiefs of staff of the national Pact armies, probably at the major-general level. And finally, Pact reforms provided for a military council that would bring together Soviet and Eastern European general officers to discuss the smooth functioning of forces in peace as well as in war. A special committee to promote the coordination and standardization of Pact equipment was also in place by the end of the decade.[6]

Perhaps the most effective means of Pact integration was the creation of a common Pact strategic doctrine that transcended and precluded the creation of separate national doctrines of defense by individual Pact members. While information on such integrated planning necessarily remains scarce, evidence recently presented by American military expert Christopher Jones suggests that a prime function of harmonizing strategic doctrine was to ensure that no individual Pact country could draft a defensive strategy capable of warding off or contesting a possible Soviet invasion of Pact countries.[7] While conclusions on this point remain tentative, the existence of such a "supranational" strategic plan embracing all Pact states and precluding their individual defense efforts would constitute a most effective means of continuing Soviet control in Eastern Europe.

Side by side with the refurbished Warsaw Pact, the sixties witnessed the expansion of another Soviet-dominated means of Eastern European integration: the Council for Mutual Economic Assistance (CMEA). This institution was created in 1949 largely to ward off the pernicious influences of the Marshall Plan. Embracing all members of the Warsaw Pact, in addition to Mongolia, CMEA functioned initially as a means to further intrabloc trade between nations whose economic development heretofore had followed separate and highly individualistic plans. No plans for specialization accompanied the foundation of CMEA, and in the early fifties, each member pursued its own self-centered (autarkic) plan of economic development.[8]

In the second half of the fifties, a new component was added to CMEA as part of the new effort of the emerging Khrushchev leadership to replace terror with national self-interest as the binding force in the satellite area. Given the gigantic demands of the Soviet market and the increasing need to provide at least a modicum of satisfaction for the Soviet consumer, it seemed reasonable to hope that mutual economic development might bring about closer feelings between Eastern European states. In 1957 a joint planning committee was added, and each constituent state began formulating tentative development plans for ten- and fifteen-year periods. The State Bank of the Soviet Union was charged with functioning as a clearinghouse to increase trade and to ensure that debts accumulated by one member would be paid from revenues earned by another. At a plenary meeting of the CMEA states in early 1958, a plan was discussed to increase regional specialization so that each country might produce a given line of products that, in turn, would advance intrabloc trade. The objective of this plan was the termination of individualistic national five-year plans and the integration of all participants through specialized production and expanded trade.[9] With the USSR constituting by far the largest single market for specialized items, success of this approach would provide an effective weapon of economic control, a means as effective as terror but less noticeable.

While the Soviet objectives were never fully reached partially due to objections by the lesser-developed members of CMEA who feared that specialization would doom them to continued production of less profitable agricultural goods, considerable strides were made toward an integrated market. Coordination at the supranational level through compulsory membership in planning committees was replaced by voluntary agreements between factories and respective states. The high point of this bilateral and multilateral coordination of production came by the end of the decade with the draft of a Complex Plan of Integration, which was approved in the early seventies. Under its provisions, each CMEA state would begin its five-year plan at the same time, attempting to coordinate its requirements as well as its marketing plan with other CMEA members. [10]

Hand in hand with intrafactory and intranational production and integration agreements, CMEA, in the sixties, increased efforts aimed at true regional integration. The highest organ within the association remained the CMEA Council that met at least once a year to decide major issues of policy. The Executive Committee of the council, composed of deputy prime ministers of each state, convened every two months to oversee implementation of CMEA Council proposals. Standing commissions, to which all members sent representatives, were established to promote unity in such areas as common standards of production, monetary conversion, and exchange of economic statistics. A secretariat was created to handle negotiations with nations and associations outside of CMEA such as the West European Common Market or economic agencies of the United Nations. [11]

The sixties also saw the creation of an International CMEA Bank of Economic Cooperation, which was designed to replace the State Bank of the Soviet Union as the main clearinghouse for intrabloc trade. Since each member-state possessed its own currency, an artificial unit known as the transferable ruble was to be used in calculating each nation's debits and gains at the end of a trading cycle. Each member would contribute a specified sum to the bank either in such rubles or in gold or convertible currency to ensure future payment to its trading partners. In 1970 an International Investment Bank made its appearance, capitalized at 1 billion transferable rubles received by national subscription and designed to assist multinational investments in joint CMEA projects. Benefiting from these institutions and aware that products produced within CMEA states rarely met international standards of quality, the Eastern European nations directed well over half of their respective exports and imports to fellow CMEA states. In conjunction with the Warsaw Pact, CMEA was making its contribution to the stability and endurance of Soviet domination of the Eastern European region. [12]

While the consolidation of Soviet authority in Eastern Europe appeared to undermine a key assumption of the politics of containment, it had a more immediate impact upon another member of NATO: West Germany. Emerging as an independent state in the first decade after the war, West Germany possessed authority over a country twice divided with respect to its prewar frontiers. Not only was there a rival government calling itself the German Democratic Republic with its capital in a suburb of Berlin, but a significant portion of prewar German territory lay under Polish administration in the so-called Oder-Neisse region. This latter band of territory had grudgingly been acknowledged as temporarily subject to Polish authority at the Potsdam Conference of 1945, with final resolution of ownership to await a general peace conference with Germany. But since a general peace conference never convened, the Polish government quickly made itself master of its "temporary" acquisition.

By throwing in its lot with the Western democracies, postwar West Germany had anticipated that Soviet rule to its east would eventually prove unaccommodating to the rump East German state, leading in time to a union within the prewar frontiers. The Marshall Plan, and the subsequent West German Economic Miracle (*Wirtschaftswunder*) that raised the West German standard of living to unparalleled levels, functioned as a basis for continuing hope of a future German reunion, a hope further intensified by the more than 3 million East Germans who fled to the West by the end of the fifties. Yet with the construction of the Berlin Wall in 1961 and the increased consolidation of communist power throughout Eastern Europe, chances for a reunion soon appeared to dim. Against all expectations, East Germany itself now experienced rapid economic expansion, leading to its entrance into the top ten industrial nations of the world as measured by output despite having less than 20 million people. Perhaps this amazing economic recovery should have been expected, for as an East German Communist once confided to this author, "No one, not even the Russians, have been able to devise a system which prevents Germans from working."[13]

The rivalry, indeed hatred, between the West German government in Bonn and its East German opponent in Pankow expressed itself in many ways, not the least of which were diplomatic. The Hallstein Doctrine annunciated in Bonn warned that West Germany would break diplomatic relations with any state that recognized its East German rival, while the Ulbricht Doctrine in Pankow pledged to follow a similar course for those who recognized Bonn. Throughout the fifties meetings of the Eastern European and Soviet leaders were frequently accompanied by appeals for recognition of East Germany by the West as a required first step to any fruitful East-West dialogue. At the beginning of the sixties, only one communist state had extended recognition to West Germany—the Soviet Union itself. By now it was clear that East German approval was needed if the diplomatic freeze between West Germany and its Eastern European neighbors was to be broken.[14]

The failure of Eastern Europe to break away from Soviet tutelage as many had anticipated and the growing authority of communism in East Germany produced a deep reevaluation among many West Germans as to the wisdom of their approach to the entire issue of reunion. Particularly within the West German Social Democratic party that had played a minor role in establishing West Germany's postwar foreign policy, this reevaluation produced a dramatic set of conclusions regarding the preferred policy for the future. To continue the existing stalemate would simply play into communist hands, for it promised little West German influence in East German affairs in the foreseeable future and presented Pankow a lengthy breathing space for further consolidation. Pressure and threats alone seemed unlikely to end the existing stalemate, for any military effort to "liberate" East Germany would surely be resisted by the 20 Soviet divisions on regular station in that country. Clearly, moves toward eventual reunification could only be successful during periods of relaxed tensions when each West German move was not subject to close scrutiny as to its pernicious effects. Equally obvious, the road to Pankow lay through Moscow and perhaps through the other Eastern European states that might have an interest in better relations. Perhaps the recent and unexpected consolidation of communist rule in the East could be turned to West Germany's advantage because the Eastern European leaders, feeling more secure in their own right, would have less to fear from normalization of relations with Bonn.[15] These notions, associated especially with Willy Brandt who became West Germany's first socialist prime minister in 1969 and with his state secretary, Egon Bahr, lay at the basis of the new *Ostpolitik* (Eastern Policy).

The new West German interest in pursuing a normalization of relations with the communist lands was fortunately matched by a similar Soviet desire in the late sixties. In the middle of that decade, the faltering Soviet economy underwent a major reform that failed to deliver the promised expansion of industrial and agricultural output by the end of the decade. The alternative to internal economic reform was utilization of Western technology in an attempt to breathe life into an economy that seemed incapable of satisfying the needs of a major power. By 1969 Poland and Hungary, both concerned with diminishing rates of economic growth, approached West German banks and concerns for possible assistance. Thus, a shift in political assumptions by Bonn and a need for Western technology in conjunction with diminished worries about the political fragility of the satellite nations came together as a bridge for states long separated by the Cold War.[16]

In early 1970 exploratory discussions seeking to discover points of common interest were begun between West Germany and the Soviet Union. The result was a major economic accord in which West Germany promised to provide 1 billion marks in credit (about $300 million) that Moscow would repay through the shipment of natural gas to West German consumers. Yet the economic accord was, to Bonn, merely the prelude to improved political relations that might allow expanded influence upon its East German rival. The political agreement reached between Bonn and Moscow in August 1970 was in essence a renunciation-of-force convention in which both parties promised to use peaceful means only to settle outstanding issues of dispute. The Soviet Union renounced future reference to certain articles in the United Nations Charter that, arguably, could be invoked to justify armed intervention on German soil. Bonn, for its part, declared it had no territorial claims against anyone and that the frontiers of existing states should not be changed by force.[17] In essence, this constituted West German recognition for Polish retention of the Oder-Neisse region. Yet renunciation of force in no way affected Bonn's continued interest in a peaceful reunification with East Germany—the only type of reunification the Soviets were ever likely to allow. On the day the agreement was signed, the West German foreign minister delivered a note to Soviet authorities that affirmed that the treaty "does not conflict with the political objective of the F[ederal] R[epublic] G[ermany] to work for a state of peace in Europe in which the German nation will recover its unity in free self-determination."[18] Four months later, in December 1970, a similar renunciation-of-force agreement was signed with Poland, an agreement that also recognized existing frontiers.[19] The *Ostpolitik* was fast becoming the replacement for decades of antagonism and distrust.

The rapid negotiation and approval of West German treaties with the Soviet Union and with Poland paradoxically now threatened to isolate East Germany from the main course of European political development. In May 1971 longtime East German party chief Walter Ulbricht resigned, showing Pankow would also join the swelling climate of détente. By now the main focus of East-West negotiations had shifted from West German–Soviet discussions to direct America-Soviet exchanges aimed at a comprehensive arms control agreement. The apparently firm foundation that communism had struck in both Eastern Europe and in the USSR left little alternative but to discuss differences instead of hoping that one day both the problems and the communist states that caused them would somehow go away.

14

Strategic Planning under Nixon

By the time of the 1968 national elections and the victory of the Republican party, nearly a quarter of a century had elapsed since the end of the last world war and its replacement by a protracted period of East-West global competition. While the doctrine of containment still had numerous proponents, the world in which it would henceforth be applied had undergone significant change. A fundamental anticipation of this doctrine had centered upon the likelihood of a shift in Soviet attitudes and abilities in response to a determined defensive policy from the West. But by the close of the sixties, it was increasingly apparent that not only the USSR was subject to change and that the United States had shifted in disturbing ways from its previous postwar position of unmatched international power and prestige. It was the growing awareness of America's more circumspect ability to affect the international scene that prompted an agonizing reappraisal of foreign and strategic policies within the new administration. In this endeavor both Pres. Richard Nixon and his special assistant for national security, Dr. Henry Kissinger, played the main role.

The change in America's international capabilities possessed a domestic as well as an international dimension and could be broken down into six categories. First, and most obvious in 1968, the failures of American policy in the Vietnam War had led to such divisions within society that consensus foreign policy was all but impossible. Campus teach-ins at colleges and universities throughout the nation were commonplace, and student violence erupted on the floors of the Democratic Convention in Chicago in spite of heavy police protection. It must be recalled that a central aim of national security planning is to create an environment in which important domestic values can exist and prosper. The campus disturbances and the growing counterculture among even the sons and daughters of leading political figures raised important questions as to whether a common agreement on preferred values was still possible.

The reexamination of values so evident upon college campuses found an echo within the Senate and House of Representatives by the end of the decade. The bipartisanship previously so evident on key issues of foreign policy gave way to bitter disagreements in Washington between respected political figures. Whereas in 1968 President Johnson's call for funding of an antiballistic missile system (ABM) had passed the Senate 46 to 27, one year later the new vice-president was needed to cast the deciding vote for approval of the Nixon version for the same weapon. That year, 1969, the Senate voted 70 to 16 that henceforth no national commitment to defend an American ally could be binding without action by both the executive and legislative branches. That same year the Senate voted 80 to 9 that funds contained in the defense appropriations bill could not be used to finance the introduction of American ground forces into Laos or Thailand.[1]

Senate reluctance to permit the continued autonomy of the White House in prosecuting the Vietnam War, in turn, reflected a significant shift in public attitude toward the entire notion of warfare and violence. Public opinion surveys reveal that the American willingness to sanction the use of force to defend other nations was lower in the 1969-to-1975 period than at any time during the Cold War. Increasingly, American attitudes and interests focused upon the resolution of domestic problems to the near exclusion of foreign ones. The following question was asked randomly each year from 1964 to 1976: "We shouldn't think so much in international terms but concentrate more on our own national problems and building our strength and prosperity here at home; do you agree or disagree?" In 1968 fully 60 percent of individuals polled expressed agreement; 73 percent, in 1972.[2]

These "subjective" indications of the declining willingness to accept the responsibilities of a great power were accompanied by clear objective signs. By 1968 America's postwar fiscal dominance of world finances was in jeopardy, largely because of the Johnson administration's refusal to raise taxes to support the Vietnam War. The new administration faced rising inflation and a record budget deficit of $25 billion. By 1970 America was mired in a depression with 5 percent unemployment. In 1971, faced with an impossible demand by foreign holders of American dollars for conversion of their bills to gold, the Nixon administration suspended convertibility, thus voiding once and for all the monetary arrangements that had bound the noncommunist world since 1945.[3]

In the international arena, equally drastic changes compelled America to reconsider her decades-old policies. From possession of 200 vulnerable intercontinental missiles (ICBMs) in 1964, the Soviet Union, by 1969, was reaching parity with the United States. By this date the Soviets had deployed 1,060 ICBMs, including 800 modern SS-11s and SS-9s in hardened sites. And yet even this achievement left considerable ambiguity as to the actual balance of terror between the two major powers since Soviet weapons gains were offset by the defection of China from the communist camp. By 1969 not even the most convinced American skeptic could deny the existence of the Sino-Soviet split, especially after the shooting along the Ussuri River that left a number of Soviet soldiers dead and wounded. In August 1969 President Nixon told a stunned cabinet that America would not allow her one-time enemy, China, to be defeated in a war with the Soviet Union.[4]

The domestic and foreign problems, so obvious by 1968, gave rise to a new vision of the international order in which the American role would be substantially different, certainly more modest, than in the preceding administrations. On the eve of joining the Nixon team, Henry Kissinger, the prime architect of America's new strategy toward friend and foe alike, reflected on the crisis of the times. "The twentieth century has known little repose. Since the turn of the century, international crises have been increasing in both frequency and severity. The contemporary unrest, although less apocalyptic than the two world wars . . . is even more profoundly revolutionary in nature. . . . The international system which produced stability for a century collapsed under the impact of two world wars. The age of the superpowers, which temporarily replaced it, is nearing its end. *The current international environment is in turmoil because its essential elements are all in flux simultaneously.*"[5]

For Kissinger three general factors accounted for the revolutionary nature of the present moment: (1) The number of major participants in the international order had increased, and the nature of their influence had changed; (2) the technical ability of each participant to affect the others had greatly expanded; and (3) the scope of each country's goals had enlarged.

In more detailed terms, the new era possessed four vital characteristics that America must henceforth reckon with. First, a multipolar order had replaced the bipolar relations of the immediate postwar period. When the ability to inflict maximum violence alone was considered, a bipolar world appeared yet to exist, with American and Soviet nuclear arsenals unchallenged in size and destructive capability. But when the influence exerted by economic might and example was considered, there were now five independent centers of power: America, the Soviet Union, Western Europe, Japan, and communist China. If one considered the influence of ideology alone, several third world states proudly offered their paths of development to more recently emerging states as ideals to emulate.[6]

A second disturbing (hence "revolutionary") characteristic of the current era was the absence of common agreement over what constituted a preferred world order. Differing values and beliefs, especially between the industrial West and the Soviet Union and China made fruitful discussions and problem solving most difficult.[7] The Soviet Union and China, in fact, were by their beliefs profoundly antagonistic toward the international order and its rules as they now existed. Both communist states perceived international law and the normal customs of international relations as weighted toward bourgeois values and as temporary. To both, classes and not states constituted the central items in the international arena, and hence, both saw no contradiction in negotiating treaties with a given state while at the same moment conspiring with that state's domestic enemies to overthrow the government in question.

A third confusing aspect of the contemporary world was the shifting nature of power as the nuclear arsenals dramatically grew year by year. In the atomic age, the capacity to destroy a given foe had become of questionable value even when one was confronted with enemies without nuclear weapons. Few, if any, rational political objectives could be attained by a fratricidal conflict that might leave the entire globe in much worse shape than before hostilities broke out. As a result, the room for maneuvering, even within the respective military blocks, had expanded as demonstrated by the increasingly autonomous foreign policies of France and Romania. The age-old approach to security by forming balances of power was of equally doubtful use since territory traditionally constituted the prizes of war, and the goal of defensive alliances had been to deny the expansion of hostile states. But in the modern age of growing nationalism, annexation of new territories often brought more losses than gains.[8] China had expanded its war-fighting potential more by exploding its first atomic bomb than it would have by incorporating all of Southeast Asia. A nonnuclear Soviet Union in possession of Western Europe would be significantly weaker than the nuclear-capable USSR of the sixties.

With the traditional notions about balance of power now of slight use, the nature of defensive alliances as well had changed—the fourth key characteristic of the postwar era. To be effective, Kissinger maintained, today's alliances would have to meet four criteria: They would have to have (1) a common objective; (2) a joint policy at least adequate to determine when war would be declared; (3) technical means of cooperation that would be present for use in common actions; and (4) an effective penalty that would exist for states that failed to honor their commitments. Viewed in this fashion, Kissinger was forced to conclude that such basic conditions for an effective alliance existed only within NATO.[9] "In the system of alliances developed by the United States after the Second World War, these conditions have never been met outside the North Atlantic Treaty Organization

(NATO). In the Southeast Asia Treaty Organization (SEATO) and the Central Treaty Organization (CENTO) to which we belonged in all but name, there has been no consensus as to the danger. Pakistan's motive for obtaining U.S. arms was not security against a Communist attack but protection against India. The Arab members of CENTO armed not against the USSR but against Israel."[10]

During the first eighteen months of the new administration, these views and assumptions about the changing nature of the world were examined for their likely impact upon preferred American policies. It was clear from the beginning that America's relationship with the Soviet Union was due for a change since the United States no longer possessed the economic and military power to engage in worldwide containment. The key question soon became whether or not the Soviet Union itself could be integrated into the existing international system, thereby acknowledging the system's legitimacy and hence abandoning at least some of the revolutionary demands for change. Clearly, this goal could not be met if America's military strength, relative and absolute, declined still further, for in such a case, the Soviets would stand little to gain by substituting negotiations for brute confrontation. Equally, the Soviets would need to be convinced that actual benefits would flow toward Moscow as a result of a more peaceful and diplomatic demeanor. In the meanwhile, America's relations with her many allies would bear reexamination and, where required, modification.[11]

The practical strategic planning and strategic programs resulting from this fundamental reappraisal of American policy in a changing world were sketched in the first foreign policy report delivered by Nixon to Congress. Three central objectives would henceforth direct both weapons procurement and diplomatic initiatives in the new administration: strength, partnership, and meaningful negotiations.[12] Each of these objectives underlay one or more policy decisions aimed at defining a new American position.

While there was no question that America's relative military power had diminished since 1945, her absolute strength still made the United States the world's most powerful state. To the new administration, the retention of such strength was a prerequisite for global security as well as the protection of American interests. Henceforth, America would no longer seek superiority—an objective many believed unattainable—but rather "sufficiency" in force acquisition. The criteria for sufficiency included (1) maintaining a strategic retaliatory capability sufficient to deter an attack upon the United States; (2) a reduction of vulnerability for U.S. strategic forces; (3) the procurement of sufficient weapons to ensure America could always inflict as much damage upon the USSR as it could inflict upon the United States; (4) an increase in the flexibility of use for American forces; and (5) efforts to ensure that the psychological perception of strength did not suggest an American inferiority. [13]

These criteria were to be met by the judicious use of military dollars to purchase weapons adequate for defense. The antiballistic missile (ABM) program of the Johnson administration, which foresaw the construction of such defenses around American cities, was examined and significantly modified. The feared development of a Chinese nuclear threat to America had not emerged with the speed the Johnson people had anticipated, and the cost of a city-based ABM system grew yearly. In its place the Nixon planners proposed to substitute an ABM system that would protect America's retaliatory ICBMs. The new program, known as the Safeguard System, which passed by one vote in the Senate in 1969, was consistent with maintaining an assured deterrence against nuclear attack since it would ensure that even in a worst-case scenario some American ICBMs would survive to devastate the attacker in a return. Knowing this, no rational nation would engage in a sneak attack. [14]

To maintain an effective offensive force, a new means of placing a number of independently targeted warheads on each American missile began testing in 1969 and 1970. Known as multiple independently targeted reentry vehicles (MIRVs), these new warheads would drastically multiply the number of bombs America could explode on Soviet targets without increasing the number of American missiles. Each MIRV fraction—it was possible to place ten or more fractions on each missile—could be aimed at a separate target, thus promising nearly unimaginable damage in a retaliatory strike. By the mid-seventies the deployment of MIRVs on both land-based (ICBMs) and sea-based (SLBMs) American missiles was in progress. [15] And yet attention was not confined just to the missile component of America's strategic potential. Since the beginning of the sixties, America's defense had rested with a so-called triad of defenses: ICBMs, SLBMs, and manned aircraft. Programs were now implemented to disperse bombers in case of attack and to decrease takeoff times. A new bomber, the B-1, was ordered into development to replace the aging B-52s. [16]

The cited list of weapons procurements and plans formed the tangible proof that America's strength would be maintained at high levels. But there was also an intangible aspect. In an age of overkill, mere possession of destructive power was of limited use without clear indications of a will to use it. Odd as it may now seem, President Nixon consciously cultivated the public image of a man whose precise response to a crisis could never be predicted with confidence, an image of plausible instability. Long an admirer of South Korean president Syngman Rhee who had made a fetish of unpredictability, President Nixon frequently dropped suggestions that certain, unspecified communist actions might elicit an asymmetric response as an expression of his uncontrollable rage. Such an image, it was hoped, would retard communist expansion in a crucial period of global transition. [17]

The principle of partnership as conceived by the Nixon administration embraced the twin goals of diminishing the extent of America's commitment to regional allies in combination with efforts to promote stabilization by reducing past rivalries with former foes. The most pressing area in which change was required lay in Southeast Asia where pledges of support and finally outright involvement of American troops had led to the existing stalemate in Vietnam. Under President Johnson, America had taken responsibility for conducting the conflict, and by the advent of the new administration, over 500,000 U.S. troops were engaged in regular operations. In the presidential campaign of that year, Nixon proclaimed he held a secret plan for terminating America's participation on an honorable basis, and his election that fall required some action to fulfill his promise. Following a series of high-level studies, the course of a gradual withdrawal of American troops was selected, with the Pentagon announcing in March 1969 that the first 25,000 American soldiers would be brought home. [18] That December another 100,000 were earmarked for withdrawal.

The need to diminish America's direct involvement in Vietnam was just one example of the problems Kissinger had foreseen in the numerous alliances that past American administrations had constructed. Thus, the rationale for the withdrawal of troops from Vietnam was cast in broad terms so as to serve notice that outside the NATO area America would expect much greater local effort than before. Henceforth, emphasis would be placed upon regional and local defense forces if the threats of communist subversion were to be met. The precise formulation of this new partnership approach came in the Nixon or Quam Doctrine announced by the president in the summer of 1969. America, Nixon pledged, would keep its existing treaty commitments. To do less would be to deny the reliability of America's promises to defend freedom, an act that would seriously undermine America's defense position throughout the world. But henceforth, to complement America's providing a nuclear umbrella over her allies and offering military equipment and economic assistance, the primary burden for regional and local defense would lie with the states directly concerned. America would no longer send manpower to halt foreign aggression with the ease with which troops had been dispatched to Southeast Asia. [19] The efforts to place more of the burden upon the South Vietnamese army by withdrawing American troops—a policy now known as "Vietnamesation"—was fully consistent with this new approach. It was hoped that the Nixon

Doctrine would maintain America's credibility while reducing defense costs, the number of troops abroad, and the growing domestic disputes that made governing America increasingly difficult.

The specific goal of the Nixon Doctrine and Vietnamesation was to establish a more stable balance in Asia that would not require future commitments of American troops. It was, therefore, not totally surprising that steps were soon taken to negotiate an end to outstanding problems with the most important regional state: China. Long before 1969 both Kissinger and Nixon had realized that China was the key to Asian stability, with the latter noting in a 1967 article in *Foreign Affairs* that "any American policy toward Asia must come urgently to grips with the reality of China. . . . We simply cannot afford to leave China outside the family of nations."[20] In July 1971 Nixon informed the American public that he intended to visit Peking the following year. That fall America removed its long-standing objection to the seating of Red China in the United Nations.

The presidential visit to China in February 1972 ushered in a new era in American-Chinese relations although a number of problems remained. Full normalization of relations was postponed until the end of the decade, and disputes over America's policy toward Taiwan continue to this day. The important Shanghai Statement issued at the end of Nixon's visit attempted to gloss over outstanding issues in the interest of promoting closer relations. In it both sides recognized "that all Chinese on either side of the Taiwan Strait maintain there is but one China and that Taiwan is a part of China."[21] This statement was purposely left vague to retard objections from opponents of the new friendships.

These first steps toward the normalization of relations with China held great promise in the Nixon effort to diminish America's military commitments abroad. With China entering the United Nations, it was hoped that discussions would replace armed conflict as the forum in which legitimate Chinese interests and goals would be accommodated. On a much more practical level, China's status as a regional power might be elevated as a means of retarding the expansion of Soviet influence in the area. The improvement of ties with Peking soon allowed defense planners to move from a two-and-a-half-war strategy—the strategy that had foreseen a possible conflict in Europe and Asia in conjunction with a small war in some other part of the world—to a one-and-a-half-war strategy.[22] It was now concluded that China would no longer act in military tandem with the USSR.

The centerpiece of the Nixon-Kissinger approach to a changed world was meaningful negotiations with America's primary enemy—the USSR. While the partial neutralization of China undoubtedly would promote stability in Asia, only a drastic improvement in relations with Moscow held promise of removing the main impediment to global harmony. The sole means of achieving this end appeared to be the partial dismantling of containment and the West's willingness to recognize certain Soviet claims and interests as legitimate given the great power status Moscow had achieved. Recognizing the legitimacy of Soviet interests, in turn, would require America to treat Moscow as a near equal, bargaining and trading for concessions in the normal fashion long enshrined within conventional diplomatic practices. Perhaps through a carefully constructed package of concessions, recognitions of interest, and penalties for nonfulfillment of pledges, a system of linkages could be created that would circumscribe Soviet activities within commonly accepted bounds of action.[23] In short, by providing clear evidence that bargaining and exchange could bring actual gain, the Soviets might be persuaded to abandon their heretofore revolutionary attitude toward Western capitalism and to join in supporting an international system of treaties and understandings from which they might also benefit.

If such an integration of the USSR into the established diplomatic order could be accomplished through a combination of concessions and penalties, the very revolutionary nature of the Soviet threat would diminish and perhaps one day cease. In the past revolutionary states had been integrated into the existing order only through war, the example of revolutionary eighteenth-century France being a case in point dear to Henry Kissinger. But in the nuclear age, such a means of integration held the potential to destroy the international order forever, and a substitute means had to be found. Nothing less than this reversal of past historic precedent, made necessary by the technological advancements of the modern age, lay at the basis of the new American approach toward Moscow. And the present moment did indeed seem propitious for such an attempt. As Henry Kissinger later explained to the U.S. Senate Foreign Relations Committee, a series of stark challenges to Moscow's position as head of the world communist movement in the sixties and seventies had prompted a move toward similar accommodation with the West. The Soviet claim to provide the sole experience that other communist states must follow had been opposed both within Eastern Europe and by China. The Soviet economy was facing unprecedented problems urgently requiring modernization, such modernization being nearly impossible without increased trade with the West. Both these challenges to Soviet preeminence might have led the USSR to withdraw into itself and to increase hostility toward its main rival, the West. But instead, the Soviets had shown new interest in reaching an accommodation with the industrial powers.[24] Now was the time to see if behind the continued revolutionary rhetoric lay a willingness to promote détente.

15

The Foundations of
Soviet Foreign Policy

As suggested in the preceding chapter, the advent of the Nixon administration marked a major shift in postwar American policy toward the Soviet Union. Since 1946 the normal American approach had relied upon the premises contributed by George Kennan that were loosely known as containment. It was assumed in Washington that the Soviet leadership required an aggressive posture so as to maintain its small degree of legitimacy in the eyes of its subjects and that a relaxation of East-West tensions would expose this tyrannical form of government to the just criticisms of its people. The sole hope for improved relations lay with a future modification of Soviet totalitarianism that might one day emerge as the Soviet leaders realized their foreign policy goals were unattainable.

In sharp contrast, the new republican security advisers in Washington, who were led by Henry Kissinger, argued that the Soviets had to be more tightly integrated into the international scene precisely because they represented a revolutionary power in an era when war could no longer be used to promote international realignment. The Soviets had to learn that they, too, could achieve desired objectives by entering normal diplomatic intercourse, and their legitimate interests had to be recognized as important. In this manner, it was hoped, the long-desired change in Soviet behavior might occur *after* and *during* the period in which Moscow became a regular participant in the existing international border. In charting such a course, both Nixon and Kissinger had to be aware of the declared assumptions the Soviets held about the existing world order, assumptions that, if truly maintained, would probably preclude such a peaceful transformation of Soviet foreign policy. The major uncertainty in Washington remained whether the Soviets were true to their often-asserted Marxist principles or whether such mouthings were more for show, derived from a revolutionary tradition that had lost its hold upon the Soviet leadership. If only to grasp the boldness of the Nixon-Kissinger effort, it is necessary to examine these principles in some detail.[1]

In traditional Western political theory, the state is perceived as the main international actor. Agreements, treaties, disputes, and even wars occur between such entities, with each state assumed to be a cohesive and independent unit. The activities of states in the international arena are motivated by national interests, and their interactions result in unequal gains and losses depending upon raw power and plain good luck. In the worst cases, states will cease to exist after being on the losing side of an armed dispute; the collapse of Austria-Hungary in 1918 is a prime example. The general rules that govern international relations in both peace and war have emerged by tradition and by common consent are enshrined in international law and custom. And yet, in the absence of an international government, the national, sovereign state remains at the center of the international system, with serious disputes between such entities often leading to war as the means of settling conflicting claims. Alliances shift as states pursue their own goals as they perceive them. And as the source of its own activity, a given state possesses no permanent allies, only permanent interests. Such, in brief, is the conventional theory of international relations as one might hear it in a typical American college course devoted to this topic.

The theory of international relations and the role of the state within it are quite different in the USSR. To a Marxist the state is not a cohesive entity somehow representing a nation's unchanging national interest. The nation-state, in fact, is a relatively recent addition to the world scene with such states being rare before the eighteenth century. In the medieval world, political entities (states) were not based upon "national interests" or even upon the rule of the dominant national or linguistic group (French, Spanish, etc.). What mattered in this era was one's religious preference since the rules of religion provided the main justification for state organization and legitimacy. To a Marxist the nation-state as we know it today emerged only with the rise of the middle class to power first in Europe and later throughout the world.

Such arguments reflect well the fundamental Marxist notion that what is important in national *or* international politics is not the state per se but the social classes that create and support it. To a Marxist not only the nation-state but all states are unnatural phenomena, arising to aid certain class aims and eventually destined to extinction. A Marxist believes that in ancient times no states existed, the state emerging only after social-economic classes of unequal power arose in society. The role of the first state, and all states hence except the socialist state, was to allow a minority of exploiting individuals to dominate the more numerous but less powerful majority.

The actual governments of such states, that is the institutions of a congress, a president, etc., that one finds in contemporary Western states, are collectively termed the *superstructure*. The type of institutions depends upon which class of exploiters dominates at that stage of a peoples' historic development. In the present period, it is the middle class that presides over conflict-ridden, class-divided Western states, using its hold on govenmental institutions to advance the interests and riches of its members with little regard for its fellow man. Thus, to say that a state has permanent interests but no permanent allies is, to a Marxist, absurd. Interests lie with the dominant class, with the institutions of the state being but a mask behind which this class pursues its goals. As an example, Marxists note that Britain and France were sworn enemies for most of the Middle Ages due to the fierce competition of the two feudal classes for the major means of production of the era: land. In the more modern period, however, as wealth shifted from agriculture to industrial production and as class domination began to reside in the hands of the middle classes, France and Britain became allies against the more pressing threat of an industrialized Germany. Such examples, Marxists maintain, clearly show that it is not states but rather classes that have well-defined interests to protect.

The Soviet view of international relations and the normal rules of diplomacy vary in tandem with their peculiar interpretation of the role of the state in history. In every era one or more states have exercised hegemony over the international arena, dominating other states in matters of war and peace. Currently, it is the United States that holds prime position over other capitalist-based states of the world. But today's unique feature is that a state deriving its power from the working class—the Soviet Union—has also assumed a position of power. Traditionally, the class struggle has been played out within states, as workers and capitalists, peasants and feudal lords battled for control. While internal class struggle is still a characteristic of capitalist states, the emergence of a workers' state in Moscow means that international relations have also become the field of such class antagonisms. In short, the class struggle that usually occurs in societies has been transposed horizontally into foreign affairs, with each victory for Moscow actually being a victory for the world's working class; each defeat, a loss for possible workers' dominance. Since the class struggle cannot be ameliorated short of the victory of one antagonist over the other, any long-term peaceful arrangement between East and West is impossible. This rejection of harmony in international relations follows directly from the basic Marxist theory that finds class struggle to be an innate and unchanging constituent of nature, its termination coming only with the final victory of the working class.

In the current century, Marxists maintain that the class struggle now dominating East-West relations has gone through three stages. The first stage occurred between the two world wars, with its most important characteristic being the birth of the first workers' state centered in Moscow. The second stage occurred after 1945 and witnessed the birth of additional socialist states in Eastern Europe and Asia. Thus, by 1950 the Soviets also stood at the head of a block of states ruled by the interests of the working class. The third stage began in the fifties and is still in progress. Its salient features include a general crisis of the capitalist order marked by decolonization and increased competition among capitalist states for a shrinking world economic market. The correlation of forces—a measurement of the relative strengths as charted by comparing political, economic, ideological, and military traits of various states—suggests the rise of the East and the decline of the West. American military power, unparalleled at war's end, has given way to parity as Soviet defense programs have reached new heights. And in the end the victory of the working class will become apparent to all. As Nikita Khrushchev announced to a startled America in the fifties, "Your grandchildren will live under communism." By this he meant no more than that by the latter years of this century, the superiority of the East over the West would become so evident that rational people everywhere would freely adopt a socialist or communist form of rule.

Since international relations are the domain of class struggle, there is no reason for a Marxist state to accord sanctity to those rules governing diplomatic intercourse already in existence. International relations constitute a tactical area in which the struggle for historic overlordship is played out, and hence, the normal, everyday rules, laws, and conventions of international behavior must be evaluated as to their effect on the horizontal class struggle. Since nearly all such international laws and conventions have arisen in the period when capitalist states dominated diplomacy, their efficiency on behalf of Soviet interests is always in doubt. This does not mean that socialist states always violate international laws or signed agreements, in fact, the socialist record is very good in this respect. Rather, each agreement and convention must stand on its own merits and be judged on how well it meets the requirements of the socialist signatories. Laws and conventions arising in the bourgeois period of international relations do not deserve respect simply because they exist.

The future, Marxists hold, will see the inevitable triumph of the working class and the disappearance of the nation-state as we know it. Nationalism, an ideology emerging about the time of the French Revolution and functioning ever since as a means of capitalist domination, will be replaced by class solidarity as the means of social unity. Since the state itself was called into history to aid the exploitative minority in its struggle with the working majority, the eclipse of the exploitative capitalist class will also mean the end of the state. Following Marxist author Friedrich Engels, Lenin argued that the state will go into the museum alongside the bronze axe. It will, in short, become merely an artifact of history, an institution once required by primitive peoples until socialism proved it unnecessary to have rule over people. At this stage of man's cultural evolution, a free federation of peoples will constitute the main form of political integration. Just as Catholicism or Protestantism was the most important characteristic of early modern states prior to the French Revolution, so in the future attitudes of "working classism" will constitute the common bond that will unite all men. Cooperation, not competition, will then be the dominant ethic of the day, and political organization may well resemble the existing multinational confederation of the present-day USSR where numerous nationalities are grouped together in the promotion of working-class goals.

If one reviews the entire range of Soviet-Marxist assumptions and predictions, the following short list of key goals and viewpoints emerges. The present array of nation-states is a temporary phenomenon and doomed to extinction. The existing actors on the international stage are, in the last resort, mere expressions of classes and international relations per se but the transposition of the class struggle from within a society to without. In this struggle only one side can win, there being no gaming model in which over the long run both sides can benefit. Rules governing international relations were developed by the class enemy prior to the emergence of socialist states in the international arena and, thus, have no intrinsic value. The future rules of international relations will be very different from those of the present, since they will reflect the eventual victory of socialist forces. Until then the international arena is essentially a tactical battlefield in which each system—capitalist and socialist—attempts to advance its interests and to complete its conquest.

With this summary in mind, it is understandable why Henry Kissinger considered the Soviet Union to be a revolutionary state profoundly subversive of the existing international order and conventional rules for peaceful change. The goal of Soviet leaders, at least as stated in public pronouncements and public writings, was not integration into the present system but abolition of the system. As Kissinger well knew, such had been the posture of revolutionary France in the late eighteenth century when Jacobin Clubs abroad were fostered by Paris in an effort to undermine the then existing pillars of social legitimacy—the monarchy and the church. So too, the USSR fostered communist movements within the very states with which it negotiated in the international arena, communist movements that denied the very legitimacy of these states and their rules of political organization. But whereas France was admitted to the international order after the bloody Napoleonic wars, the advent of the atomic bomb made such a transition impossible today. Thus, the USSR had to be made to understand that peaceful acceptance and integration were to its benefit. Kissinger's main hope was that Marxist ideology had declined since the Soviet revolution and that the day-to-day problems of government had made Soviet leaders more pragmatic than ideological.[2] And history was not devoid of such changes. The medieval popes, while espousing a religious idealism that cast serious doubt upon wordly possession, maintained vast territorial holdings in Italy and negotiated within international relations as worldly princes despite their public pronouncements. Perhaps the same mental transformation was possible for the new secular priests of Marxism in Moscow. The emergence of a special category of East-West relations, entitled peaceful coexistence, suggested that the Soviets also recognized the unique characteristics of the atomic age.

The declared Soviet view as to how relations ought to be conducted with the diverse states found in the contemporary international realm is as detailed as their views on the state itself. Essentially, there exist two distinct types of states: those whose organization reflects capitalist aims and goals and those who represent the emerging working class. There are, in turn, two general principles of foreign relations: proletarian internationalism and peaceful coexistence. Proletarian internationalism, however, comes in three stages, with its highest expression being socialist internationalism. In its basic rules, proletarian internationalism stems directly from the days of Karl Marx himself and arose in the second half of the nineteenth century.

Proletarian internationalism was the manner in which the early Marxist parties and working-class movements related one to another long before the birth of the USSR. Its fundamental premise was that class solidarity transcended national differences and that all workers of the world must unite on behalf of common goals and to end oppression. This camaraderie found expression in meetings of European workers organized into the First International in 1864 and the Second International whose birth occurred in the late 1880s. Workers from the various nations were to put aside their national distinctiveness, reject the nationalistic pleas of their respective societies, and work together to end capitalist rule once and for all. The outbreak of World War I, however, and the intense nationalism that accompanied it overrode frequent worker pledges never to fight one another in the interest of their respective nation-states, the result being the disruption of the Second International and the birth of a Third International in Moscow.

The world war also spawned the first self-proclaimed workers' and peasants' state in the newly emerged Soviet Russia. A second stage of proletarian internationalism now appeared with the Soviet state taking the position of the workers' vanguard and demanding the allegiance of all those "truly revolutionary." A newly created Third International took charge of organizing workers' movements throughout the bourgeois world, with the prime test of loyalty being whether a foreign worker would support his own government or the USSR in times of trial. As Joseph Stalin himself proclaimed, "He is an internationalist who unreservedly, unhesitatingly and unconditionally is prepared to defend the USSR, because the USSR is the basis of the world revolutionary movement, and it is impossible to defend, to advance this revolutionary movement without defending the USSR."[3]

The third stage in the evolution of proletarian internationalism came with the emergence of a group of fraternal socialist states in the wake of World War II. For the first time in history, relations could be established between states, each of which was alleged to represent the working class. Such relations were to be based on complete equality, respect for territorial integrity, state independence, and sovereignty, as agreements between the USSR and its neighbors today assert. And yet even here, in relations between states openly proclaimed as socialist, the direct ties between the workers of each country, sometimes independent of the wishes of the respective governments, are most important. The clearest expression of this superiority of worker-to-worker connections came in the 1968 invasion of Czechoslovakia by the USSR and four other Eastern European states. As announced in the Brezhnev Doctrine, it is the duty of all members of the socialist community to assist the workers of their respective countries to fight the intrigues of imperialism and capitalism even if the government of the threatened state does not seek assistance.[4] Proletarian internationalism, often called socialist internationalism when applied to relations between two or more socialist states, supersedes any mere pledges of respect for sovereignty in cases where the very rule of socialism is in question. National governments, in the last resort, are remnants of the past era of bourgeois rule; direct ties designed to promote common interests between workers without respect to nationality are the traits of the communist future and even now are considered as of a higher order.

In addition to forming the basis of ties between socialist states, proletarian internationalism plays a major role in influencing the various national liberation movements dotting the third world. The original goal of proletarian internationalism was to assist the revolutionary pursuits of diverse oppressed movements, and in the modern period, struggles for political and/or economic independence still claim the attention of Marxists everywhere. A reading of the main Soviet press in any given month shows the number of revolutionary leaders who appear in Moscow for discussions at the highest level—a pattern repeated in each of the Eastern European capitals. Proletarian internationalism thus remains the key relationship principle between socialist states and workers, an indication and a promise of how one day all peoples will relate one to another in the expected communist world of the future.

In sharp contrast to proletarian internationalism stands the principle of peaceful coexistence. This latter form of international relations is not derived from common class aspirations and is but a grudging concession to the still remaining nonsocialist states temporarily inhabiting the globe. The need for such a principle of interaction emerges from the dangerous characteristics of the nuclear era in which a wrong step might lead to the extinction of all states—capitalist and socialist alike. Thus, the eventual communist victory must come without the assistance of a global war. In the main, peaceful coexistence is a tactical retreat, forced upon the socialist states by the vicissitudes of history. It is temporary since history itself assures the victory of communism and is perceived as distinctly inferior and subordinate to the higher principles of proletarian internationalism. More important, peaceful coexistence is not perceived as an acknowledgement of the status quo but as a distinctive means of class struggle from which the socialist states will emerge victorious.

The class struggle between East and West, in the present era, occurs in three separate but interrelated areas: the economic, the political, and the ideological. Peaceful coexistence governs, Moscow proclaims, in the first two fields of competition. Economically, both systems compete to demonstrate their superiority in providing for the actual needs of their respective citizens. At least in theory, there is no doubt in the mind of a Marxist that the socialist form of economic organization, devoid of strikes and competition, will outproduce capitalist societies in the long run. In the realm of politics, the goals of peaceful coexistence include limiting capitalist aggressiveness so as to preclude the outbreak of wars. The development of considerable socialist military capability aids this effort since it reveals to the capitalist states the dangers of provoking conflict. Efforts to gain increasing support from one's own citizens is also included in the political competition. In the area of ideology, however, no competition, peaceful or otherwise, can be allowed, and any bourgeois efforts to undermine the appeal of Marxism must be met with singular resistance. The fundamental goals of a future, classless, and socialist society holding sway throughout the world must be proclaimed and persistently sought.

While the destructive power of the atomic bomb and its equal ability to destroy socialist and capitalist societies alike is usually cited by Marxists as the main reason for a policy of peaceful coexistence, there are other explanations of equal importance. In the Soviet view, the West, too, is a strong advocate of limiting prospects of war due to its recognition of the shifting balance of power in a socialist direction. Thus, this new form of East-West interaction emerged, in part, from the West's acknowledgment of its increasing vulnerability to the socialist challenger. Since socialism is indeed fated to win the "peaceful" competition, no true Marxist would support a continuation of the status quo one moment beyond what is required to avoid outright war. Consistent with beliefs about the future victory of socialism and the superiority of proletarian internationalism over the time-limited policy of peaceful coexistence, Soviet support for the revolutionary movements in the third world and even in the capitalist West have not diminished. Like the nation-state, peaceful coexistence will also one day find itself in the garbage heap of history since the anticipated demise of capitalism will remove the need for any policy except proletarian internationalism within a world of socialist states.

Given these well-developed and frequently enunciated Soviet beliefs, prospects for a peaceful integration of the USSR into the existing international order might seem dim indeed. But in the minds of President Nixon and Henry Kissinger, a glimmer of hope remained. The Soviet leadership of the seventies was a far cry from those revolutionary idealists who had created the state in 1917; the current leadership was composed mainly of pragmatic engineers who showed interest in economic exchange with the West. Perhaps a significant gap had developed between rhetoric and reality, a gap that might allow much closer East-West ties. And even in the worst case, in the event peaceful coexistence was a considered and firm Soviet policy, the duration of such a period might be extended well into the next century with the ensuing time of peace being used by the West to further modify Soviet beliefs. Whether either of these two interpretations would turn out to be accurate could only be determined with time as the carefully crafted policy of integrating the Soviets into international life proceeded. And when the first term of the Nixon administration ended in 1972, the accumulated evidence suggested that the Soviets had indeed sacrificed revolutionary goals for the more tangible gains achieved through regularized contacts with the West.

16

The Strategic Arms Limitations Talks

While the Nixon-Kissinger officials negotiated numerous agreements and understandings with the Soviet Union, the high point of the first Nixon administration was the completion of Strategic Arms Limitation Talks I (SALT I) in May 1972. For the first time, the two superpowers seemed to recognize their unique responsibility for the peace and survival of mankind, pledging to restrict the most destabilizing forms of arms competition and to consult regularly if arms issues came into dispute. At the same May 1972 meeting, a detailed statement of common principles was accepted to guide future interactions in the hope of settling serious disputes before they threatened to produce conflict. In retrospect five key factors resulted in the SALT agreement: (1) the Nixon-Kissinger decision to involve the USSR in a web of international treaties and covenants; (2) the pace of the Soviet nuclear buildup following the Cuban Missile Crisis that led to near parity in nuclear weapons by 1968; (3) the changing Soviet strategic doctrine that increasingly acknowledged the superiority of offensive over defensive weapons; (4) the Limited Test Ban Treaty of 1963 that established the pattern of partial arms accords; and (5) the development of spy-in-the-sky satellites that allowed continuous surveillance of each side's national territory without violation of airspace.[1]

The SALT I negotiations had a considerable history prior to the signing of the agreement in the spring of 1972. As early as January 1964, President Johnson had proposed such an understanding with Moscow, suggesting a "verifiable freeze of the numbers and characteristics of strategic nuclear offensive and defensive vehicles." As was perhaps anticipated, the Soviets declined to give a positive response, no doubt a result of their then inferior position in the nuclear arms race. Possessing only about 200 ICBMs against a total of over 800 deployed in the United States, the Soviets were involved in developing a defensive system adequate to the American challenge.[2]

In the immediate postwar period, the USSR, confronted by the threat of nuclear attack, deployed an extensive and expensive national antiaircraft system against U.S. heavy bombers. The advent of the missile age forced consideration of a new defensive system, and in 1962 a limited antiballistic missile (ABM) complex was established around Leningrad. Two years later it was dismantled as a failure, but a follow-on system dubbed the Galosh System was set up around Moscow.[3] The explosion of the first Chinese atomic bomb in 1964 gave new impetus to defensive measures in both America and the USSR. In 1966 the U.S. Congress voted funds for an American antiballistic missile system, and the following year Johnson announced he would approve a limited ABM deployment if no agreement were reached with Moscow.[4]

In June 1967 Johnson and Soviet prime minister Aleksey Kosygin convened a meeting at Glassboro, New Jersey, to discuss a possible ABM agreement. Kosygin, however, clearly indicated that his nation's strategic policy still perceived such defensive weapons as both positive and stabilizing. "I believe," Kosygin stated, "that defensive systems, which prevent attacks, are not the cause of the arms race, but constitute a factor preventing the death of people."[5] Such sentiments were at odds with American perceptions of the arms race in that the procurement of defensive systems appeared to act as a further stimulus to acquire additional offensive weapons to override them. American strategists had long before concluded that in the atomic age the offensive was both superior to and cheaper than any defensive system possible under existing technology. If, for example, a Soviet or American ABM site was capable of destroying 20 percent of incoming warheads, the opposition would simply deploy 20 percent more forces to ensure the same total got through. Since offensive weapons were much cheaper than defensive weapons, such a competition would always favor the offense. In short, there seemed to be no adequate defense against a determined atomic opponent.[6] The refusal of the Soviets to accept this conclusion, however, placed strong political pressure upon the Johnson administration to follow suit, and that fall Johnson announced America would also field an ABM system. Not until the following spring did the Soviets suggest that they were finally willing to begin strategic arms talks— no doubt a result of their own rapidly developing arsenal of weapons that threatened to overtake the Americans in sheer numbers within the next two years. The Soviet invasion of Czechoslovakia in August 1968 once again doomed any talks for the moment.

Despite a call for continued American nuclear superiority in the 1968

Republican platform, newly elected President Nixon soon realized that such a posture was unreachable short of major outlays in defense spending. In March 1969 a reevaluation of arms control strategies was begun by the new administration, and in June Washington informed Moscow it was prepared to initiate serious talks. The negotiations started in November 1969 with the participants meeting in Helsinki and Vienna over the next four years as slow progress was made. In his own unique fashion, Kissinger himself took a direct, if often concealed, hand in the negotiations, maintaining a "back channel" to Moscow for the discussion of crucial issues. By the spring of 1972, just in time for Nixon's announced visit to Moscow, the main outlines for SALT I were in place. With a few last-minute changes during the Nixon visit, the agreement was signed by the two leaders on May 26.[7] The resulting accord was in two distinct parts: a permanent treaty governing the deployment of antiballistic missiles by both sides and a temporary, five-year, interim agreement detailing the permitted number of offensive weapons each side might possess.

The ABM treaty pledged that neither side would construct a nationwide ABM system nor the radars attending such a system. Each side was permitted two separate ABM sites, one to be located around the respective capitals and the second to be placed at least 1,300 kilometers from the first. The reason for these separations of sites was to ensure that neither side could link its two systems together to cover a significant part of its overall national territory. Each site was allowed a maximum of 100 ABM launchers for a total of 200 per side plus 15 more that might be placed at a testing ground for experimentation. A subsequent agreement signed in 1974 restricted the deployment of ABMs to one site. Verification of compliance was to be by national-technical means and would not require on-site inspection. National-technical in this case meant satellites placed by each power above the land mass of the other plus other nonintrusive means of detection such as radars located in third countries.[8]

A special problem confronting the negotiating teams had been the exclusion of radically new ABM systems if and when such became available. Uncertain of what future technology might bring, both sides did their best to limit development, testing, and deployment of systems whose outlines they could but barely perceive. Thus, an ABM was defined as "a system to counter strategic ballistic missiles or their elements in flight trajectory." Development, testing, or deployment of sea-based, air-based, space-based, or mobile land-based ABMs was forbidden as was development, testing, or deployment of ABM launchers capable of firing more than one missile. Modernization of existing systems was allowed within reason, but the development of systems "based on other physical principles" would require consultation between the signatories. This latter clause was seen as a hedge against future systems deriving their power from lasers or particle beam weapons.[9]

The ABM Treaty provided for a Standing Consultative Committee composed of American and Soviet representatives who would regularly meet to consider problems raised as to treaty enforcement or interpretation. It would also discuss modifications of the treaty if such appeared necessary. The treaty was to be of indefinite duration but was subject to review every five years. Either party could withdraw from the treaty by giving six months' notice of such intent in case "extraordinary events related to the subject matter of this Treaty jeopardized its supreme interest."

The second component of SALT I was termed the Interim Agreement in recognition of the fact that it would bind the two signatories for only a five-year period or until a permanent offensive treaty could be negotiated. During the five-year period, the offensive nuclear capability of each side was subjected to certain limits as to the number of weapons each could possess. Both sides were forbidden to begin construction of additional fixed intercontinental ballistic launchers after July 1, 1972. The use of the term *launcher* was important here, since the prohibition applied to the *means* by which nuclear warheads were hurtled into space and toward targets in the enemy country. The number of warheads atop each launcher, however, was not restricted. Although the Soviet side refused to give precise details about the number of launchers it possessed or had under construction, the figure of 1,618 was accepted by the United States. Since construction sites for launchers were relatively easy to discover with the satellite technology of the period, there appeared little problem in not having exact Soviet data on this issue. America, which had completed its deployment of ICBMs earlier, had 1,054 launchers. To ensure that the Soviets would not convert their smaller ICBMs to heavier missiles under the guise of modernization, the agreement forbade the conversion of light ICBMs to heavy. In effect, this capped the number of very large Soviet ICBMs at 313; America, in contrast, had no launchers in this "heavy" category.[10]

The restrictions on ICBMs were central to the agreement, since this type of strategic weapons was considered the most accurate of all delivery means in the respective arsenals. But by the time of SALT I, both sides were deploying strategic launchers at sea in an effort to secure their respective weapons from surprise attack. The restrictions placed upon submarine-launched ballistic missiles (SLBMs) permitted America to have 710 SLBMs on 44 modern ballistic missile submarines and the Soviets to possess 950 on 62 such submarines. As of the date of the agreement, neither side had this number of SLBMs, and the document's phrasing included a penalty if such a number were attained. Thus, as of late May 1972, the

Soviets were considered to possess 740 SLBMs either in operation or under construction. America had only 656 SLBMs in operation. To reach the higher permitted figure of 950, the Soviets would have to dismantle an equal number (210) of ICBMs. America would need to give up the difference between 710 and the existing 656, payable also in dismantled ICBMs. In part, this rather odd provision, nicknamed the "one way trade-off to sea," was designed to promote crisis stability in times of future East-West tension.[11] It was assumed that missiles hidden beneath the sea in submarines would be invulnerable to a sneak attack and that the mere possession of such invulnerable assets would give a nation a sense of calm and assurance in moments of crisis since no sneak assault could destroy such means of retaliation. Knowing the other side would retain credible second-strike ability regardless of how great the surprise of the initial attack, the likely attacker would be dissuaded from firing the opening shots of a nuclear war.

At the time of the Interim Agreement, America was in the process of placing several warheads upon each of its modern ICBMs. These warheads were known as multiple independently targeted reentry vehicles (MIRVs), and the American weapon allowed a package of three such warheads to sit atop some 550 of its Minutemen 3 missiles. Despite clear indications that the Soviets would also one day place such warheads upon their ICBMs, no provisions in the agreement dealt with restrictions on what was then the advanced edge of warhead technology.[12] Since it was deemed easier to verify changes in the launchers than in the smaller warheads atop each rocket, a restriction was placed upon modernization of each side's ICBMs. The dimensions of each side's launchers could not be increased by more than 10 to 15 percent in the event future modernization occurred.

The Interim Agreement was perceived by both sides as but one stage in a continuing effort to achieve a final limitation on offensive weapons similar to the ABM Treaty. Indeed, Article VIII specifically noted, "It is the objective of the Parties to conduct active follow-on negotiations with the aim of concluding such an agreement as soon as possible." During the five years the agreement would be in force, verification would be through recourse to the national technical means of both sides.[13]

This first major arms control agreement between America and the USSR contained a number of major achievements. Despite the apparent numerical advantage accorded the USSR in both ICBMs and SLBMs, a rough parity was maintained. SLBMs and ICBMs formed only two legs of the three-legged triad of America's defensive forces, with the U.S. deployment of nearly three times as many strategic bombers as the USSR offsetting the quantitative imbalance in strategic missiles. In addition, two of America's NATO allies, France and Britain, possessed a nuclear capability;

none of the Soviet's Warsaw Pact associates had similar weapons. Even the greater number of permitted Soviet SLBMs was counterbalanced by virtue of geography; the Soviets were able to maintain a much smaller percentage of their submarines on patrol at any one time compared to the United States. [14] To Nixon and Kissinger, the very signing of SALT I provided a key indication that their hopes for a deeper integration of the USSR into the normal fabric of the international order were justified. Regular discussion would now occur between the superpowers within the boundaries of the accord just signed, and the Standing Consultative Committee provided for would further Soviet acceptance of dispute resolution within conventional limits. All in all, SALT I seemed an important step in resolving East-West disagreements by means short of open conflict.

Since the ABM agreement was designated a treaty, its approval by two-thirds of the American Senate was required by law. The Interim Agreement, in contrast, was submitted for a majority vote in both the Senate and the House. To ensure passage with the greatest number of votes, the administration accepted a reservation demanded by Sen. Henry Jackson that insisted that in any future SALT agreements the number of offensive missiles allowed each side would be roughly equal. This amendment served notice that the next round of negotiations would be more complex. [15]

While SALT I was the high point of the Nixon-Kissinger effort to immerse the USSR in a web of agreements and negotiations, it was but one of many such accords signed by the end of Nixon's first term in office. By 1972 the United States and the USSR had approved a Seabed Treaty prohibiting weapons of mass destruction on the ocean floor beyond the three-mile limit, an Accident Measures Agreement increasing safeguards against accidental nuclear explosions, a Hotline Modernization Agreement improving the emergency ties between the two capitals, and a Biological Weapons Agreement. In the area of trade, a bilateral U.S.–USSR Commercial Commission was formed, and a Grain Agreement was signed as well as two trade agreements. [16] By now such progress had been made in making the Soviet Union a constituent part of the normal diplomatic world that efforts were in order to codify the rules that would henceforth bind interaction between the superpowers. It can be argued that the resulting Basic Principles Agreement of May 29, 1972, was as important as SALT I in ushering in a new era of peaceful East-West relations. Oddly, this agreement received less attention in the Western media despite the fact that it, and not SALT I, symbolized the apparent success of the Nixon-Kissinger game plan for full Soviet integration into the peaceful pursuits of international life.

The Basic Principles Agreement consisted of twelve chapters and began with a mutual acknowledgment that both powers would seek strengthened peaceful relations in line with the pledges and obligations of the United Nations Charter. Both sides agreed that in the nuclear era there was no alternative to peaceful coexistence and that differences in ideological orientation were no bar to normal interaction based upon recognition of sovereignty, equality, noninterference, and mutual advantage. The key section of the document was contained in the second chapter, which pledged restraint by both sides in future diplomatic endeavors. The powers would do their utmost to avoid military confrontation and would be prepared to settle outstanding difficulties by peaceful means. "Both sides recognize that efforts to obtain unilateral advantage at the expense of the other, directly or indirectly, are inconsistent with these objectives." The security interests of both sides were acknowledged, and both recognized that as members of the United Nations Security Council they possessed special responsibilities for the preservation of peace. Consistent with the goal of peaceful relations, the two powers promised to exchange views on problems of mutual interest at the highest level. A special area of concern would remain arms control, with the designated long-range goal being general and complete disarmament and establishment of an effective system of international security consistent with the principles of the United Nations. Ties were to be expanded in the areas of science, culture, and trade, with commissions being formed where appropriate. Both sides denied that they possessed any special claims in world affairs, a thinly veiled reference to the old issue of spheres of influence; and both denied that they would recognize any such claims put forward by the other.[17]

In combination with SALT I and the numerous other understandings and agreements, the Basic Principles Agreement ended one of the most busy and fruitful periods of postwar East-West negotiations. Unlike past phases of such negotiations, however, this round of talks and agreements emerged from a well-thought-out game plan devised in Washington to accommodate the growing Soviet power within the traditional framework of accepted international relations. Only time would tell whether the assumptions and promises of the Nixon-Kissinger game plan would bear fruit. In the meantime, negotiations continued to construct a permanent agreement limiting nuclear offensive weapons.

The urgency with which the Nixon administration pursued a follow-on agreement after SALT I was far from fortuitous. Henry Kissinger had predicted that within eighteen months technological advances would make further negotiations much more difficult. In addition, the defense planners within the Nixon administration had voiced fears that a breakthrough in areas not covered by SALT I might be possible. Thus, America delivered notice at the time of signing that "if an agreement providing for more complete strategic offensive arms limitations were not achieved within five years, U.S. supreme interests could be jeopardized. Should that occur, it would constitute a basis for withdrawal from the ABM Treaty."[18]

In the immediate aftermath of the signing of SALT I, there were both positive and negative indications as to prospects for a future agreement. On the positive side, President Nixon appeared to retain the support of the Senate in his further efforts at negotiations. In June 1973 Soviet party chief Brezhnev visited the United States, confirming a pledge that he and Nixon would seek to conclude a new SALT agreement the following year.[19] Despite these suggestions of hope, however, sentiment against further discussions with the Soviets was gaining momentum.

Almost immediately following the May Moscow meeting at which SALT I was signed, reports circulated concerning possible duplicity by Henry Kissinger in the entire proceedings. The Interim Agreement had limited the Soviets to 950 SLBMs on 62 modern ballistic submarines. It was soon discovered, however, that this phraseology allowed the Russians to retain a number of SLBMs mounted upon earlier, nonnuclear-powered submarines of the Golf Class, which were first launched in 1958.[20] While the significance of this additional quantity of short-range SLBMs was unclear, its discovery raised serious questions about whether Kissinger had misled the American delegation on other, yet undiscovered problems as well. To add to growing fears that SALT I gave advantages to the Soviets, the CIA, on the day after the agreement was signed, detected a concerted modernization effort by the Russians that, while technically within the limits of the understandings, threatened the spirit of accommodation so necessary for future negotiations. In the words of Nixon's CIA director, James Schlesinger: "For the limitations on offensive forces to have contributed to arms stability, the Soviets would have had to refrain from exploiting through new technology, the possibilities allowed under the agreement. But starting immediately *after* the signing of the Moscow agreements in mid-May, 1972, there was a veritable explosion of Soviet Research & Development activity on all of the new generations of missiles. Apparently the Soviets had deliberately held up such activity—until the American signature was dry on the agreements."[21] Especially upsetting to intelligence analysts were the results of recent Soviet tests of their giant ICBM named the SS-9. Several times larger than the biggest American missile, the SS-9, containing a primitive multiple independently targeted reentry vehicle (MIRV), was fired in a pattern that appeared designed to destroy either American ICBM fields or their command and control centers. Such a capability, if further perfected, might allow a Soviet surprise attack upon the most accurate of America's retaliatory forces.[22]

Concerns about the Soviet military buildup coincided with a decline in good political relations with Moscow due to the surprise Egyptian and

Syrian attacks upon America's ally, Israel, in 1973. Worried about a unilateral Soviet move into the disputed Middle East, the United States placed its nuclear forces upon alert during this Yom Kippur War. And by the time tensions had cooled, President Nixon, due to the expanding Watergate investigations, found himself no longer able to gain congressional or popular support for a dramatic second breakthrough in arms discussions. When Nixon left office in August 1974, thereby avoiding impeachment, the prospects of SALT II had to be left to his successor.

Actual negotiations for SALT II began in November 1972, six months after the original agreements had been signed. Well aware of the constraints of the Jackson amendment that proposed essentially equal levels of offensive weapons in any subsequent understanding, Henry Kissinger attempted to discover a series of plateaus for various nuclear arms that would satisfy the senator.[23] When Nixon resigned, Kissinger was retained by his successor, Gerald Ford, and continued his talks with Moscow. In November 1974 his efforts appeared to bear fruit as Brezhnev and Ford met in the Soviet Pacific port city of Vladivostok to sign a new accord. True to Kissinger's earlier predictions, technology had made efforts at control more difficult, and the resulting understanding was more complex in form and content. The Vladivostok Accord was to function as the basic outline for the soon-to-be-completed new Offensive Agreement that would replace the 1972 Interim Agreement. Only a few minor points remained to be decided.[24]

The Vladivostok Accord allowed each side to retain 2,400 strategic vehicles. This latter term was defined to include ICBMs, SLBMs, and, for the first time, intercontinental bombers. Both sides were allowed to have MIRV warheads on their ICBMs and SLBMs but only to a limit of 1,320 MIRVed missiles of both categories. If no permanent agreement were immediately forthcoming, the Vladivostok Accord would cover the period from the expiration of the 1972 Interim Agreement in 1977 to December 31, 1985. During this time both sides would devote full efforts to resolve remaining difficulties.[25]

Among the problems still outstanding was the question of how one might verify any proposed limitation of MIRVed warheads. Unlike rocket launchers whose giant size made them easy targets for spy-in-the-sky verification, it was impossible to determine whether a warhead was or was not MIRVed without actually taking apart the warhead nose and inspecting the contents. In short, the possibilities of cheating appeared unlimited. The American suggestions for verification rested upon the proposition that once a given type of launcher was tested in a complete and successful series in a MIRVed mode all launchers of that type would henceforth be considered MIRVed. This seemed the only solution aside from on-site inspection, which was sure to draw objections from the Soviets. A second issue dealt with the definition of an intercontinental bomber. While it was clear that certain planes such as the American B-52 possessed such intercontinental ability, it was less clear whether the most recent Soviet bomber, the Backfire, should also be subject to restrictions. Perhaps the most technologically advanced of the Soviet bomber force, this new plane did not possess the range to hit American targets and return to Soviet bases if it flew in a normal pattern. But if it refueled in flight or if it were to bomb America and then land on friendly Cuban bases, it could deliver a nuclear assault.

The problem of what did or did not constitute a "strategic vehicle" also impinged upon a recent American technological innovation—the cruise missile. Initially patterned after the wartime German V-One rocket, the cruise was a pilotless drone that could fly over 1,500 miles and be launched from ship, air, or land. While slow by rocket standards, flying below the speed of sound, the small size of these missiles and their fantastic accuracies made them a weapon of enormous promise. As expected, the Soviets wished cruise deployments to be counted against the upper limit of 2,400 strategic missiles. The Ford administration, stressing the slow velocities of this weapon, argued that at best the cruise missile was a second-strike weapon and hence ought to be omitted from the list of dangerous offensive strategic vehicles. Clearly, the number and complexity of issues preventing a follow-on SALT accord would take both time and wisdom despite the fact that Henry Kissinger hinted that a final agreement was but a matter of time.[26]

The publication of the Vladivostok Accord gave rise to considerable discussions both in the American Congress and among concerned citizens at large. To many the ceiling of 2,400 strategic vehicles undercut the entire notion that an arms limitation agreement was being prepared. As of 1974 neither America nor the USSR had deployed such a high number, suggesting that Vladivostok might function as an arms expansion accord, at least in the short run. Similar objections greeted the proposed limitation on MIRVed warheads of 1,320 for each side. As of late 1974, America had MIRVed slightly more than 800 missiles, and the Soviets were only now starting their own programs. Equally important to many, the Vladivostok Accord had done nothing to redress the existing inequity in large missiles, a category in which Russia was vastly superior. Under Salt I the Soviets had retained 313 very large SS-9 missiles while America possessed none. Overall, this advantage meant that the Soviet missiles had the potential to deliver approximately three times as many pounds of atomic explosives as America. Such a superiority in "throw-weight" (the total weight of the warhead that a rocket can "throw" toward its target) became especially significant in an era when MIRVed warheads were becoming dominant. America, for example, had placed three warheads on its small Minuteman 3 launchers. The giant size and throw-weight of the Soviet SS-9 suggested that as many as thirty warheads, each targeted at a separate American objective, might be possible.

President Ford's defeat in the 1976 election meant that the conclusion of a SALT II agreement would fall to yet another administration, this one devoid of architect Henry Kissinger. And yet the new democratic president brought certain advantages with respect to further negotiations with the Soviets. Not only was the stability of the presidency reestablished through the national election of Jimmy Carter, but the main critic of SALT I and Vladivostok, Sen. Henry Jackson of Washington, was a member of Carter's own party. Early in the new administration, Richard Perle, Jackson's chief assistant on security affairs and later assistant secretary of state in the Reagan administration, drafted a letter to the White House. The total number of weapons allowed at Vladivostok struck Senator Jackson as excessive, and a suggestion was made to reopen this issue with the Soviets. In addition, the letter recommended that the problem of heavy missiles ought to be dealt with head-on, the American advantage in cruise missiles should be protected from restrictions, and the new Soviet Backfire bomber should be counted in the total of strategic vehicles. Perhaps the most important of Jackson's admonitions concerned the 313 heavy Soviet missiles, for this Soviet advantage was enshrined in the now five-year-old SALT I Treaty.[27]

Interested in assuring domestic support for continuing arms negotiations, the Carter administration drafted am ambitious plan for presentation to Moscow. In the spring of 1977, Secretary of State Cyrus Vance flew to the Soviet capital with a proposal to cut the total number of strategic vehicles permitted well below the Vladivostok level of 2,400 and to include a subceiling on heavy missiles that would force the Russians to scrap about half of their existing force. The fact that the outline of the new American plan was leaked to the press on the eve of Vance's departure did not improve its prospects. In Moscow Brezhnev rejected this reopening of issues long settled, remarking that he had already expended considerable political capital just to get agreement from his own military for the Vladivostok Accord.[28] Clearly, SALT II would require difficult negotiations if a common understanding were to be reached in the near future.

It soon became clear that the three years since Vladivostok had complicated the problems as each side was in the process of deploying new weapons systems. The Soviets had constructed a new generation of missiles, improved weapons with the designations of SS-17, 18, and 19. The SS-18, a follow-on for the SS-9 and hence the new "heavy" weapon, appeared to have accuracies that might allow the total destruction of

America's ICBMs, thus opening what some felt would be a "window of opportunity" for a Soviet disarming first strike.[29] America, in turn, was continuing the development of cruise missiles that, when deployed in large numbers, would greatly complicate Soviet efforts to defend their nation. And as negotiations progressed, it became apparent that not all the issues recent technology had spawned could be solved within the near future.

By 1979 both sides agreed to establish three separate categories of problems: those that could be solved now; those that remained disputed and hence were open only to limited or temporary solutions; and those that would be postponed until a future SALT III. As a result, the SALT II agreement signed in the summer of 1979 was a three-tiered document consisting of an Interim Agreement that was to expire in 1985, a Protocol that would bind each side only until 1981, and a general statement of principles that would form the basis for SALT III.[30]

The new SALT agreement was much longer and more complex than its predecessor, partly because of new technological complexities and partly because of suspicions that the Soviets had taken advantage of ambiguities in SALT I to advance their own might. ICBMs were now defined as those ballistic weapons possessing a range in excess of 5,500 kilometers. SLBMs were defined as submarine-launched ballistic missiles installed "on any submarine regardless of type," an effort to avoid the "error" in SALT I allowing additional such weapons on nonnuclear boats. Both heavy ballistic missiles and cruise missiles were specifically defined to the satisfaction of both sides.[31]

With the issue of definitions out of the way, the agreement proceeded to set specific limitations. Consistent with the past Vladivostok Accord, each side was allowed to retain/deploy an aggregate of 2,400 strategic vehicles (ICBMs, SLBMs, and bombers). But on January 1, 1981, that total would drop to 2,250. The precise mix of these three weapons systems within the agreed-upon totals would be left to each side, with the proviso that neither could build additional ICBM launchers. Both sides eschewed conversion of "light" missiles to "heavies" and in future modernizations would not increase the volume of the ICBM silos by more than 32 percent. Neither side would flight test or deploy any new types of ICBMs (modernization) not flight tested as of May 1, 1979, except that each side could test and deploy one new type of light ICBM without regard to this restriction. For the United States, this last provision allowed the building of the MX missile—a project already under development.[32]

For the first time, SALT II contained restrictions upon the modernization of warheads, placing firm limits upon the number of MIRVs permitted on each launcher. Concerned about Soviet insistence that its advantage in heavy missiles be retained at the price of any agreement, yet worried that the throw-weight advantage this gave to the Soviets might one day lead to the placing of thirty or more warheads on their heavy SS-18, the Carter negotiators produced an interesting compromise. Neither side would flight test or deploy an ICBM or SLBM with more MIRVs than had been tested as of May 1, 1979. For America this meant that the Minuteman 3 ICBM—America's most modern weapon—would continue with three separate bombs or "fractionations" within the MIRV casing (the "bus"). The American SLBM then in use on the Poseidon submarine (the C-3) would be limited to fourteen fractionations, and the follow-on D-4 designed for the next generation of submarines, the Tridents, would be restricted to seven. The "heavy" Soviet SS-18, in turn, would be allowed ten fractionations (independently targeted reentry vehicles) per rocket, with the SS-17 and 19 allowed fewer. Since it was assumed that neither side would risk deploying additional fractionations on any launcher without testing to see whether such increases adversely affected the rocket's accuracy and given that national technical means alone could adequately monitor all such long-distance rocket tests, the restrictions on MIRVs required no on-site inspections.[33]

With the restrictions upon MIRVing spelled out, the agreement continued with sublimits as to how many of each type of weapon might be deployed. While the overall number of strategic vehicles was 2,400, only 1,320 of these could fall into the categories of MIRVed ICBMs, MIRVed SLBMs, MIRVed air-to-surface ballistic missiles, and heavy bombers capable of carrying cruise missiles with a range exceeding 600 kilometers. Within this figure only 1,200 vehicles could be MIRVED ICBMs, MIRVed SLBMs, and MIRVed air-to-surface ballistic missiles. This meant an advantage for America since the difference between the 1,320 figure and the lower ceiling of 1,200 permitted deployment of 120 bombers with cruise missiles, a technology in which America possessed a significant lead. Within the 1,200 MIRVed vehicles, only 820 could be MIRVed ICBMs.[34]

Concomitant with restrictions on quantity and quality of nuclear strategic weapons went measures designed to improve the feeling of trust between the two sides. These "confidence-building measures" mandated that each side would notify the other of planned ICBM launches if the ICBM warhead was programmed to leave a nation's territory during flight. A Standing Consultative Commission was established to discuss any questions that might arise during the life of the agreement. The agreement was to become effective when ratified by both sides and to remain operative until the last day of 1985 or until completion of a follow-on SALT III accord.

While the agreement contained detailed restrictions on weapons that both sides felt were of an equitable nature, it also made reference to weapons upon which final understanding was still lacking. In the Protocol to the agreement, the two sides pledged they would refrain from various deployments or tests until the last day of 1981 at which time the Protocol, but not the agreement, would expire. Among these more limited restrictions were pledges not to deploy or flight test a mobile ICBM launcher or a cruise missile with ranges exceeding 600 kilometers based upon land or sea (air-launched cruise missiles remained unrestricted in the Protocol although they were limited under the regular agreement). Neither side would flight test or deploy air-to-surface ballistic missiles during this shorter period.[35]

The main agreement and the Protocol covered those issues that the Carter administration felt were open to either permanent or temporary understanding. Issues yet to be resolved were sketched in the Joint Statement of Principles and Basic Guidelines for Subsequent Negotiations of Strategic Arms. In this section it was agreed that the two sides would continue their negotiations "in accordance with the principle of equality and equal security, on measures for further limitations and reductions in the number of strategic arms, as well as for their future qualitative limitations." The goal of follow-on discussions was broadly described as (1) significant reductions in the number of strategic offensive arms; (2) qualitative limits of strategic offensive arms; and (3) resolution of issues included in the Protocol of this agreement.[36]

The extremely detailed agreement that constituted SALT II contained important concessions by both sides, a necessity if an understanding were to be reached. The Americans had given in on two key issues. Finally, the matter of the 300 plus Soviet "heavy" missiles appeared settled to Soviet satisfaction. The agreement did not call for a special subceiling on such large weapons as many, including Senator Jackson, had hoped, nor was the United States allowed compensation through the deployment of its own "heavy" force. The throw-weight advantage that accompanied the deployment of the heavy SS-18 would remain. A second concession involved the counting of bombers with cruise missiles within the 1,320 sublimit on strategic vehicles. And yet the Soviets, too, gave up advantages, actual and potential. The limitation of 820 MIRVed ICBMs removed fears that the USSR might place multiple warheads on a larger force of land-based missiles. Equally important, and in part offsetting the Soviet retention of heavy missiles, were restrictions upon the MIRVing of the SS-18 to a maximum of ten. It had long been a worry in Washington that the Soviets might MIRV this, their largest strategic vehicle, to as high as thirty. And in a separate statement, Leonid Brezhnev pledged that the disputed Backfire bomber would not be produced in numbers exceeding thirty per year in recognition of unassuaged American fears as to its potential intercontinental capability.[37]

All in all, SALT II appeared to be the most comprehensive accord possible at the time, divided into a long-term interim agreement, a shorter-term protocol, and a promise to continue talks until complete satisfaction was achieved and a permanent treaty signed. Only one major hurdle remained in the short run: ratification of the agreement by the Congress. And the prospects for ratification were as much a function of the shifting East-West political relations as they were of the specific restrictions contained in the agreement itself.

17

Détente to Disenchantment

The efforts of President Nixon and Security Adviser Henry Kissinger to reorient American policy consistent with the changing nature of postwar power relationships aimed at fuller integration of the Soviet Union within the existing framework of international relations. Since it was assumed that this process would require time, the Nixon administration determined certain guidelines that had to be upheld during the period of transition. Most important, America's power and influence could not be perceived as declining without the risk of a repudiation of policy by an aroused Congress and citizenry. During the era of détente, America would have to remain true to its commitments abroad, even while emphasizing the need for distant allies to contribute more to their own defensive needs. The Guam or Nixon Doctrine could not be seen as a first step to American disentanglement from the third world, and the war in Vietnam could not terminate short of victory with honor. If these last prohibitions were violated, no nation in the future would respect America's promise of mutual defense or protection. Unfortunately, despite evident success in integrating the USSR into the common international fabric during the seventies, these key principles came more and more into question. And once again Vietnam provided the initial crisis point.

The importance of maintaining American commitments in the wake of the Nixon Doctrine became obvious in the spring of 1972. In March the North Vietnamese opened a major offensive that threatened progress in pacification achieved in the first years of the Nixon presidency. Despite the nearness of the May summit, Henry Kissinger immediately called in veteran Soviet ambassador Anatoly Dobrynin, accusing the Soviet Union of complicity in the North Vietnamese attack.[1] On the eve of his final preparatory trip to Moscow the next month, Kissinger was ordered by Nixon not even to discuss the summit unless substantial progress on Vietnam was made in talks with Leonid Brezhnev, a point that was accentuated by an American bombing of Hanoi and Haiphong that damaged several Soviet ships and killed a number of Soviet citizens while Kissinger and Brezhnev were engaged in discussions.[2]

To treat the North Vietnamese assault in a milder fashion threatened to raise the specter of appeasement, a charge Nixon and Kissinger could not permit while delicate negotiations with Moscow were in progress. Kissinger, in fact, was informed by Brezhnev that Moscow was not behind the new Vietnamese challenge but, rather, those who opposed the planned U.S.–Soviet summit (Hanoi and Peking). Guns used in the offensive had not recently been supplied from Moscow but had been stored for two years in North Vietnam itself in anticipation of a future attack. Perhaps sensing the delicate position in which Nixon found himself with reference to American domestic opinion, Brezhnev promised to transmit the most recent peace proposals to Hanoi via a Soviet spokesman, dispatching a high Soviet official shortly thereafter to Hanoi.[3]

With no apparent letup in the North Vietnamese offensive, President Nixon contemplated aborting the May summit. He resolved to escalate the bombing of North Vietnam and authorized the unprecedented step of mining the North Vietnamese harbors, ignoring the fact that most ships of call were from communist nations that, in turn, would pressure Moscow to break all ties with Washington. To Nixon the sanctity of America's existing commitments was a necessary prerequisite to the reordering of international relations that he and Kissinger sought in Moscow. As Nixon cautioned Kissinger in a memo outlining the new steps he planned in Vietnam: "Our desire to have the Soviet Summit, of course, enters into this, but you have prepared the way very well on that score, and, in any event, we cannot let the Soviet Summit be the primary consideration in making this decision. As I told you on the phone this morning, I intend to cancel the Summit unless the situation militarily and diplomatically substantially improves by May 15 at the latest."[4]

The main provisions for a final agreement in Vietnam were approved by all concerned parties early in 1973. A cease-fire in place would begin as of January 28, 1973, with North Vietnamese forces located in South Vietnam allowed to remain but forbidden to receive new supplies. American forces would withdraw in sixty days, and prisoners of war on both sides would be released. An International Commission of Control and Supervision was created to reconcile disputes between the warring factions in South Vietnam, and provisions were made for general elections at a future date. While these conditions did not satisfy the South Vietnamese government as to the likely peaceful intentions of their opponents, Nixon, in a secret letter to Pres. Nguyen Van Thieu, promised America would respond with full military force if the settlement were violated and would continue assistance to Saigon during the armistice period.[5] Finally, an end to the conflict seemed in sight. And yet now more than ever the fate of Vietnam depended upon America's willingness to honor its commitments to its ally.

By 1973, the year of the Vietnamese armistice, the Nixon administration had used almost all of its political capital in promising a victory with honor in Southeast Asia. Several years earlier public opinion polls revealed growing disenchantment with this war, a disenchantment that merged with disillusionment about the president himself in 1973 due to the Watergate crisis. Between 1970 and 1973, Congress placed increasing restrictions on America's ability to bomb Cambodia, most of which were passed over presidential vetoes. In June 1973 all funds for such bombings were curtailed. In November Congress passed the War Powers Resolution that forbade the commitment of American troops for more than sixty days without legislative approval.[6] The following year, 1974, Congress spurned a White House request for $1.5 billion for Saigon, offering instead less than half this amount.[7]

In January 1975, the Khmer Rouge rebels in Cambodia opened a last offensive against the American-backed government in Phnom Penh. When Congress rejected a White House plea for $200 million in emergency aid, the Cambodian government collapsed. That same March North Vietnam sent its entire regular army south in open violation of the 1973 agreement. In April President Ford requested nearly $1 billion in emergency military and economic assistance. American monetary commitments, he was informed, would be available only to assist the evacuation of remaining U.S. personnel. On April 30 North Vietnamese forces entered Saigon. A crucial principle supporting efforts at détente had been rebuffed.[8]

While the "loss" of Vietnam and the emergence of a communist government in Hanoi appeared to reflect a real if perhaps minor shift in the world balance of forces, equally significant changes were occurring in the "perceived" balance of world power. The American disillusionment with the seemingly never-ending engagement in Southeast Asia led to congressional attempts to restrict military power through reduced appropriations. This, in turn, caused a growing disparity between the types and quantities of weapons procured by America and the Soviet Union at the very moment Washington was seeking better ties with Moscow. Indeed, the Nixon and Ford presidencies showed the largest relative reduction of American forces with respect to the Soviet Union experienced in the postwar period. In the first eight years of the seventies, the United States deployed only two new strategic systems: the MIRVed Minuteman 3 and the Poseidon submarine.

The Soviets, in contrast, put into action eight new or updated ICBMs and two SLBMs. American ground forces were reduced by over 200,000 between 1970 and 1977. Soviet military manpower, already almost twice that of the United States, grew by over 200,000 in the same period. The Soviet navy, long inferior to America's, expanded to near equality in all categories except aircraft carriers. In summary, American defense expenditures as a percentage of gross national product declined from 8.2 in fiscal 1970 to 5.2 in fiscal 1977. While the exact amount the Soviets spent on defense remains an issue of debate, the general consensus pointed to between 11 and 13 percent of gross national product—well over twice the American rate. (It must be kept in mind, of course, that the Soviet gross national product was only about six-tenths of the American at that time.) Accounting for inflation, America's defense outlays declined at an annual rate of about 4.5 percent between 1970 and 1975; Soviet outlays increased at about 3 percent per year.[9] And while it was difficult to translate such figures into precise measurements of military readiness, the *perception* of growing American inferiority soon became dominant here and abroad. Once again a prerequisite for maintaining a stable and promising relationship with Moscow had been undermined.

The magnitude of the growing spending gap between the United States and the Soviet Union in the period of détente can best be seen by viewing comparative spending figures from 1960 to 1980. The figures shown in Table 2 state total Soviet and American defense allocations excluding military pensions and funds expended for research, development, testing, and evaluation (RDT&E).

The relative decline of American military power and the "loss" of Vietnam to communism were but two of the problems plaguing efforts at developing détente with the USSR. For an era of peaceful coexistence to become a reality, both superpowers were required to approach one another with new understanding and appreciation, foregoing opportunities to best their rival in future diplomatic contests. And yet as the seventies progressed, both powers fell back to their normal pattern of suspicious diplomacy. Within a year after signing the Basic Principles Agreement of May 1972, it became apparent that Moscow and Washington had very different expectations of where the period of détente would lead.

In the summer of 1973, the two superpowers signed a new accord, the Agreement of Prevention of Nuclear War. Its terms appeared rather straightforward and perceptive, noting that both sides "agree that they will act in such a manner . . . as to exclude the outbreak of nuclear war between them and between either of the parties and other countries." It also said that "if at any time relations between the parties or between either party and other countries appear to involve the risk of nuclear conflict . . . the

Table 2. Soviet and American Defense Spending, 1960-1980
(all figures in 1982 constant U.S. dollars [billions])

	Soviet Spending (CIA Estimate)	Soviet Spending (Defense Dept. Estimate)	U.S. Spending
1960	$109.8	$101.8	$127
1962	112.6	109.3	141.1
1964	121.9	116.3	142.5
1966	128.6	124.5	146.1
1968	135.6	133.4	188.7
1970	143.3	143.3	159.1
1972	149.2	154.5	130.6
1974	159.1	170.6	122.6
1976	165.7	184.7	119.9
1978	165.1	192.8	123.2
1980	170.7	208.1	127.3

Source: Steven Rosefielde, "Soviet Arms Buildup or U.S. Arms Decline?" in Helmet Sonnenfelt, ed, *Soviet Politics in the 1980s* (Boulder, 1985), 112.

United States and the Soviet Union . . . shall immediately enter into urgent consultation . . . and make every effort to avert this risk."[10] Only with the subsequent publication of Henry Kissinger's memoirs did the world learn this accord was "about 180 degrees removed from the original proposal advanced by Brezhnev."[11]

What Leonid Brezhnev initially had in mind during these discussions was nothing less than a superpower condominium over all other nations: a bilateral understanding to guide global development in the interest of Moscow and Washington. As first discussed by Brezhnev in 1972, this special U.S.–USSR relationship would replace past American nuclear guarantees to NATO allies, promising that all threats to use nuclear weapons would be subject to superpower veto. In addition, America's growing ties with communist China would be subordinated to increasing Soviet fears of China's nuclear potential, a fear that might one day compel Moscow to launch a surgical strike against its Asian neighbor. Only by careful editing and removal of unacceptable clauses was the accord converted into a relatively innocuous agreement that both powers could sign in June 1973.[12] And yet by now, a year after the May 1972 summit conference in Moscow, it was clear that both sides had very different interpretations of what the new spirit of détente entailed. In the fall of 1973, these different interpretations and different interests once more conflicted.

Since shortly after the creation of the state of Israel in the late forties, the USSR and the United States had found themselves backing different regional allies in a bid for dominance in the Middle East. Surely here the fundamental clause of the 1972 Basic Principles Agreement, which pledged both sides to eschew "efforts to obtain unilateral advantages at the expense of the other," would experience a test. Indeed, the very signing of this agreement convinced Egyptian president Anwar Sadat that Moscow was an unreliable ally, leading to the expulsion of 20,000 Soviet advisers shortly thereafter.[13] By the summer of 1973, the Soviets were aware that Egypt intended to attack Israel, and Brezhnev dutifully, if obliquely, informed President Nixon that pacification of this region was increasingly important.

On October 3, 1973, the Soviets were informed by Egypt that war was imminent. During the next two days, the Soviets began a highly visible airlift of their civilians from both Syria and Egypt, a move that for some unexplained reason failed sufficiently to alarm or inform American intelligence.[14] On October 6 war began, with each side soon providing needed resupplies for its respective client. On October 16 Soviet prime minister Kosygin flew to Cairo and persuaded Sadat to approve a cease-fire in place. Kissinger departed for Moscow shortly thereafter to work out details, and on October 22 the United Nations Security Council adopted a joint American-Soviet resolution for a cease-fire. To this point the superpowers had acted consistent with past pledges to consult when danger threatened.[15]

Two days later, as the cease-fire collapsed in the wake of continued Israeli advances, Sadat urgently called for a joint American-Soviet force to restore the peace. By now Egyptian forces were in danger of annihilation, an event that would reveal the USSR as an unworthy ally throughout this vital region. In response Brezhnev informed Washington that if American troops failed to respond, Soviet units would unilaterally answer Sadat's plea, bringing Russian forces into direct confrontation with Israeli units. As Henry Kissinger later noted: "We had not worked for years to reduce the Soviet military presence in Egypt only to cooperate in reintroducing it as a result of a UN resolution. Nor would we participate in a joint force with the Soviets, which would legitimize their role in the area."[16] In short, when confronted by a serious challenge in which both national honor and regional prestige were involved, the superpowers quickly returned to business as usual without regard for avoiding "unilateral advantage." With American nuclear forces placed on alert and a brisk message dispatched to Moscow, direct Soviet intervention was avoided and a ceasefire finally accepted. But this first fundamental test of the Basic Principles seemed a failure for both sides.[17]

Less than a year after the Yom Kippur War, a second potential test of détente appeared with the rapid withdrawal of Portugal from its former African colony of Angola. By the time of independence in 1974, three main guerrilla forces were in a struggle for dominance, each being supported by outside powers including Russia, the United States, China, South Africa, and Zaire. In early 1975, to the surprise of many, the three disputing factions agreed to establish a coalition provisional government. But despite this agreement, the special committee of the National Security Council supervising CIA covert activities (the "40 Committee") resolved to provide $300,000 to its own Angolan ally, the Front for the National Liberation of Angola (FNLA). Shortly thereafter, Soviet arms began to arrive at the headquarters of their ally, the Popular Movement for the Liberation of Angola (MPLA). As the various Angolan groups once again engaged in warfare, outside forces stepped up their assistance. By the summer of 1975, over 200 Cuban advisers were with MPLA forces, and by August regular troops from South Africa and Zaire were engaged on behalf of anti-MPLA units. That summer the Ford administration approved $50 million in arms for anti-MPLA forces to be spent over the next four months. In the face of this concerted onslaught, MPLA forces began to falter. But in November *Operation Carlota* began in which 10,000 to 12,000 Cuban regulars were dispatched to Angola by year's end, initially in Cuban planes but later in craft flying the markings of the USSR. By early 1976 pro-American forces had been routed, and an aroused Congress, still feeling the shock of Vietnam, voted to end all covert aid. The MPLA soon claimed sole custody of the newly independent Angolan state.[18]

Although it was the U.S. Congress that ultimately terminated American involvement in Angola, the resulting MPLA victory was perceived widely as a "unilateral" Soviet gain. As Kissinger asserted, "It is difficult to reconcile this with the principles of coexistence that we signed in 1972, and this would have to be taken into account by our policy if it continues."[19] The following summer, during the hard-fought campaign for the presidency, Gerald Ford informed an audience in Peoria, Illinois, that the word *détente* henceforth would not be used in his campaign.[20] Under attack by challenger Ronald Reagan for being soft on communism, Ford increasingly stressed a program of peace through strength. Détente was clearly becoming a divisive issue.

The Carter administration entered office pledging to improve faltering relations with the Soviet Union and to complete negotiations on a SALT II agreement. Yet from the early days, the increased stress upon civil rights emanating from Washington aggravated the more traditional Russian diplomats, while Soviet adventurism in Africa continued to cause concerns in Washington. It was not until 1979, however, that the final crisis of détente unfolded, an odd coincidence since this also was the year when SALT II would be signed and almost a decade of negotiations would find fulfillment.

In June 1979, while Jimmy Carter was preparing to meet Leonid

Brezhnev in Vienna, the American National Security Agency (NSA) chanced upon the word *Brigada* during a review of Russian-language transmissions from Cuba. It was referred to the intelligence community for assessment, but no common interpretation could be reached as to what type of Soviet unit might be involved. In August American reconnaissance photographs of Cuba revealed a Soviet force complete with tanks, artillery, and armored troop carriers. When this new information was leaked to the press, Sen. Frank Church, head of the Senate Foreign Relations Committee and contender in a difficult reelection race in his home state of Idaho, postponed hearings of SALT II until the problem of the Soviet Brigada was resolved. On September 5, 1979, Secretary of State Cyrus Vance informed a press conference that he would "not be satisfied with the status quo in Cuba."[21]

The Soviet response to charges of a Russian buildup in Cuba was to assert that no change in their forces had occurred since 1962. They acknowledged that a small training mission had remained in Cuba following the earlier Cuban Missile Crisis and that its existence must have been known in Washington since that time. Privately, Moscow hinted to Washington that if American intelligence was so slipshod that it had failed to spot this unit in the intervening seventeen years this was a problem for Washington alone to remedy. Publicly, the USSR suggested that certain conservative and antidétente elements were using this "manufactured" crisis to undercut the recently signed SALT agreement. On October 1, aware that little assistance would come from Moscow, the Carter administration announced certain unilateral measures designed to return East-West relations to as normal as possible. America would expand its surveillance flights over Cuba, and a new Joint Caribbean Military Task Force would conduct maneuvers in Cuban waters. With calm returning the Senate Foreign Relations Committee returned to work, finishing its debate on SALT II in November and requesting space on the full Senate calendar for final discussion and vote.[22] Before such a vote could occur, however, the Soviet invasion of Afghanistan ended détente once and for all.

Afghanistan, a nation of between 15 and 18 million people located on the southern border of the Soviet Union, had traditionally been the scene of Great Power rivalry. In 1978 a revolution installed a pro-Soviet government in the capital of Kabul, and Russian assistance and Russian advisers were quickly dispatched. In December of the same year, the Soviet Union and Afghanistan signed a Treaty of Friendship that formalized their increasingly close relations. But the revolutionary government in Kabul soon lost the support of the conservative, Muslim peasantry, and uprisings began throughout the land.

In March 1979 a major disturbance in the city of Herat in which a whole division of Afghan troops defected to the rebels produced numerous casualties among Soviet advisers stationed in the area. Impaled Soviet heads were carried through the streets. In October another division defected, again with significant Soviet casualties. By now even the Soviet press reflected clear concerns over instability on the southern frontier. Of equal importance, the prestige and honor of the Soviet military was in question. In December 1979 over 100,000 Soviet troops crossed the border, occupying Kabul and assassinating the Afghan ruler.[23]

To the Carter administration, just recovering from the crisis of the Cuban Brigade, this new action constituted a decisive change in East-West relations. On December 28 President Carter informed Soviet leader Brezhnev that the invasion was "a clear threat to the peace" and "could mark a fundamental and long-lasting turning point in our relations." The American demand for immediate Soviet withdrawal went unheeded, and President Carter told ABC News, "This action of the Soviets has made a more dramatic change in my own opinion of what the Soviets' ultimate goals are than anything they've done in the previous time I've been in office."[24] On January 2 Carter recalled the American ambassador from Moscow; on January 3 he requested the Senate to postpone indefinitely further consideration of SALT II.

The dramatic conclusion of an era of détente required substitution of a new policy designed to rebuff resurgent Soviet expansion, and the Carter administration fell back upon an updated version of containment. Uncertain as to precise Soviet objectives and deeply concerned about potential threats to the oil-producing states of the Persian Gulf, Carter identified the Middle East, not Europe, as the likely focus of Soviet aggression. In his State of the Union Address of January 1980, the president announced what came to be known as the Carter Doctrine. "Any attempt by any outside force to gain control of the Persian Gulf region will be regarded as an assault on the vital interests of the United States of America, and such an assault will be repelled by any means necessary, including military force."[25] To show its resolve, the White House requested a 5 percent real increase in defense spending and the reinstatement of draft registration. A "Quick Reaction Force" capable of rapid movement to distant portions of the globe was also organized.

When the diverse responses to the Soviet invasion of Afghanistan were placed in perspective, it was obvious that one era had ended and another had begun. America's new containment policy included pledges to halt further communist expansion in the Persian Gulf, in conjunction with efforts to improve relations with Russia's eastern neighbor, China. American military forces would bear the main burden of the new approach. In the diplomatic arena, past efforts at relaxing East-West tensions were concluded. SALT II was withdrawn from consideration, and existing trade agreements with Moscow were scrapped. In 1980 alone U.S.–Soviet trade diminished 60 percent. Cultural agreements were allowed to expire, and the president forbade olympic participants to travel to the 1980 games in Moscow. Clearly, the "Grand Strategy" of Nixon and Kissinger had given way by the end of the decade to renewed Cold War and containment.

18

The Evolution of
U.S. Strategic Doctrine

In the first five years following World War II, nuclear weapons were considered within the general strategy of long-range bombing established in the preceding conflict. In 1947 the Strategic Air Command numbered only twenty trained air crews and six weapons-assembly specialists within its ranks. Consistent with past experience, the primary targets for future nuclear strikes were enemy urban areas since critical war industries were located there. The destruction of urban populations in collateral damage would bring results as well, lessening enemy morale. It was widely conceded that Japan's exit from the war in the summer of 1945 had been the result of anticipated urban destruction on an atomic scale. Such fears would produce proper results in the next conflict as well.[1]

Since the main delivery system for nuclear bombs was the relatively slow B-29 bomber, concentration on the enemy's capability to launch an assault in the initial moments of a future conflict was impossible. Not until the advent of long-range rockets would either side be able to focus attention upon the offensive power of the other. Until then the slow speed of bombers meant the opponent would have adequate time to put his own forces in motion. In addition, until the first Soviet nuclear explosion in late 1949, the Russians did not possess a nuclear capability to threaten the United States in the event of war. In the spring of 1948, the strategic plans of the Joint Chiefs of Staff called for the use of 50 bombs to be dropped upon 20 Soviet cities with the goal of destroying 50 percent of Soviet industrial production.[2]

The fifties brought new possibilities and new problems. The explosion of a Soviet bomb in 1949, several years ahead of the most pessimistic American predictions, opened the prospect of counterforce strategic targeting. Such counterforce targeting would be directed against Soviet bomb depots and Soviet airfields from which planes with atomic cargoes might be launched against America. The Korean War also caused Western strategists to revise past assumptions that the USSR would avoid conventional war in the face of Western atomic superiority. If Korea was but a prelude to a general Soviet assault upon Western Europe as many in Washington feared, atomic attack against Soviet cities and Soviet industrial capabilities would do little to immediately retard the advancing Russian armies. The Harmon committee analysis ordered by Secretary of Defense James Forrestal asserted that while an atomic attack upon Soviet cities as then planned would produce as many as 4 million casualties, its impact upon Soviet industrial output would be temporary and uncertain. The Soviet conventional advance into Western Europe and the Middle East would not be significantly affected.[3] Clearly, a new targeting option was required.

As the fifties advanced, the new targeting approach soon came to focus upon three sets of objectives: industrial facilities, retardation targets (railheads designed to facilitate movement of Soviet troops westward, supply depots, etc.), and counterforce installations (targets associated with the Soviet ability to deliver an atomic response).[4] With America rapidly expanding its own atomic potential in response to the Soviet atomic bomb and later the Soviet hydrogen bomb, pressure from the air force forced an expansion of targets to be hit, with emphasis upon counterforce targets that would hinder the Soviet ability to fight a nuclear war. Unfortunately, coordination between the services and even within each service lagged behind as new targets were identified. Only with the advent of the navy's own nuclear weapon—the Polaris submarine—was a concerted effort made to coordinate targets so that the three services would not, by mistake, waste valuable nuclear weapons upon targets already destroyed by another branch of the U.S. military.[5]

The new coordination effort resulted in the first Single Integrated Operations Plan (SIOP) of December 1960. Primary and secondary targets were assigned to every nuclear warhead in the American inventory regardless of which service possessed control over a given weapons use. Delivery of each warhead was fine-tuned to ensure that the weapons would land in the proper sequence and that the premature firing of a weapon would not give warning of impending attack. Under this first SIOP, the entire American nuclear arsenal would unload in a giant spasm, thus avoiding the destruction of unfired American weapons in any return Soviet nuclear strike. According to Pentagon declarations, the United States would respond to unambiguous warning of an impending attack, a position that left unclear whether such a warning might be perceived in deepening political tensions or only in the event that Soviet forces were already on their way toward American targets. Pentagon estimates were that the execution of the 1960 SIOP would produce about 400 million deaths within communist-controlled countries stretching from Albania through China. No middle ground existed within the first SIOP; all three types of targets would be struck at once, producing unprecedented casualties.[6] In part, it was the size of anticipated destruction and the continued growth of American nuclear weapons that gave rise to reconsiderations of strategy in the sixties.

The stategic environment of the sixties was significantly different from that of the preceding decade. In response to a perceived Soviet superiority in nuclear-tipped rockets (the so-called missile gap), the Kennedy administration accelerated the strategic buildup begun by Eisenhower. In 1950 the United States possessed 520 intercontinental bombers. In 1960 there were 1,735; in 1965, over 2,000. In 1950 America had no intercontinental ballistic missiles (ICBMs). In 1960 it possessed 42; in 1965, 854. In 1950 the United States had zero submarine-launched ballistic missiles (SLBMs). In 1960 it had 32; in 1965, 496. American regional forces assigned to Europe and the Far East in 1960 possessed over 700 planes and missiles able to deliver nuclear warheads on Soviet targets.[7]

This major advance in available nuclear assets had a downside as well. By 1960 the USSR possessed nearly 1,500 medium-range bombers able to attack targets among American allies in Europe; by 1965, over 1,700. Soviet intercontinental forces in 1960 were set at 149, of which 4 were ICBMs and the rest long-range bombers. By 1965 the total was 434, of which 224 were ICBMs and 15 were SLBMs.[8]

To complement the vastly expanded power of destruction, the new Kennedy administration developed a different manner of thinking about nuclear war than its predecessors. Secretary of Defense Robert McNamara relied heavily upon academic strategists, individuals who had spent much of their lives in institutes, such as RAND in southern California, that were devoted to analyzing alternative nuclear strategies and approaches to targeting.[9] In 1962 McNamara announced the new strategic doctrine that he hoped would provide a secure environment during his tenure at the Pentagon.

The goal of American strategic forces, McNamara proclaimed, henceforth would be twofold. The United States would procure and deploy sufficient forces to ensure that even in the worst possible case of sneak attack enough strength would remain untouched to guarantee the devastation of the USSR in a return strike. Force would also be deployed with accuracies and numbers sufficient to destroy Soviet nuclear forces that might be directed against America in a third phase of an attack.[10] Consistent with these goals, the new SIOP drew a clearer distinction between cities (countervalues) and military forces (counterforces). Three categories of targets were identified: nuclear threat targets, other military targets, and urban-industrial sites. The nature of the American assault was now graduated so that some degree of flexible response was possible once the president determined the scope and magnitude of the Soviet attack. Under the 1960 SIOP discussed above, the sole presidential choice had been to fire all nuclear assets or to fire none. The 1962 SIOP provided one program (menu) of firing designed to destroy enemy nuclear forces, a second and third menu that combined military and nonmilitary targets, and a final menu that focused upon industrial and urban targets.[11] From what is presently known, it does not appear that gradations existed within each program; the president was required to fire all warheads committed within a given program if this option were selected.

The emphasis upon striking Soviet nuclear targets instead of going for urban populations engendered significant criticism as the sixties progressed. Conservative politicians maintained that this new strategy demonstrated a lack of American will, an effort to keep a nuclear war "clean" and with limited casualties. European critics charged that avoiding urban targets would make conventional war more likely since neither side would expect total devastation in future wars; conventional wars were likely to be fought in Europe itself. Liberal critics suggested that procurement and deployment of missiles accurate enough to destroy Soviet weapons on the ground as foreseen in the first program might give America the ability to destroy all Soviet nuclear capability in its own sneak attack. If America approached this threshold of weapons required to eliminate all Soviet missiles and bombers, it would destabilize the existing arms balance and push the USSR toward a policy of preemptive nuclear firing in cases of growing political tension.[12]

Perhaps more important than the mentioned criticisms, the objective of possessing sufficient force to ensure destruction of Soviet nuclear weapons was almost impossible to quantify since all possible scenarios of how a war might start had to be taken into account. It was relatively easy to calculate how many survivable nuclear weapons were needed to devastate, for example, 50 percent of the Soviet urban population in a return strike. Cities have the disadvantage of not moving, not being "hard," and not suddenly expanding in size and number. Soviet nuclear forces, unfortunately, possessed all those characteristics as the USSR continued to expand its forces, harden its silos, and place an increasing number of missiles at sea in submarines difficult to locate. From 1966 to 1970, the USSR deployed over 1,000 ICBMs in hardened sites, which were difficult to destroy with any degree of assurance.[13] And as early as 1963, the American air force asked for a minimum of 10,000 ICBMs if all Soviet nuclear forces were to be targeted.[14]

As the sixties continued, the McNamara Pentagon slowly shifted emphasis to a nuclear strategy that would promise the devastation of Soviet urban targets to such an extent that Moscow would never contemplate a sneak atomic assault. Such a strategy helped pacify critics who charged that McNamara's initial strategy had sought to acquire sufficient weapons to allow a surprise first attack by America. But more important, the new strategy, increasingly known as mutually assured destruction (MAD), provided a rational criterion that permitted precise calculation as to how many weapons of which kinds America ought to deploy.[15] By the end of the Johnson administration in 1968, the main tenets of the MAD strategy had been worked out and the needed weapons either deployed or ordered. Interestingly, despite the change in *declared* nuclear policy, the guidelines that stated how American nuclear weapons would actually be used continued to stress Soviet military targets and not cities. In short, a significant gap developed between what is known as declaratory policy and actual nuclear strategy.[16]

The MAD declaratory policy consisted of five tightly integrated assumptions/predictions about human behavior. First, it assumed that making war was a rational activity engaged in by rational men with specific objectives in mind. If the losses expected in a potential conflict were significantly greater than the gains to be achieved, rational men would not initiate conflict. Second, MAD assumed that Soviet leaders highly valued the lives of their citizens and the continued functioning of their own society. If America deployed an assured second-strike capability that could destroy these values (McNamara gave several figures as to what such a capability would be, with the figures of assured destruction of 20 to 25 percent of Soviet population and 50 percent of Soviet industrial capability being typical), the Soviets would surely avoid provocative behavior. Third, MAD emphasized that America's ability to target Soviet cities was matched by a Soviet ability to do likewise. Since cities could not be defended nor "hardened" against atomic assault and given the relatively crude nature of antiballistic missiles (ABMs) of the period, this situation would continue for the foreseeable future. This premise entailed the fourth assumption that held that a war-fighting ability was functionless in the atomic age since both sides possessed the ability to destroy the other. Even limited nuclear war was irrational since (1) there was no way to ensure such a conflict would remain limited; (2) the ability of each side to control its use of limited options undoubtedly would be destroyed early in the conflict; and (3) limited war would place a premium upon going to full-scale attack as soon as possible so as to destroy the other side's ability to escalate the conflict to its advantage. Fifth, the terror of nuclear war and the uncertainty about the exact strategic plan of one's opponent would dissuade either side from attempting a conventional war since a conventional provocation might bring on total destruction of both.[17]

These basic premises were crucial in determining which weapons and how many of each America ought to procure in the sixties. The Pentagon ordered 1,054 ICBMs of several different varieties since even in a worst-case scenario this number would ensure destruction of a significant portion of Soviet industry and population. The same assumptions prompted McNamara to expand the number of missiles placed upon submarines since these were the most likely weapons to survive a surprise Soviet attack. Bombers were retained to diversify the basing mode of America's nuclear might, making it even more difficult for the USSR to destroy a significant number of retaliatory weapons in surprise attack. Thus, by the end of the decade, the notion of a triad of basing modes (ICBMs, SLBMs, and bombers) was firmly entrenched in Pentagon strategy as the best means of complicating Soviet targeting problems.[18] Since retaliation was to be the preferred policy, the largest number of American warheads were placed in submarines despite the fact that SLBMs were the least accurate of America's nuclear weapons. Deception remained more important than accuracy as long as the MAD strategy dominated procurement and deployment.

By the end of the sixties, critics of the MAD strategy discerned new reasons for their opposition. The relentless Soviet nuclear buildup following the Cuban Missile Crisis continued unabated, with the total number of Soviet missiles bypassing those deployed in the United States. Such an expansion suggested that regardless of American nuclear strategies the USSR was pursuing an objective that would permit a war-winning strategy if conflict erupted. The Soviet deployment of the giant SS-9 missile in 1967, a rocket nearly five times larger than the American Minuteman missile, raised fears that Moscow might be seeking a first-strike capability that would effectively end any American ability to retaliate. Flight tests of this new Soviet missile, as monitored in the West, suggested the targets for its warheads were the 100 launch-control sites attached to the Minuteman missile fields in the United States.[19]

The Soviet missile growth raised basic questions concerning the entire strategy of mutually assured destruction (MAD). The unexamined assumption of this strategy presupposed that the Soviets thought as we did, that Soviet views on war and survival were a mirror image of those held in the West. But the new Soviet capability for nuclear war fighting put these assumptions in doubt. In the fifties Chinese communist leader Mao Tse-tung had confided to Nikita Khrushchev that even in the event of a global nuclear war in which China suffered 300 million dead, millions of Chinese would remain to dominate the postwar world. What if Soviet views on casualties and conflict more nearly approximated those of Mao than those of the MAD strategists? In such an event, a Soviet nuclear attack upon America remained possible. More frightening, in the event of such an attack, the American president would be confronted with few real choices about how to respond. To do nothing in the face of such an attack would be to surrender. But to respond by destroying Soviet urban targets would be to invite the Soviets to fire an even more devastating third round of rockets that would end American society once and for all. While no one could predict how an American president would respond, it was possible that the MAD strategy would deter him, thus producing defeat instead of devastation.

The dilemma of how to provide alternate nuclear responses for the president in case the Soviets failed to adhere to the constraints of MAD became a major issue in the Nixon administration. And while concerns about this problem were evident early on, the revision of nuclear strategy away from MAD is usually associated with James Schlesinger, who became secretary of defense in the last year Nixon was in Washington. A former strategic analyst for RAND in California, Schlesinger had also been bothered by limited nuclear options available in case of war. Under the existing SIOP, even the smallest menu of options would cause millions of Soviet deaths, inviting a massive Soviet response that would obliterate America; in essence, all American responses promised total war. What, Schlesinger wondered, would be the American response if the Soviets fired, let us say, five missiles at targets designed to minimize U.S. casualties and then called for Washington to surrender. Clearly, America required "selective response options" to cover the numerous scenarios that the opening salvos of nuclear war might follow.[20] When Schlesinger became defense secretary, the smallest nuclear option America could use in case of limited strike was to fire 2,500 warheads at Soviet targets, a response that would surely bring a full Soviet third strike. As Schlesinger stated in his Annual Defense Department Report for Fiscal 1975, "What we need is a series of measured responses to aggression which bear some relation to the provocation, have prospects of terminating hostilities before general nuclear war breaks out, and leave some possibility for restoring deterrence."[21]

Following considerable study, the new nuclear strategy was codified in a document entitled NSDM 242 (National Security Decision Memorandum) that provided for limited or selective use of nuclear forces. The same basic types of targets remained as were designed in the McNamara era, with Soviet military sites and assets being primary, but smaller proportions were identified that might avoid a general nuclear war until the last possible moment. The new strategy also strove to provide America with escalation dominance and an ability to conduct a protracted limited nuclear war. This meant that regardless of the level of attack America had to possess the ability to inflict slightly more damage in its response, maintaining this ability right up to the usage of all remaining nuclear assets. In short, a strategy (MAD) that called for deterrence by the horror of nuclear war was being replaced by a strategy that foresaw the extension of deterrence into the war-fighting period itself, with America possessing sufficient capability to conduct a series of strikes and responses until the enemy called it quits. At the highest level of escalation—the final firing of American missiles— the United States would attempt to target its forces so that the reconstruction of a Soviet industrial society would be delayed as long as possible.[22]

While the new Nixon strategy made important breaks with the past, the period of the early seventies was not propitious for rearranging American forces consistent with Schlesinger's new ideas. In the first six years of the decade, American defense spending, adjusted for inflation, actually declined, as did the relative balance between American and Soviet nuclear forces. Not until the Carter administration did the spending curve turn around, and by then several new modifications in strategic doctrine were under consideration. As announced by Secretary of Defense Harold Brown in August 1980, the Carter strategy formalized by PD-59 (Presidential Directive) was intended to convince the USSR that no use of nuclear weapons, regardless of the scale of attack, would lead to victory, however victory might be defined. This directive emphasized the limited options provided the president under the preceding NSDM 242 and thus was an evolutionary, not a revolutionary, modification. But the number of targets were drastically expanded, and their nature was changed. Based upon extensive studies as to exactly what types of things the Soviet leadership considered most valuable, and hence was least willing to risk, the new targeting approach stressed political assets and means of social control. While the precise details of the Carter targeting plan remain highly classified, it appears that four new groupings of targets were added to the SIOP: targets that would (1) threaten Soviet domination of the Eastern block; (2) open the Soviet Union to an invasion by communist China; (3) undermine Russian control over the multinational USSR; and (4) destroy the Soviet Communist party's rule in Soviet society. Major emphasis was to be placed on locating and targeting leadership facilities, bunkers, control centers, and party headquarters.[23]

The innovations of PD-59 moved America even further along the road of a nuclear war–fighting strategy and further away from the older assumption of mutually assured destruction. The possibility of a protracted nuclear conflict inherent in the new strategic planning placed a premium upon not only procurement of accurate, hard-kill weapons but upon secure command and control installations as well. Possession of sufficient weaponry would be of little use if no one survived the first round of nuclear explosions to give the order to launch a limited retaliation or if all communication lines were destroyed. With American targeting strategy firmly established on new assumptions foreseeing the possibility of limited and protracted nuclear war, the debate quickly shifted to determining the types and numbers of weapons needed to fulfill the new objectives. With the return of the Republicans to the White House in 1980, this responsibility fell to Pres. Ronald Reagan.

19

The Soviet Threat
of the Eighties

By the eighties the Soviet military, once restricted in capabilities to a powerful land force, had blossomed into a major multifaceted threat. While the ground forces remained, after China, the largest in the world, an oceangoing navy had been added as well as the largest missile force on the globe. Ten thousand antiaircraft surface-to-air missiles (SAMs) protected key military targets, and military equipment advanced even by Western standards was in common use. Given nuclear parity between the super-powers, it was not merely the missile forces of the USSR that demanded close attention but the other service branch as well.[1] Gone were the days when a conventional Soviet assault could be deemed unlikely due to America's unmatched ability to retaliate with devastating atomic weapons. Now, under the common umbrella of mutual nuclear deterrence, the prospects of conventional war appeared enhanced.

The Soviet threat was composed of two relatively distinct although interrelated elements: capabilities and intentions. *Capabilities* referred to the hardware that Soviet troops possessed as well as to the quality of training. *Intentions* considered how such equipment might be used, in short, the overall Soviet defense plan that would guide Soviet forces in times of war. Clearly, the second category, intentions, was most important. But it was also the most difficult to determine. In part, this difficulty arose from the extreme secrecy that surrounded Soviet military planning. And yet even if a Western spy gained access to the most secret of Soviet strategic documents, it would not ensure that the West could predict Soviet responses in the event of conflict. If, for example, a Soviet spy had gained access to the recesses of the Pentagon on the eve of the Korean War, his discoveries would have provided overwhelming evidence that America had no plans to defend that small and distant land. But within a day after the North Korean invasion, the American commander in chief, President Truman, had revised all plans, and troops were readied to leave for the Far East. Thus, any general overview as to how the Soviets are likely to dispose of their ample military forces in the event of war cannot provide answers about how a given Soviet party leader might modify, update, or even interpret existing military mandates in case of conflict. The best basis for predicting Soviet military behavior and gaining insight into overall Soviet defense planning is to examine the recent past when Soviet forces have been involved in defense of the homeland. From such surveys certain general principles of defense doctrine can be extracted.

The overall global Soviet objective is to secure an international environment in which the Soviet brand of socialist values and organization can prosper. Since imperialism (the present stage of capitalism according to Soviet theorists) and Soviet or "real" socialism are by their nature antagonistic, the Soviet global purpose is to diminish and replace imperialistic power. Such diminishing is measured through the correlation of forces, a multiindex guide to relative power in the areas of politics, economics, ideology, and the military.[2] Until imperialism and capitalism are so weakened that they are virtually powerless, the threat of war remains great despite Western protests of peaceful intentions. Traditionally, from Lenin through Stalin, Soviet theorists held that military conflict between socialism and capitalism was inevitable, with the more progressive social system (socialism) destined to win. The advent of atomic power, however, forced a modification of views, and in 1956 Nikita Khrushchev announced that war was no longer an ever-present certainty. Numerous Soviet writers and political leaders since that time have suggested that war would be one of the worst possible means of securing the global rule of socialism, although some Soviet spokesmen seem confident that socialism would still emerge victorious. Yet as long as imperialism exists, Soviet theorists maintain that war is still possible and that the primary purpose of Soviet military doctrine is to plan defense against such a prospect.[3]

In its broad confines, Soviet defense strategy seeks to dominate politically and militarily the geographical regions adjacent to the USSR: Eastern Europe, China, and Afghanistan being among the most important. These regions must not be used as launch points for a Western invasion of the Russian heartland. Given the destructive power of atomic weapons and the long distances over which they may be hurled, Soviet defense doctrine also emphasizes the threat to the heartland constituted by missiles located deep within capitalist states (United States, Britain, and France). The way in which this threat might be handled will be discussed later. The third world also figures in defensive doctrine in its larger sense, in that any decline of capitalist economic interest in this region of the world will diminish the economic viability of capitalism in general and hence further shift the correlation of forces in a Soviet direction. As a result, Soviet military equipment frequently finds its way to national liberation movements fighting for national independence or fledgling third world socialist groups that seek to end their country's economic dependence upon the West.[4]

The Soviet military forces developed in support of these broad goals are divided into five distinct services. The oldest of these is the Ground Forces that, in 1983, consisted of approximately 1.8 million individuals, about 1.4 million of whom were draftees.[5] These forces were arranged in 50 armored divisions, 134 motor rifle divisions, 7 airborne divisions, 15 artillery divisions, plus other, smaller units. The divisions, in turn, were organized according to the percentage of men and equipment present during peacetime. Category one divisions possessed 75 to 100 percent of both; category two divisions were at 50 to 75 percent strength; and category three held 50 percent or less of required strength as well as equipment and fighting vehicles of older types. Estimates vary as to how many of which category are present in any given Soviet military district. The 30 divisions the Soviets maintain on duty in Eastern Europe, most of which are in East Germany, are clearly category one and are ready to go on relatively short notice. Thirty-five percent of the divisions in the European parts of the Soviet Union and deployed in the Far East are considered in category one and two. Most divisions located in Soviet Central Asia appear to be category three. While the combination of the three categories yields an apparent strength of nearly 200 divisions, it must be recalled that most divisions are significantly below wartime levels of men and equipment and that no separate national guard or organized reserve system exists as a basis for fielding additional divisions in case of conflict. In the event of war, the category-three divisions would swell with veterans requiring training prior to dispatch for combat.[6]

The newest Soviet service, the Strategic Rocket Forces established in 1959, is currently the most prestigious. Often referred to as the "Primary Service," its commander takes precedence at official functions over those of the remaining services. All Soviet land-based missiles with a range exceeding 1,000 kilometers are assigned here. Short-range missiles remain part of the ground-forces inventory.[7] The fact that missiles of less than 3,000-kilometer range though more than 1,000 are combined with missiles capable of striking targets as far away as America reveals the persistent Soviet concern with military objectives in Europe and Asia. While the number of such shorter rockets underwent considerable change in the early eighties as the USSR modernized its medium-range ballistic missiles (MRBMs) and its intermediate-range ballistic missiles (IRBMs), about 500

MRBMs and IRBMs remained deployed against European and Asian targets. These complemented nearly 1,400 ICBMs aimed at more distant objectives. Supplementing this respectable nuclear capability, the Soviet navy retained control over nearly 1,000 submarine-launched ballistic missiles (SLBMs) while the Soviet air force retained over 100 long-range bombers able to strike targets in the Western Hemisphere and return to home base.[8]

The Soviet National Air Defense Forces, usually referred to by their Russian name of PVO-Strany, constitute a substantial Soviet investment in defending the homeland against air or missile attack. Since the initial postwar threat to the USSR arose from American strategic bombers, the investments in this service have been extensive and diverse. By the mid-fifties two concentric rings of surface-to-air missiles (SAMs) had been placed around Moscow at an estimated cost of billions. In the sixties, as the primary threat to Soviet cities shifted from bombers to missiles, an anti-ballistic missile system (ABM), the so-called Galosh System, was placed around the Soviet capital. Currently, the Galosh System is being refurbished to include the 100 ABMs permitted under the 1972 SALT I Treaty.[9] Following Soviet practice, the SAM sites, designed initially against a much earlier threat, remain in place and, in fact, have been expanded. In the first half of the eighties, an estimated 10,000 SAM launchers were deployed, with the most recent additions possessing a limited ABM ability as well. PVO-Strany held control over about 1,300 interceptor aircraft and possessed an extensive warning system deployed throughout the USSR and above the atmosphere.[10]

Aside from the Strategic Rocket Forces, the expansion of the Soviet navy by the eighties best revealed the emergence of a global Soviet threat. Traditionally small and confined to coastal activities in support of ground forces, the Soviet navy underwent a drastic increase in the sixties, and by the following decade, a force capable of challenging America on the open seas (a "Blue-Water Navy") existed.[11] The Soviet navy is seriously constrained by factors of geography and is divided into four main fleets. The Northern Fleet is based behind the Scandinavian Peninsula with headquarters at the Russian city of Severomorsk. To exit its port facilities and engage Western fleets in the North Atlantic, this fleet must pass through a relatively narrow gap running from northern Norway through Britain, an area in which NATO has placed numerous detection devices on the sea bottom. The Baltic Fleet is positioned in the upper end of the Baltic Sea, with its main base located at Kaliningrad. Leaving its home sea to engage NATO forces, this fleet must pass by three NATO members: West Germany, Norway, and Denmark. The Black Sea Fleet, positioned in the large, landlocked sea along the southern border of the USSR, has its headquarters at Sevastopol and must exit its peacetime domain through narrow straits controlled by NATO-member Turkey. The Pacific Fleet, with headquarters at Vladivostok and Petropavlovsk in the Far East, remains open to surveillance units deployed in and around Japan. Aside from the SLBM-carrying Soviet submarines, the Soviet navy possesses about 70 cruise missile–carrying subs and about 200 attack submarines. By the early eighties, almost 300 principle surface combatant ships formed the heart of the surface navy, including 3 Kiev-class aircraft carriers (37 tons in size) and 2 smaller Moskva antisubmarine warfare (ASW) helicopter carriers. There were also 819 minor surface combatants that rounded out the forces available for conflict. Besides units on the seas, the Soviet navy also had a respectable land-based air arm, possessing nearly 800 aircraft that included almost 100 of the modern TU-22 intermediate-range bombers, nicknamed the Backfire. In case of war, these bombers would be assigned to seek out and destroy Western naval units at great distances from Soviet soil. [12]

The Soviet air force should not be viewed as an equivalent of Western air forces since the control of missiles ranging over 1,000 kilometers as well as antiair and antimissile forces are assigned to other services. The Long-Range branch of the Soviet air force combines nuclear and conventional bombing as its primary mission. The Frontal Aviation branch would engage in tactical troop support as the ground forces advanced against the enemy. In total, by the early eighties, the Soviet air force had disposed of almost 6,000 combat aircraft, 2,300 helicopters, and 600 transport planes of varying vintage and sophistication. [13]

The total number of troops under arms by 1983, excluding some 400,000 border guards but including 1.5 million command and general support troops, was slightly in excess of 5 million. A draft remained in force, with all Soviet males upon reaching the age of eighteen eligible for call. Service in the army and air force was set at two years; in the navy and border guards, three. [14]

While the expansion of Soviet forces in all branches and services caused increasing concern in America during the seventies, it was the dramatic increases in both quantity and quality within the missile branches that remained of most concern. In that decade the Soviets deployed their fourth-generation ICBMs, the SS-17s, SS-18s, and SS-19s. Several modifications of these weapons appeared to have accuracies as good as the best American ICBM, the Minuteman 3. In 1977 the Soviets began emplacement of a new and very accurate IRBM, the SS-20, capable of striking targets as far away from Soviet soil as the Western edges of Portugal and Britain. By the end of the decade, some American analysts were suggesting that Soviet willingness to constrain the total number of ICBMs within SALT II reflected an increased and justified Soviet confidence in the

Table 3. Soviet Warhead Development, 1960-1980

	1960	1965	1970	1975	1980
Total warheads	294	381	1,403	1,875	6,156
ICBMs	4	224	1,220	1,537	5,140
SLBMs	0	15	41	196	874
Bombers	290	142	142	142	142

Source: Robert P. Berman and John C. Baker, *Soviet Strategic Forces: Requirements and Responses* (Washington, D.C., 1982), 138.

enhanced destructive power of their remaining missiles due to improved accuracy. In short, the era when America could counterbalance the larger number of Soviet missiles with superior technology and accuracy appeared to be at an end. Given this expanded Soviet ability to strike American targets, it is easy to understand why the pattern of Soviet missile expansion, as shown in Table 3, caused great concern in Washington as the eighties began.

Although each new Soviet ballistic missile increased anxieties in the West, it was the SS-20, which began deployment in the western military districts of the USSR in the second half of the seventies, that provoked the most immediate concern. An extremely accurate weapon carrying three separately targeted warheads (MIRVs) and with a range of 3,000 miles, this mobile missile contained state-of-the-art technology perhaps as good as anything in the West. While the Soviets had deployed IRBMs before, the sophistication of this new weapon plus its augmented number of warheads marked a major shift in the balance of nuclear missiles in Europe. At one stroke the new weapon threatened to make obsolete the NATO doctrine of flexible response that had guided the alliance since the late sixties. Flexible response was premised upon the ability to escalate fighting to higher and higher levels so as to dissuade the enemy from ever opening the first phase of conflict. But with Soviet superiority in theater nuclear weapons, it would now be NATO that would cringe before the prospect of expanded levels of violence. A turning point seemed in the offing.[15]

After nearly a decade of decline in preparedness as measured by procurement, the Carter administration initiated a response to the growing Soviet buildup. In May 1977 America prompted the NATO Defense Planning Committee to agree to a 3 percent per year increase in member outlays after inflation. One year later a meeting of NATO heads of state confirmed the 3 percent pledge and agreed upon a ten-point program for further modernization. The new Long-Range Defense Program focused upon improvements in key areas including readiness, reinforcements, reserve mobilization, maritime response, air defense, communications, command and control, electronic warfare, logistics, and theater nuclear modernization.[16] As a stopgap measure against the new Soviet theater nuclear capability, the United States assigned 400 of the most modern SLBMs aboard Poseidon submarines to NATO. The number of American F-111 long-range figher bombers stationed in Britain and able to deliver nuclear weapons on Soviet targets in all types of weather were soon doubled to a new total of 164.[17]

A more permanent solution to the threat of the SS-20—the "Two-Track Decision"—was approved by NATO ministers in December 1979. NATO resolved to combine defense with diplomacy in meeting the Soviet challenge; America would deploy 572 medium-range missiles in Europe. Of these weapons 108 would be the new theater ballistic rocket, the Pershing Two with a range of about 1,100 miles. All Pershings would be deployed in West Germany so as to allow access to targets in the western portion of the USSR. In addition, 464 ground-launched cruise missiles would be placed in Britain, Italy (Sicily), Belgium, and the Netherlands. These latter weapons, while flying only at the speed of sound, were extremely accurate and very difficult to detect. Deployment of both missiles would commence in 1983 unless an agreement with the Soviet Union made such action unnecessary. This promise of discussions prior to deployment constituted the second track.[18]

The capabilities of the Soviet military establishment, the number of men under arms, and the quality and quantity of equipment available are much easier to determine than the overall plan that would guide the use of such forces in battle. In the broadest sense, the Soviet objectives of promoting a world safe for socialist values and of dominating the land masses adjacent to the USSR have been mentioned. But to translate such general goals into operational terms is much more difficult. What is required is an understanding of how—according to what principles—the Soviet Union decides what forces to purchase and how they would be used in the diverse scenarios of potential conflict that the future might bring. In this narrow sense of procurement and usage, the term *strategic doctrine* is more appropriate than intentions per se. And in an excellent definition of this term, American security analyst Fritz Ermarth notes that "strategic doctrine [is] a set of operative beliefs and principles that in a significant way guide official behavior with respect to military research and development, weapons selection, deployment of forces, operational plans, arms control, etc."[19]

It is clear from a reading of Soviet sources that nuclear war is perceived as a catastrophe for both socialist and capitalist states; it is something that the Soviets seek to avoid. But coupled with this perception goes a Soviet belief that under certain circumstances the West may well initiate such a fateful conflict. To a confirmed Marxist, the values an individual holds and those that a nation collectively espouses arise in a definite environment and from definite class relations. As capitalism-imperialism perceives its outdated way of life in decline—as socialism more and more dominates the correlation of forces—it is possible Western leaders will refuse to surrender peacefully to the verdict of history. Thus, war may be the final response of a doomed capitalist society.

Those who might rebut this Soviet concern and suggest that no rational person would invoke world conflict simply to avoid inevitable defeat fail to note the lessons of history. Recent analyses of the Japanese decision to attack Pearl Harbor in 1941 reveal that *no* members of the Japanese cabinet considered an American defeat as possible. The best hope, perceived as equally uncertain, was that America, following a series of surprise Japanese victories, would be willing to negotiate outstanding problems between Tokyo and Washington in a more lenient manner. Without war the stranglehold America had placed upon crucial Japanese imports promised to weaken daily Japan's ability to resist future American pressures. Better to fight while the army and navy still retained significant capability than to wait and slowly give way to new demands. Once in decline the future held only more dismal prospects.[20]

The combination of a desire to avoid war with the recognition that war with the capitalist states may nevertheless erupt has produced a Soviet strategic doctrine usually termed deterrence through victory denial plus war-fighting ability. Deterrence, the primary goal of a socialist philosophy that is certain history is on its side, remains the most important task of the Soviet politicians. This goal is advanced through negotiations, arms control agreements, treaties pledging to avoid conflict in preference for direct discussions of problems, propaganda, etc. The mission of the Soviet military, in contrast, is to prepare for the worst possible scenario—war. Unlike America where numerous intellectuals and sometimes "not-so-intellectuals" join in the general discussion of what ought to be Washington's military policy, in the USSR such discussions are limited to official participants. The task of the military is to prepare for war at the same time the politicians attempt to avoid it.[21] In a sense, a clear distinction between politicians and military leaders is more difficult to draw than this. The military promotes a coherent doctrine and procures certain types of weapons, in part to convince the West that war would be suicidal. But since history already proclaims the "self-death" of capitalism due to *internal* and unavoidable class contradictions, war remains a real prospect. In such an event, the military must be guided by a strategy that will ensure that the USSR will never leave the battlefield in a position inferior to its capitalist opponent(s). In certain circumstances the Soviets appear to believe that victory in nuclear war might be possible.

The Soviet deployment of nuclear and nonnuclear forces is designed to limit damage to Soviet society while assuring the West that war would bring destruction to capitalist civilization. It combines a damage-limitation ability designed to destroy American and other enemy missiles and key targets if war begins, a countervalue component whose likelihood of exterminating Western urban life ought to give "war mongers" pause for thought, and provisions for protecting urban Soviet centers. These latter defensive measures include an extensive civil defense system, the only functioning ABM site in the entire world, and numerous SAM sites around key areas. Victory denial, in short, requires some ability to attack your opponent, especially his offensive power, and to ensure by passive and active defense that your society will emerge from conflict second to none. The war-fighting aspect of Soviet doctrine arises from the deployment of weapons that would have specific targets in the event of war, targets that would undoubtedly include enemy missile sites, submarine pens, military and political command centers, etc. Victory, in some meaningful sense, would occur when the enemy acknowledged its exhaustion following the destruction of its remaining offensive power. [22] In other words, in sharp contrast to the MAD strategy discussed earlier, Soviet weapons would be used for an identifiable military purpose; they would not simply be fired in a last-ditch response once war had begun. With judicious use of increasingly accurate nuclear weapons, the Soviets appear to retain some hope that an atomic conflict could be terminated on grounds more favorable to Moscow than to its antagonists. In any event, this is the objective that appears to drive Soviet strategic behavior when it is not concentrating on demontrating the futility of such conflict in general.

If the contrast between the Soviet strategy of deterrence through victory denial plus war-fighting ability and the former American doctrine of mutually assured destruction is quite stark, the changes in Washington's approach to nuclear war in the seventies and eighties seemed to narrow the differences. PD-59 and the follow-on Reagan administration modifications to be discussed subsequently contained plans for damage limitation through accurate targeting of enemy missiles and command centers, as well as some notion of leaving a future war in a position not inferior to the enemy. And yet some dissimilarity in doctrines seems to remain. Washington continues to compare its strategic forces against Moscow's as they exist in peacetime. But for the Soviets what is of utmost importance is not the number of weapons at the beginning of the war but the number remaining once the first blow is struck. As a result, as political tensions rise and war becomes more likely, there is increased pressure within the Soviet doctrine for a preemptive strike that will catch enemy missiles and planes still on the ground.

The combination of a greatly expanded military capability and a doctrine that emphasized victory denial by means of a war-fighting ability convinced many in the West that the eighties would reveal an unprecedented Soviet challenge to the full array of Western values and security concerns. The republican administration that was elected in 1980 entered power with a pledge to restore America's military might and to block any Soviet plans for world expansion.

20

Offensive and Defensive Planning under Reagan

The Reagan administration entered office with an expressed promise to refurbish the American defense capability and to regain military superiority over the USSR. As with any new group of officeholders, the Reagan people presented numerous and diverse ideas about how these goals might best be accomplished. The strategy eventually adopted was by and large evolutionary, building upon the precedents of the past Carter White House with the exception of a startling shift in defensive planning that foresaw the possibility of a strategic defense initiative (SDI) that might shield the United States from future missile attacks. But aside from SDI, or "Star Wars" as its detractors quickly named it, the main effort in the first Reagan administration was directed toward procuring the weapons and other types of equipment necessary to implement the plans for a more flexible approach to nuclear war initiated by Reagan's predecessors. Buoyed up by ever-increasing budgets, significant progress was soon made in bringing America's ability to wage protracted nuclear war into line with the accepted nuclear strategy. By mid-decade the United States was bumping up against the limitations decreed in the SALT II agreement and those in the Salt I agreement on anti-ballistic missiles.

In a lengthy article in *Foreign Affairs*, Secretary of Defense Caspar Weinberger labeled America's defensive strategy as deterrence but deterrence with a slightly unconventional twist. "Our strategy is simple," he wrote. "We seek to prevent war by maintaining forces and demonstrating the determination to use them, if necessary, in ways that will persuade our adversaries that the cost of any attack on our vital interests will exceed the benefits they could hope to gain. The label for this strategy is deterrence.[1]

To be effective, American forces would have to meet four distinct tests.

First, survivability referred to the ability of America's military forces to ride out a surprise attack by a large enough margin to promise a retaliation of such magnitude that enemy losses would exceed any possible gain. Second, credibility concerned the acquisition and deployment of American weapons in such a manner that the enemy would be assured that the United States would respond to any assault. Third, clarity dealt with identifying the types of enemy behavior that America's arsenals were intended to deter. Fourth, safety involved minimizing the possibilities of accidents and/ or miscalculations in the use of nuclear forces.

Rejecting pointedly the sixties doctrine of mutually assured destruction (MAD), Weinberger asserted that deterrence in the present era rested upon a three-tiered American response to the outbreak of future conflict with a nuclear foe. The first tier, defense, concerned America's ability to respond to enemy attack or threat of attack with the appropriate level of response. America had to have and display the weapons that would allow it to engage in limited war fighting with the goal of quickly restoring peace on terms not unfavorable to the United States. While the possible selective responses would include the use of nuclear weapons, they would also embrace conventional components, sea assaults on Soviet land targets, etc. Should a prompt and limited response fail, American strategy would move to implement the second tier of deterrence, escalation. This would involve raising the destructiveness and, most likely, the duration of the conflict. As the classified Five-Year Defense Guidance, leaked to the press in 1982, stated, "The United States must have plans that assure U.S. strategic nuclear forces can render ineffective the total Soviet military and political power structure."[2] If the destruction accompanying escalation still failed to dissuade the foe from further hostile activity, the third tier, retaliation, would come into play. As the Defense Guidance noted, "The U.S. must also possess . . . force that will maintain, throughout a protracted conflict period and afterwards, the capability to inflict very high levels of damage against the industrial/economic base of the Soviet Union."[3] The use of retaliation when all else had failed was designed to ensure that the postwar recovery of Soviet society would progress at a pace slower than recovery in the United States.

Although Weinberger's comments in combination with injudicious statements by other top defense officials brought protests that America now sought means to fight and win a nuclear conflict, the secretary of defense stubbornly reiterated that the goal of this strategy was deterrence. If America convinced the USSR that it was prepared for all contingencies through a well-thought-out program of measured response, the Soviets would be less likely to test the American resolve. And if war nevertheless erupted, this more flexible approach to the use of nuclear weapons stood the best chance of minimizing the resulting damage and terminating the conflict at lower levels of violence.

In terms of doctrine, the accent upon flexible use of nuclear and nonnuclear responses was far from new. The task of the Reagan administration was to provide the wherewithall by means of which the strategy could be made creditable and effective. For this two distinct goals had to be met. First, America's nuclear weapons needed to possess the accuracy and the hard-kill potential to target those Soviet installations that were of greatest significance to the leaders in Moscow. These would include Soviet nuclear weapons, missile command sites, Soviet party and government centers, lines of communications between military units, and basic elements of the Soviet economy. But the mere ability to destroy such objectives was insufficient. Equally important was the ability to ensure such specific destruction in a nuclear war environment. In short, the second prerequisite for the flexible strategy was the ability to conduct a protracted nuclear war that might last days, weeks, or even months.

While these two requirements of a flexible nuclear strategy were perceived by the Carter administration as well, the short period between the issuance of PD-59 and Carter's defeat in 1980 restricted the earlier administrations' ability to procure the needed equipment and weapons to bring doctrine and assets into line. This task fell to the Reagan planners. The new administration soon began the job, focusing upon procurement of accurate and survivable nuclear weapons and upon improved command, control, communications, and intelligence (usually known as C^3I) so necessary to fight a protracted nuclear war. In 1982 the Reagan administration proposed spending $222 billion in the ensuing five years on these two broad categories of defensive acquisitions. This would be broken down into $78 billion for bombers and cruise missiles, $51 billion for sea-based strategic weapons, $42 billion for land-based ICBMs, $29 billion for strategic defenses, and $22 billion for C^3I.[4]

The objective of spending large amounts of money on offensive weapons was to refurbish the basic triad of nuclear forces that America had possessed since the sixties. The land-based leg of the triad was to be updated by delivery of a new, large (100 ton) missile named the MX that carried a MIRVed warhead with ten bombs, each of which was more accurate than those on any other American missile. Unofficial reports suggested that the MX warheads could land within 100 yards of their targets. This combination of size and extreme accuracy made the MX a perfect complement to the strategy of selective and optimum response to a future nuclear attack.

The greatest problem in the first Reagan administration over this missile concerned the preferred basing mode that might protect it against a feared Soviet surprise assault. The Carter administration, faced with the same problem, had elected to deploy the missile along a lengthy circular route with multiple aiming points (MAPs) spaced at regular intervals in which a small number of MX missiles might be hidden. A total of 4,600 MAPs would exist to conceal 200 weapons that would shuttle between them concealed from Soviet eyes. In theory, to assure the destruction of all 200, the Soviets would have to use a minimum of 4,600 warheads or, since conventional wisdom suggests that 2 warheads are required to ensure the "kill" of a target, 9,600. Given the constraints of the SALT II agreement upon Soviet missiles and their warheads, this number would constitute virtually the entire Soviet warhead stock, thus diminishing the odds that the Soviets would ever select this option. When the Reagan administration abandoned the MAPs basing strategy, it was left without a creditable means of deploying a weapon considered vital to the new nuclear strategy. By the end of the first Reagan administration, the problem of an adequate basing mode had yet to be solved, and congressional funding for the MX remained limited to far fewer missiles than requested.[5]

The sea-based leg of the nuclear triad was to be improved by increasing the range and the accuracy of submarine-launched ballistic missiles (SLBMs). Retrofitting of the older Poseidon submarines with the more modern Trident C-4 missiles was completed by 1984, and by that date 4 of the newest, larger Trident submarines were on duty. A fifth began sea trials in early 1985. The target number of Tridents was set at 20, with funding for the first 12 approved by 1984. Equally important, the follow-on Trident D-5 missile was readied for deployment in 1988 or 1989. The D-5, when placed aboard the submarine fleet, would combine high accuracy with an enhanced capability against hardened, smaller targets. Being fired from below the seas, it could maintain a high degree of survivability as well.[6]

In tandem with plans to improve the land- and sea-based aspects of the American triad went efforts to replace the aging B-52 force with new and more able aircraft. The Reagan planners reversed a previous Carter decision and opted to deploy a small, fast, penetrating bomber, the B1-B. The first new bombers entered service in 1986, with a total of 100 foreseen by the end of the decade. Plans to field another bomber, difficult if not impossible to detect on enemy radar due to its radar-absorbing exterior coating and the absence of sharp angles, the so-called Stealth Bomber, were carried over from the Carter administration. Delivery of the first such planes, however, was not expected until the early nineties.[7]

While not strictly part of the nuclear defense triad, the Reagan administration enhanced its ability to retaliate selectively to an enemy nuclear attack by the deployment of theater nuclear weapons in Europe in 1983. Under the 1979 NATO "Two-Track Decision," a total of 108 very accurate,

1,800 kilometer–range Pershing Two missiles were scheduled for delivery to West Germany, and 464 ground-launched cruise missiles were planned for other NATO countries. With the failure of East-West arms talks and despite a major mobilization of Western European peace groups, deployment began before President Reagan's first term ended. While designed to assure NATO allies of America's resolve to defend that continent even at the risk of a world war, the Pershings especially contributed to the overall strategy of selective options. With pinpoint accuracy such missiles, while incapable of reaching targets as far away as Moscow, could destroy important military, party, and governmental sites in the western USSR.[8]

The first half of the new decade also witnessed deployment of cruise missiles in a variety of locations. While such weapons are too slow to destroy time-sensitive targets in the early phase of a nuclear conflict—they fly only at about 600 miles per hour—the weapon is considered functional for retaliation and total devastation of the Soviet economy because of its high degree of accuracy. In December 1982 15 B-52 bombers were outfitted with cruise missiles having a range of 1,500 miles. With such weapons the bomber would not have to penetrate Soviet territory prior to launch and, in essence, became a mobile rocket launch platform. By the end of 1984, 90 B-52Gs possessed such missiles with plans to expand the number of missile-equipped B-52s to 200 by 1988. Plans called for deployment of 4,000 to 5,000 sea-launched cruise missiles by 1988, with approximately 750 being outfitted with a nuclear warhead.[9]

Deployment of accurate and adequate survivable missiles and bombers was but one part of the requirement for a deterrence strategy based on defense, escalation, and retaliation, that is, a strategy foreseeing the possibility of limited nuclear war. America also had to possess adequate facilities to detect enemy missile launches against the United States, as well as a capability to determine whether or not responding American missiles had or had not struck their targets. Clearly, this lay within the category of intelligence. But hand in hand with intelligence went the ability to take command of the nuclear battlefield, measure out the appropriate response, and transmit orders to units already under fire. This capability refers to command, control, and communications that, when combined with intelligence, is usually abbreviated to C^3I. In the broadest outline the American system consists of four interrelated components.

The first line of defense in the event of nuclear threat would be the defense support satellites (DSS) positioned high above the earth to detect ICBM and SLBM launches. These satellites are supported and supplemented by extensive networks of land-based detection systems: the Ballistic Missiles Early Warning System (BMEWS), Distant Early Warning (DEW Line), and other installations. In case of attack, such facilities would provide key intelligence as to the number of missiles launched and their probable impact points. The Reagan administration, in its first term, undertook to harden the DPS against the possibility of future Soviet laser attacks that might destroy them or leave them blind. By the end of the decade, air force planners anticipated the establishment of additional satellites, primarily smaller units equipped with decoys so as to fool any Soviet antisatellite weapons.[10]

Once the satellites/sensors picked up indications of an attack, the information would be relayed to U.S. command centers and from there to decision-making authorities who would then order the appropriate response. Planned improvements in the C³I system include hardening the airborne command posts that would take charge if the White House and Pentagon were destroyed. Very low-frequency communications equipment is being installed to ensure continued control of and communication with American forces on the nuclear battlefield. Communications would also be enhanced by future deployment of Military Strategic, Tactical, and Relay System (MILSTAR) composed of four satellites that would be used to transmit battlefield details from diverse command posts. To facilitate control over weapon uses as the battle developed, the Reagan planners anticipate future launching of the NAVSTAR Global Positioning System, some eighteen or more satellites that would provide intelligence about where nuclear weapons had exploded as well as their nuclear yields. Based on such information (intelligence), relayed through an increasingly secure command, control, and communications network, American decision makers could calculate the damage America's selective response had produced, as well as retarget remaining missiles in case further firings would be required.[11]

Whether the extensive efforts to provide secure C³I facilities, able to function in a nuclear environment, are adequate to the task remains a topic of much debate among experts. Many believe that the unparalleled confusion and destruction accompanying mankind's first nuclear war with two or more participants would undermine all peacetime attempts to construct a foolproof C³I system. If, for example, the satellites and sensors that provide much of American intelligence were blinded or destroyed, a strategy of selective and measured nuclear response would be extremely difficult. Unclear as to enemy intentions or even missile launches, the temptation would be great to fire all American assets before they were also destroyed. While this scenario haunts many strategists, it is clear that the Reagan people are attempting to provide as much insurance of C³I survival as current technology and budgetary constraints will allow.

The most novel aspect of Reagan's overall nuclear strategy remains the strategic defense initiative (SDI), which the administration hopes one day may make atomic war a near impossibility. While considerable doubt as to the technological feasibility of SDI remained among scientists and laymen alike, Secretary of Defense Weinberger provided three justifications for the program's continuation. First, since the Soviets were researching the component parts of such a system, they might achieve a breakthrough that would put America at risk. Second, the historical record clearly demonstrated that the USSR had never accepted the premises of mutually assured destruction that underlay the SALT I Treaty. Therefore, one could anticipate that if it became possible, the USSR would abrogate that treaty and break out of its restrictions to the harm of the United States. In such an event, America should be technologically prepared to follow the Soviet example. "The third, and in my view, most conclusive argument for our strategic defense research program," the secretary of defense concluded, "is the very real possibility that science and technology can in fact create a future in which nuclear missiles become less and less capable of their awful mission."[12]

By the mid-eighties, the broad outlines of what might form an effective SDI system had become known although it remained uncertain which of the suggested possibilities would prove technologically adequate or be adopted. The final system would likely be a layered, defensive one designed to destroy incoming warheads as well as Soviet rockets shortly after launch. Its first layer of defense would operate during the initial moments following detection of Soviet missile firings. This so-called boost phase when the missile slowly rises from earth to an altitude of from 120 to 180 miles lasts between three and five minutes and is a time of maximum vulnerability. Three means of attack appear possible: space-based lasers, pop-up rockets, and relay mirrors.[13]

A space-based laser would be deployed on numerous orbiting platforms, some of which would at all times lie above the Soviet land mass. Upon detection of missile firing, such lasers would fire a highly organized beam of light that would focus on the rocket surface itself. A rough parallel might be made with the use of a magnifying glass to burn a piece of wood by focusing the sun's rays at a small point on the wood's surface. Needless to say, the problem of destroying a missile would be much more complex. If one second of direct light contact were required, the beam of laser light would have to maintain a shifting focus through a four-mile change in the rocket's altitude. Such laser space platforms, in turn, would be highly vulnerable to Soviet countermeasures. An alternate means of destroying Soviet missiles in the boost phase would employ pop-up rockets. Such missiles would be fired through the atmosphere after a Soviet launch had been detected and would send a laser beam at the Soviet target before falling back to earth. Since lasers cannot penetrate solid earth, such rockets could not fire their beams over the horizon and hence would have to be located near the USSR. A third means of accomplishing the same task would be the use of mirrors floating through space on large platforms. These mirrors might reflect laser beams originating on earth, focusing the deadly rays against the rising Soviet rocket. Such mirrors, however, would be highly susceptible to Russian countermeasures.[14]

Boost-phase interception would be complemented by devices designed to destroy remaining Soviet weapons missed in the initial state of defense. Midcourse defense would occur after the Soviet missiles had disengaged their warheads that would now be on their way to U.S. targets. This phase would last between twenty and twenty-five minutes. Since the individual warheads would be much smaller than the missile itself and since the Soviets would be capable of launching "decoys" that looked like warheads to fool any defensive system, interception at this stage would be equally trickly. The three intercept possibilities mentioned above— spaced-based lasers, pop-up rockets, and mirrors—would be used in midcourse defense as well.

The final intercept phase known as terminal defense would take place as the attacking warheads and decoys were falling through the upper reaches of the atmosphere and approaching their targets. This intercept phase would be somewhat easier than the other two since the effect of the earth's atmosphere would allow better discrimination between true warheads and decoys. It is also at the terminal stage that the majority of research projects have traditionally been aimed. But even here difficulties present themselves. While it appears feasible to design a fairly adequate terminal defense around a restricted number of "hard targets" (missile fields, command centers, etc.), it would be most expensive and extremely difficult to extend this protection to the country as a whole.[15]

As can be seen, the problem of creating a leak-proof system of antimissile defense is extremely difficult and remains most problematic. If a three-phased defense system similar to what has been described were put in position and if each phase destroyed 90 percent of its potential targets, this would allow only one-tenth of a percent of total Soviet warheads to strike their American targets. But since the Soviets by 1985 possessed numbers of warheads approaching 10,000, this would allow 10 to reach their targets. Thus, a system with 90 percent efficiency in each phase, a technological accomplishment far beyond man's present ability, would still permit devastation unparalleled in world history, a situation in which the term *war victory* would have little or no meaning.

The Reagan administration's efforts to revitalize America's defense posture also embraced objectives less tangible but no less important than the major weapons systems already described. And in some areas distinct progress was evident. Clearly, the American people became more self-confident, and the legacy of defeat attending the Vietnam War waned. In part this improved attitude about America's rightful place in the world stemmed from the sparse use of armed might in the first years of the eighties. Secretary of Defense Weinberger showed himself very reticent to employ American troops in pursuit of foreign policy objectives unless the American public showed itself firmly behind such deployments. Henceforth, Weinberger maintained, six criteria would govern the application of force. First, the vital interests of the United States would be clearly involved. Second, if troops were to be committed, it would have to be in numbers sufficient to win the declared objective. Third, clear political and military objectives would initially be identified. Fourth, the commitment of troops once made, reassessment of means and goals would constantly be made. Fifth, prior to employment of force, American public opinion would first be assessed to discover whether there was a reasonable chance of public and congressional support. Sixth, "the commitment of U.S. Forces to combat should be a last resort—only after diplomatic, political, economic and other efforts have been made to protect our vital interests."[16]

The problems that had plagued recruitment into the peacetime U.S. military ever since conscription was abandoned during the Nixon administration seemed to have found solutions. In 1980, on the eve of the new republican presidential victory, the chief of staff of the army used the term *hollow army* to describe the then existing deficiencies. By then half of the entering recruits scored in the bottom category on tests that established eligibility for service. Between fiscal year (FY) 1975 and FY 1979, active duty strength in the military fell by about 3.5 percent, and civilian strength fell by 8 percent. In 1980 only 68 percent of new service members were high school graduates. Career reenlistment rates declined during the same period, and by FY 1980 the shortfall of navy pilots stood at over 25 percent.[17]

The national campaign platform of the Republican party in 1980 contained twelve separate planks designed to remedy this situation, and from the first days of the new administration, a concerted effort was mounted. A pay raise in the last year of the Carter administration was followed by a new increase in 1981 that, for the first time, made military salaries competitive with those in the civilian sector. Skills in especially short supply were specifically and differentially targeted through bonuses for reenlistment and special postservice educational benefits. An added factor in the soon-noticed improvement in military ranks was the high civilian unemployment in 1981 and 1982 that made a service career more desirable. The removal of the stigma attached to such service in the eyes of many since the Vietnam conflict also boosted military enlistments.

Between FY 1980 and FY 1984, active military strength increased by almost 100,000, or roughly 5 percent. Force levels in FY 1984 stood at their highest since FY 1974. Civilian strength attached to military assignments rose by 95,000, or almost 10 percent. In the same period, the military reserves expanded by over 175,000, or about 20 percent. Impressive as these raw figures of growth might seem, they were more than matched by significant improvements in the quality of the new military. Between FY 1980 and FY 1984, the number of high school graduates among new recruits increased from 68 to 93 percent. The portion of recruits now scoring in the top three categories in military admission tests exceeded 90 percent. Retention rates also began to rise as the new pride and augmented compensation made a military career more desirable. In FY 1984 the retention rate was 21 percent greater than four years earlier. The shortage of naval pilots was cut by 50 percent by FY 1982.[18]

If the new pride in being an American and the increase in both the quantity and quality of military manpower were obvious gains in U.S. national security, the Reagan policies in the field of arms control were of a more uncertain nature. Traditionally, the pattern of each new administration had been to accept the achievements of its predecessors and to seek further arms records. But the Reagan administration entered office convinced that SALT II was fatally flawed due to alleged advantages conceded the Soviets. While agreeing to abide by the restrictions of SALT II as long as Moscow did the same, Reagan refused to resubmit the agreement for ratification. Not until 1982 were the outlines of a replacement arms control policy announced, with the Reagan planners preferring the acronym START (Strategic Arms *Reduction* Talks) to show displeasure with past agreements that merely restricted the growth of each side's arsenals instead of reducing the total numbers.

The new U.S. arms policy was designed to bring about deep and selective cuts in total American and Soviet missiles and warheads. The initial goal was mutual reduction to a common level of 5,000 warheads on each side. In 1982 Washington estimated that both sides possessed about 7,500 such warheads. Besides cutting warheads the U.S. proposal required that neither side field more than 850 ICBMs and SLBMs together. In 1982 America possessed about 1,700 ICBMs and SLBMs while the Soviet total was estimated at 2,500. There was also to be a sublimit on warheads so that neither side could position more than 2,500 of the allowed 5,000 warheads on ICBMs. Since America possessed only 2,150 such warheads on ICBMs, it would not be directly affected. The Soviet total, however, was 5,500 warheads on its ICBMs, fully 73 percent of the total number of Soviet warheads deployed. As a final point, America would not be willing to grant the Soviets any "offsets" for the nuclear weapons in the hands of America's NATO allies.[19]

Once the first phase of START objectives was completed, a second round of cuts would focus upon specific and, from the American point of view, especially threatening weapons. The 300 plus "heavy" Soviet missiles permitted by earlier agreements (the SS-18) would be reduced with about two-thirds of them being replaced. The goal of this phase would be to equal the total throw-weight of each side's land-based missiles so that each side could launch the same weight of destructive power against the other. But since the Soviets had always emphasized their land-based force at a time when America was diversifying its strength consistent with the triad deployment of forces, this limit on land-based throw-weight would disproportionately affect the USSR.[20] In addition, as the number of U.S. and Soviet missiles declined, the importance of missiles in the hands of other Soviet foes (Britain, France, and China) would increase. To further complicate the issues, in 1983 President Reagan announced that henceforth America would devote great efforts to a strategic defense initiative (SDI) that, if successful, would allow America a defense against Soviet offensive forces. As might have been predicted, the combination of required deep cuts in Soviet forces in tandem with a major American defensive effort designed to shield the U.S. from all offensive nuclear weapons produced uncertainty and then stagnation in East-West strategic arms discussions. At the close of Reagan's first term, talks had been suspended.

The Reagan administration's approach to the issue of theater nuclear force (TNF) negotiations with the Soviet Union as mandated under the two-track decision of 1979 was equally path breaking and initially fruitless. Dubbed the "zero-option" approach, the American proposal for arms discussions stipulated that the 572 as yet undeployed American missiles would not be positioned in Europe as planned *if* the Soviets would dismantle their new SS-20 intermediate-range ballistic missiles (IRBMs) as well as the older SS-4s and SS-5s that were also capable of striking European targets. Redeployment of removed Soviet missiles to positions in the Soviet Far East would not be allowed, while British and French missiles able to strike Soviet targets would not be affected by the American proposal. American aircraft capable of carrying nuclear weapons would be excluded from restrictions as would nuclear-capable submarines attached to NATO. As Alexander Haig, American secretary of state at the time the zero option was advanced, subsequently noted, "It was absurd to expect the Soviets to dismantle an existing force of 1,100 warheads, which they had already put into the field at the cost of billions of rubles, in exchange for a promise from the United States not to deploy a missile force that we had not yet begun to build and that had aroused such violent controversy in Western Europe."[21]

As anticipated, the initial Soviet response was negative, advising that any agreement about theater nuclear weapons in Europe ought to include all such weapons in and near the continent. All nuclear-capable missiles and aircraft, including those possessed by America's European NATO allies, should be subject to restrictions, with both East and West to be limited to 300 such carriers on each side.[22] When the United States and the NATO allies rejected the Soviet counterproposal and began deployment of the first Pershing Two missiles and land-launched cruise missiles in later 1983, the Soviet representatives walked out of the arms control discussions. Thus, by the close of Reagan's first term, no new arms agreements had been achieved, no talks were in progress, and increasingly strident voices within and without the administration were calling for abrogation of past accords such as SALT I and SALT II. Not until late in Reagan's second term did a major shift in Soviet policy associated with the reformist program of the new Soviet leader, Mikhail Gorbachev, facilitate a TNF accord.

Among the most troubling aspects of the Reagan defense strategy was the growing uncertainty as to continued full funding of the ongoing massive military buildup. In early 1985 President Reagan requested a total federal budget of $974 billion, $314 billion of which would be in total obligatory authority for the Department of Defense. In constant dollars (spending adjusted for inflation), this represented a 40 percent increase in defense appropriations over the last full year of the Carter administration.[23] While the general American consensus supported an expanded budget, increasing concern was evident as to how the new money was being allocated. By now stories about $400 toilet seats and $800 wrenches being purchased by the military were rampant. But much more disturbing was the shifting balance between funds spent for new weapons and research, on the one hand, and monies assigned to keep existing forces at high operational levels of preparedness. The procurement of weapons benefited from a monetary increase of 75 percent in the four years between FY 1981 and FY 1986; research, development, testing, and evaluation increased 86 percent. In sharp contrast, operations and maintenance of equipment as well as pay for military personnel expanded by only 17 percent. The possibility of a military force heavily armed with the fruits of the most advanced weapons technology yet inadequately trained in their use troubled a number of military critics.[24] When the 1986 congressional elections placed control of both the House and the Senate in the hands of the Democratic party, it became likely that future defense appropriations would receive much closer scrutiny.

Conclusion: The Future as a Function of the Past

If a lengthy examination of America's diverse postwar efforts to maintain a posture of effective national security offers any certainties, surely among them is the lesson that the plans and perceptions of any given administration exert a major influence upon its successor, be the latter of the same or of a different political persuasion. Thus, as America stood on the threshold of the nineties, it became important to assess what the lasting impact of Ronald Reagan's eight years in the White House would be. While only time would tell how significantly this administration had altered the basic ingredients of national security planning, several major shifts in purpose and strategy were already visible. Among them, clearly the most important was the significant reversal in the previous balance between offensive and defensive military planning. Where this administration had inherited a tradition of reliance upon a defensive conventional strategy in the postwar confrontation with the USSR, the Reagan people took pains to craft a series of offensive plans that they believed offered more reliable assurances of America's continued defense. In the realm of nuclear weapons, the Reagan administration attempted to substitute a defense strategy premised upon an effective antiballistic missile network (SDI) for America's earlier reliance upon its ability to destroy the USSR in case of nuclear war. Even the decades-old doctrine of containment was not spared by the strategists' pen as the Reagan Doctrine, with its emphasis upon rollback, soon found expression in expanded arms support to rebels from Afghanistan to Nicaragua. Each of these alterations represented significant changes with which future administrations would have to deal.

A hallmark of the Reagan years was the effort to build a 600-ship navy adequate to fulfill the numerous tasks required by America's worldwide commitments. Yet the announced purpose of this augmented fleet showed significant variance with the tasks traditionally assigned. Past defensive emphasis upon ferrying American troops to Europe in case of war and maintaining "defensive sea control" of vital supply lines was replaced by a new doctrine entitled the "maritime strategy." Under its provisions the navy would assume an offensive posture even before the actual outbreak of conflict. With political tensions increasing, the navy, in a show of resolve, would sail into waters north of the Scandinavian Peninsula, prepared to block any outward surge of Soviet submarines from their bases in northern Russia. In this way a possible Soviet threat to allied shipping in the North Atlantic would be met in Soviet home waters. American nuclear-powered "killer" submarines would be the main naval component assigned this deadly task. Once war had broken out, additional naval missions would commence. American naval forces would threaten various exposed areas of the Soviet land mass through the use of naval airpower and the landing of small units of marines. This mission, entitled Horizontal Escalation, would force the USSR to remain constantly on guard even in global areas where no conflict had yet occurred. It would remove the offensive initiative from Moscow, forcing the Soviets to shift forces from their offensive efforts to the more routine duties of guarding the extensive Soviet border. Finally, America's naval offensive would quickly focus upon Soviet nuclear ballistic submarines, attempting to destroy them before they had sailed to pre-assigned firing points. Success in this endeavor would certainly reduce the number of missiles that the Soviets could rain down upon American targets. And yet, that was not to be its primary objective. In a world of complex if dangerous balance between the nuclear might of the USSR and America, it was postulated that a concerted threat to diminish the relative Soviet nuclear capability in the early, preferably conventional, phase of a conflict might convince Moscow that little hope remained of successfully terminating the struggle. Loss of a significant portion of its nuclear ability might force Moscow to the peace table even before the employment of nuclear weapons. [1]

The shift from defensive to offensive missions for the navy was comple-mented by a similar alteration in plans for America's ground forces assigned to the defense of Europe. Traditionally, these units expected to wage a war of position and attrition against any invading army from the Warsaw Pact. This would allow American-NATO forces the advantage accruing to the defense in contemporary combat, with the goal of persuading the Eastern bloc that unsustainable casualties would greet any communist offensive westward. Consistent with a defensive doctrine, America in past decades had attempted to offset expanding Soviet offensive capabilities with corre-sponding defensive remedies. The dramatic growth in Soviet–Warsaw Pact tank numbers, for example, was offset by the expanded deployment of defensive antitank weapons. But during the Reagan administration, a clear shift toward a more offensive doctrine occurred. While the new American doctrine entitled "airland battle" and the revised NATO strategy of "follow-on-force attack" (FOFA) have yet to be fully harmonized, the common feature of a shift to the offensive is the most obvious feature.

The innovative element in the airland battle approach to conventional warfare was the emphasis upon an "active defense" that replaced the static defense of the past. No longer could an enemy plan his own route of attack assured that defending forces would focus solely upon disrupting his pre-selected line of advance while failing to launch independent strikes against the enemy's vulnerable rear lines. Henceforth, American units would be free to undertake a war of maneuver aimed at disrupting the enemy by concentrating upon the weakest links in his overall position. Such a strategy might naturally include taking the offensive, sending units of the defending forces across the prewar frontier to seek the foe's vulnerable rear. As a recent monograph published by the United States Army Training and Doctrine Command stated, "Offensive operations were to be characterized by aggressive initiative on the part of subordinate commanders, by speed and violence, by seeking the soft spots, by rapid shifts in the main efforts to take advantage of opportunities, by momentum, and by the deepest, most rapid destruction of the enemy defenses possible."[2] In this use of "active" defense, a combination of land and air forces, as well as diverse methods of destruction, would be brought to bear so as to ensure the enemy's rapid destruction. "The deep battle in its defensive aspect would take full advantage of air-delivered weapons, field artillery fires, tactical nuclear weapons—should their use be approved, air maneuver units, and unconventional warfare forces."[3]

To America's allies in Europe, the most startling aspect of the airland battle approach was the apparent abandonment of NATO's traditional and persistent protestations that the Western Alliance was designed strictly for defensive purposes. Public adoption of airland battle would require creation of offensive units within NATO and might both increase tensions with the East and engender a revival of the peace movement, especially in West Germany. Yet NATO could not simply ignore the significant improvement in Warsaw Pact forces during the seventies that had given rise to the new American approach to conventional warfare. Especially worrisome were NATO studies that showed that although Western forces might fend off an initial conventional attack by Eastern forces, the tide of battle would turn some thirty to forty days out when the full force of Soviet reserves entered the fray. By then America and Germany would already have committed their full reserve strengths, and only the much larger Soviet army would possess fresh and decisive additional troops. A defensive strategy of static position and attrition would be ineffectual against the growing imbalance of opposing forces.

The NATO doctrine of follow-on-force attack, approved by the NATO Defense Planning Committee in 1984, was designed to engage the Soviet–Warsaw Pact second and third echelons before their arrival at the front. This plan carefully avoided the use of allied ground troops in offensive maneuvers, preferring instead to rely upon missiles and airpower. Yet despite understandable sensitivity to allied fears of blurring the differences between a defensive and an offensive plan of battle, FOFA clearly proposed to expand the length and breadth of the battlefield to include attacking enemy units and installations deep within the Warsaw Pact countries. Once again, the emphasis was upon the "active" defense.[4]

The distaste for a strictly defensive posture when confronting the Soviet Union extended to the political realm as well. Since the late forties, America had, with rare exception, practiced a form of containment aimed at restricting Soviet expansion outside its immediate postwar shere of influence. The Reagan administration, however, proposed that the time was now ripe to threaten exposed bastions of worldwide communist influence, thereby drastically increasing the "costs of empire" for a USSR already in serious domestic economic turmoil. Under the Reagan Doctrine, America stood ready and willing to provide economic, political, and military assistance to rebel movements resisting pro-Soviet governments or contesting regimes deemed likely to fall under the Soviet sway. The most noticeable example of such "rollback" activities by Washington was Afghanistan where resistance groups received increasing supplies of sophisticated weapons both from America and from its Middle Eastern allies. Similar supply programs were arranged for rebel forces in Angola and Nicaragua. As one well-known analyst of American strategic thought aptly noted: "The Reagan strategy for dealing with anti-American Communist regimes in the Third World may be summed up in this proposition: The United States will attempt to overthrow Marxist-Leninist regimes where this can be done with little danger to U.S. lives and little expenditure of U.S. resources."[5]

The new emphasis upon offensive activities in the conventional realm was accompanied by an equally startling shift toward a more defensive posture in the area of nuclear weapons. Traditionally, America had placed primary reliance upon its extensive nuclear arsenal to dissuade the Warsaw Pact from even contemplating aggression. Refusing to pledge never to use such weapons first, Washington left little doubt that a successful conventional Warsaw Pact advance in Europe faced the likelihood of unleasing an offensive nuclear strike both from America's atomic weapons stationed in

Europe and from those positioned in the American heartland itself. This pledge to initiate a nuclear offensive rather than to see NATO go down to defeat was viewed as the backbone of its allies. Consistent with this pledge, successive administrations took pains to modernize America's strategic weapons, keeping up with state-of-the-art technologies.

The first indication of a shift in emphasis came with the announced Reagan arms control approach entitled Strategic Arms Reduction Talks (START). While the early years of the eighties saw little clarification as to the dimensions of reduction the administration sought, the summit meeting of 1986 between Ronald Reagan and Mikhail Gorbachev revealed that America was willing to forgo its entire offensive strategic rocket force in exchange for equal Soviet reductions. With the important proviso that SDI not be seriously constrained, President Reagan suggested that an agreement to reduce all strategic weapons (missiles and bombers) by 50 percent in five years be extended to embrace the scrapping of all missiles in ten. And there is some suggestion that Mr. Reagan in fact agreed to destroy all strategic weapons, including bombers, within the longer time frame.[6]

While the meeting at Reykjavik ended without any agreement, a similar proposal for the destruction of both sides' nuclear offensive missiles in Europe gave clear signs of success. Dubbed the "double zero" approach, the United States and the Soviet Union agreed that the so-called intermediate-range nuclear weapons (INF) possessed by both sides would be dismantled. Celebrated as a triumph of the Reagan administration's insistence that the American Pershing Two and cruise missiles would not be removed without a commitment by Moscow to remove its ominous SS-20s, negotiations soon broadened to include all missiles with ranges from 500 to 5,000 kilometers. And once again, America promised to destroy hardware once considered important in light of past promises to take the nuclear offensive in the event of possible conventional defeat in Europe.

The continued emphasis upon the defensive strategy associated with eventual deployment of a comprehensive antiballistic missile shield (SDI) confirmed this administration's reevaluation of past balances between offensive and defensive nuclear weapons and strategies. And while SDI functioned as a "flashpoint" for debates between supporters and opponents of the Reagan nuclear strategy, the broader implications of extensive shifts in offensive and defensive doctrine and deployment still awaited a detailed debate.

While policy shifts in the Reagan administration had a direct influence on America's defense posture, changes occurring on the other side of the globe also promised to exert a major influence on security planning in the next decade. In the spring of 1987, *Foreign Affairs* celebrated the fortieth anniversary of George Kennan's famous Mr. X article that introduced the

Table 4. GNP of the Industrialized Nations
(in billions of U.S. Dollars)

	1960	1970	1980	1986
USA	509	990	2,602	4,200
European Community	191	480	2,765	3,400
Japan	43	205	1,040	1,800
USSR	223	435	1,050	1,230
China	40	122	400	600
USSR as ratio of other four blocs	28%	24%	15%	12%

Source: "Perspective," *German Tribune* 1258 (January 18, 1987): 5.

American public to the strategy of containment.[7] A key aspect of Kennan's approach was the hope that in time the Soviet Union might modify its intense hatred for the West, transforming itself into a more traditional state capable of functioning within the bounds of normal diplomatic relations. In the seventies, the Nixon administration sensed such a change in Soviet behavior, responding with a series of proposals for extended détente. The combination of continued East-West rivalry in the third world and the unanticipated Soviet arms buildup later in the decade, however, soon returned relations to their former icy state. But by the late eighties, the Soviet Union was again giving indications of a wish to harmonize its security policy with those of its Western foes. And this time there were signs that internal Soviet changes, as once hoped for, were producing modifications in Soviet views of the contemporary world. At stake was nothing less than the survival of the Soviet Union as a major economic power. And while arguments abounded about which branches of Soviet industry were most backward and whether the problem was one of investment or attitude, a simple glance at the drastically diminished Soviet economic share in world output clearly revealed the sad state of affairs confronting the leadership of Mikhail Gorbachev.

While clearly suggestive, economic statistics were not the sole indication of a sincere Soviet desire to reach accommodation with the West. Throughout 1987 the Soviet press published political and economic essays arguing for a fundamental Soviet reappraisal of the nature of the international world. One theme in particular ran through such studies: The revolutionary potential of the modern era had diminished to the point at which hopes for significant upheavals in Western states were banished to the far horizon. Evgenii Primakov, director of the prestigious Moscow Institute of World Economy and International Relations argued in the party daily, *Pravda*, that the expansion of the multinational corporations and the efforts of capitalist governments to coordinate their economic policies meant capitalism was still far from reaching its inevitable end.[8] Aleksandr Bovin, a well-known analyst for the government daily, *Izvestia*, was even more blunt as to prospects for revolutionary change. "Above all, it should be acknowledged that the ability of capitalism to adapt to the new historical setting has surpassed our expectations. The prospects of Socialist trans-formation in the developed Capitalist countries has receded indefinitely."[9] In short, the USSR was stuck with the world as it now existed for at least the foreseeable future and would have to adapt its policies accordingly.

The result of this philosophical reappraisal of the world's diminished revolutionary potential was a series of Soviet suggestions for improved East-West relations under the common rubric of "The New Political Think-ing." Proposals for the destruction of all Soviet and American intermediate-range nuclear weapons in Europe and for the destruction of both sides' intercontinental ballistic missiles by the mid-nineties were only the most publicized of the radical Soviet initiatives. Western fears that such "denuc-learization" might leave NATO exposed to the existing Soviet superiority in conventional weapons were met by Russian calls for negotiations on chemi-cal weapons including strict on-site inspections and discussions aimed at reducing conventional forces in Europe by one-quarter by the early nine-ties.

While the new Soviet stance on age-old issues of arms control offered hope of both an internal evolution of Soviet politics and a world less susceptible to armed conflict, it also posed major problems for America's relations with its allies. The Reagan administration's willingness to with-draw American missiles from Europe renewed European fears that Wash-ington was distancing itself from the future and fate of that continent. More threatening, if less appreciated, were Soviet efforts to promote European neutralism by offering concessions to the individual NATO members. For example, Soviet party chief Gorbachev offered the Scandinavian states a series of agreements consistent with common desires to reduce tensions that included possible withdrawal of Soviet ballistic missile submarines from the Baltic, mixed companies designed to explore and exploit the energy riches of the region, a limitation on military exercises in the waters surrounding Scandinavia, and mutual cooperation on common environ-mental issues.[10] Each of these suggestions contained points of interest to America's allies, and each was capable of causing some degree of friction within the NATO alliance. Thus, the new Soviet policy of détente will be a two-edged sword in the coming decade: a possibility for a less dangerous world and a threat of increased disruption within the decades-old NATO pact.

A final example of how policies of the late eighties may change the basic contours of four decades of national security planning lies in the fiscal profligacy of the Reagan administration. As mentioned in the first sections of this book, the fundamental objective of all national security planning is to preserve a way of life, a set of values and interrelationships that a given sociey finds intrinsically worthwhile. In the past Americans have shown overall satisfaction regarding the balance between "guns and butter," believing that the perceived threat could be adequately met while maintaining domestic programs designed to advance the well-being of each citizen. But the unprecedented budget deficits of the eighties and the inability of the legislative and executive branches to agree on domestic and foreign monetary proposals suggest that the consensus on priorities is past. The passage of the Gramm-Rudman Bill with its provisions for automatic reduction of the budget deficit threatens to remove the question of priorities from the common debate. It would be ironic indeed if the last decade of the twentieth century witnessed not only a major shift in Soviet internal politics but also the end of the postwar American consensus about what social values lay at the very foundation of the American way of life.

Notes

INTRODUCTION

1. Thomas Hobbes, *Leviathan, Parts I and II*, ed. by H. W. Schneider (Indianapolis, 1958), 86.
2. George Kennan as quoted in John Gaddis, *Strategies of Containment: A Critical Appraisal of Postwar American National Security Policy* (New York, 1982), 27.
3. Paul Nitze, "U.S. Foreign Policy, 1945–1955," *Foreign Policy Association Headliner Series* (March–April 1956): 54.
4. Louis Morton, "War Plan Orange: Evolution of a Strategy," *World Politics* 11 (January 1959): 221–50; and Maurice Matloff, "The American Approach to War, 1919–1945," in M. Howard, ed., *The Theory and Practice of War* (Bloomington, 1965), 215–43.
5. Morton, "War Plan Orange," 231.
6. Maurice Matloff and Edwin M. Snell, *Strategic Planning for Coalition Warfare, 1941–1942* (Washington, D.C., 1953), 2–3.
7. Matloff, "American Approach to War," 221–22.

1. PREWAR AND WARTIME PLANNING

1. Henry G. Cole, "War Planning at the War College in the Mid-1930's," *Parameters* 15 (Spring 1985): 52–64.
2. Matloff, "American Approach to War," 230–31; and Maurice Matloff, "Prewar Military Plans and Preparations, 1939–41," *United States Naval Institute Proceedings* 79(July 1953): 743–44.
3. Matloff and Snell, *Strategic Planning for Coalition Warfare*, 6–7.
4. Ibid., 13–14.
5. Quoted in Matloff and Snell, *Strategic Planning for Coalition Warfare*, 25.
6. Ibid., 27.
7. Quoted in Mark S. Watson, *Chief of Staff: Prewar Plans and Preparations* (Washington, D.C., 1950), 375.
8. Ibid., 379–80.
9. Matloff and Snell, *Strategic Planning for Coalition Warfare*, 44–46.
10. Watson, *Chief of Staff*, 403.
11. Ibid.
12. Ibid., 402.
13. Matloff and Snell, *Strategic Planning for Coalition Warfare*, 55.
14. Ibid., 59.

15. Ibid., 58–62.

16. Watson, *Chief of Staff,* 331–66.

17. Ibid., 343–46.

18. Matloff and Snell, *Strategic Planning for Coalition Warfare,* 99–101.

19. Ibid., 101–07.

20. Ray S. Cline, *Washington Command Post: The Operations Division* (Washington, D.C., 1951), 98–100.

21. Ibid., 143–63; and Matloff and Snell, *Strategic Planning for Coalition Warfare,* 217–65.

22. Matloff and Snell, *Strategic Planning for Coalition Warfare,* 266–67.

23. Mark A. Stoler, "The Pacific-First Alternative in American World War II Strategy," *International History Review* 2 (July 1980): 434–38.

24. Quoted in Ibid., 439.

25. Ibid., 442–47. See also Matloff and Snell, *Strategic Planning for Coalition Warfare,* 266–306.

26. Cline, *Washington Command Post,* 215–18; and Wesley F. Craven and James L. Cate, eds., *The Army Air Force in World War II: Europe: Torch to Pointblank, August 1942 to December 1943* (Chicago, 1949), 300–307.

27. Cline, *Washington Command Post,* 219–22.

28. Ibid., 222–33.

29. Ibid., 334.

30. Ibid., 334–46.

2. FDR AND U.S. WARTIME PARTICIPATION

1. See the concluding bibliographical essay for a selection of works dealing with Franklin Roosevelt's foreign policy.

2. James MacGregor Burns, *Roosevelt: The Soldier of Freedom* (New York, 1970), 129–30.

3. Michael M. Boll, *Cold War in the Balkans: American Foreign Policy and the Emergence of Communist Bulgaria* (Lexington, 1984), 14–17.

4. Dean Acheson, *Present at the Creation: My Years in the State Department* (New York, 1969), 27–39.

5. See Robert Dallek, *Franklin D. Roosevelt and American Foreign Policy, 1932–1945* (New York, 1979), 399–400.

6. Ibid., 432.

7. Boll, *Cold War in the Balkans,* 15–16, 23.

8. Dallek, *Roosevelt and American Foreign Policy,* 436.

9. Quoted in Warren Kimball, "Naked Reverse Right: Roosevelt, Churchill, and Eastern Europe from *Tolstoy* to Yalta—and a Little Beyond," *Diplomatic History* 9 (Winter 1985): 1.

10. Adam B. Ulam, *Expansion and Coexistence: Soviet Foreign Policy, 1917–73,* 2d ed. (New York, 1974), 321–22, 340–45.

11. Dallek, *Roosevelt and American Foreign Policy,* 400.

12. Herbert Feis, *Churchill, Roosevelt, Stalin: The War They Waged and the Peace They Sought* (Princeton, 1967), 283–87.

13. Dallek, *Roosevelt and American Foreign Policy,* 436.

14. Diane Clemens, *Yalta* (New York, 1972), 59.

15. Albert Resis, "The Churchill-Stalin Secret 'Percentages' Agreement on the Balkans, Moscow, October 1944," *American Historical Review* 83 (April 1978): 386.

16. Winston Churchill, *Triumph and Tragedy* (Boston, 1953), 227.

17. Ibid., 368, 387.

18. Feis, *Churchill, Roosevelt, Stalin,* 518–29.

19. Ibid.

20. Burns, *Roosevelt: The Soldier of Freedom,* 572.

21. Feis, *Churchill, Roosevelt, Stalin,* 550–58.

22. Burns, *Roosevelt: The Soldier of Freedom,* 573–77.

23. Boll, *Cold War in the Balkans,* 81–82.

24. Ibid., 82.

3. THE BIRTH OF CONTAINMENT

1. Churchill, *Triumph and Tragedy,* 454.

2. Daniel Yergin, *Shattered Peace: The Origins of the Cold War and the National Security State* (Boston, 1977), 69–80.

3. Joseph C. Grew, *Turbulent Era: A Diplomatic Record of Forty Years, 1904–1945,* 2 vols. (London, 1953), 1:456.

4. Boll, *Cold War in the Balkans,* 130.

5. Yergin, *Shattered Peace,* 83.

6. Michael M. Boll, *The American Military Mission in the Allied Control Commission for Bulgaria, 1944–1947: History and Transcripts* (Boulder, 1985), 23.

7. Harry S. Truman, *1945: Year of Decision* (New York, 1955), 283.

8. Alvin Z. Rubinstein, *Soviet Foreign Policy since World War II: Imperial and Global* (Boston, 1981), 43–45.

9. Walter Millis, ed., *The Forrestal Diaries* (New York, 1951), 192.

10. Truman, *Year of Decision,* 606.

11. Steven L. Rearden, *History of the Office of the Secretary of Defense: Volume I, The Formative Years, 1947–1950* (Washington, D.C., 1984), 4–5.

12. Herbert Feis, *Between War and Peace: The Potsdam Conference* (Princeton, 1960), 181–89.

13. Ibid., 349.

14. Ibid., 235–52.

15. Ibid., 253–58.

16. Boll, *Cold War in the Balkans,* 153.

17. Truman, *Year of Decision,* 606.

18. For biographical details on Kennan, see George F. Kennan, *Memoirs, 1925–1950* (Boston, 1967). See also his "Retrospective," in *Foreign Affairs* 65 (Spring 1987): 885–90.

19. Kennan, *Memoirs,* 557.

20. A selection of Kennan's papers can be found in Thomas H. Etzold and John Lewis Gaddis, eds., *Containment: Documents on American Policy and Strategy, 1945–1950* (New York, 1978); in Kennan's *Memoirs;* and in the spring 1987 issue of *Foreign Affairs.* For an excellent interpretation of his ideas, see Gaddis, *Strategies of Containment,* 25–53.

21. Kennan, *Memoirs,* 535–43.

22. Ibid., 560–65.

23. F. Roy Willis, *France, Germany, and the New Europe, 1945–1967* (New York, 1968), 7–25; and Robert A. Pollard, *Economic Security and the Origins of the Cold War, 1945–1950* (New York, 1985), 94–99.

24. Willis, *France, Germany, and the New Europe*, 25–53.

25. Stephen E. Ambrose, *Rise to Globalism: American Foreign Policy, 1938–1970* (Baltimore, 1973), 166–68; and Lucius Clay, *Decision in Germany* (Garden City, 1950), 362–92.

26. Ulam, *Expansion and Coexistence*, 432–35.

27. Hadley Arkes, *Bureaucracy, the Marshall Plan and the National Interest* (Princeton, 1972), 153.

28. Pollard, *Economic Security*, 133–53.

29. Ibid., 156–67.

30. Acheson, *Present at the Creation*, 217–25.

31. Pollard, *Economic Security*, 107–32; Rearden, *History*, 147–69.

4. EMERGENCE OF THE NATIONAL SECURITY ESTABLISHMENT

1. Rearden, History, 1–27; Paul Y. Hammond, *Organizing for Defense: The American Military Establishment in the Twentieth Century* (Princeton, 1961), 186–226; and Tyrus G. Fain, ed., *The Intelligence Community: History, Organization, and Issues* (New York, 1977), 13–17.

2. Etzold and Gaddis, *Containment*, 1–23.

3. Rearden, *History*, 118–23.

4. John E. Endicott, "The National Security Council," in John F. Reichart and Steven R. Sturm, eds., *American Defense Policy*, 5th ed. (Baltimore, 1982), 521–27; and John Tower et al., *The Tower Commission Report: The Full Text of the President's Special Review Board* (New York, 1987), 6–15.

5. See Anthony Cave Brown, *The Last Hero: Wild Bill Donovan* (New York, 1982).

6. *Commission on CIA Activities within the United States, Vice President Nelson A. Rockefeller Chairman, Report to the President* (Washington, D.C., 1975), 45–46. (Hereafter *The Rockefeller Report*.)

7. Ibid., 46.

8. Rearden, *History*, 141–43.

9. Etzold and Gaddis, *Containment*, 12.

10. Rearden, *History*, 143–65; Fain, *Intelligence Community*, 216–18.

11. Fain, *Intelligence Community*, 329–30.

12. Ibid., 324–29.

13. Rearden, *History*, 29–88.

14. Ibid., 132–40.

15. John G. Kester, "The Future of the Joint Chiefs of Staff," reprinted in Reichart and Sturm, *American Defense Policy*, 527–45.

16. Ibid.

17. Kenneth W. Condit, *The History of the Joint Chiefs of Staff: The Joint Chiefs of Staff and National Policy, Volume 2, 1947–1949* (Wilmington, 1979), 116.

18. Ibid., 165–84.

5. STRATEGIC PLANNING UNDER TRUMAN

1. For an account of early U.S. planning against a Soviet threat, see Michael S. Sherry, *Preparing for the Next War: American Plans for Postwar Defense, 1941–45* (New Haven, 1977).
2. Russell F. Weigley, *History of the United States Army* (Bloomington, 1984), 496–98; and idem, *The American Way of War: A History of United States Military Strategy and Policy* (Bloomington, 1973), 369–70.
3. Weigley, *History of the United States Army*, 498– 99.
4. Ibid., 486–87.
5. Ibid., 486, 501–02; and Rearden, *History*, 11–15.
6. Gregg Herken, *The Winning Weapon: The Atomic Bomb in the Cold War, 1945–1950* (New York, 1982), 196–97.
7. David Alan Rosenburg, "The Origins of Overkill: Nuclear Weapons and American Strategy," reprinted in Norman A. Graebner, ed., *The National Security: Its Theory and Practice, 1945–1960* (New York, 1986), 128–31.
8. Herken, *Winning Weapon*, 219–21.
9. Ibid., 219–23; and Rearden, *History*, 203.
10. Herken, *Winning Weapon*, 228.
11. Ibid., 229.
12. Ibid., 270–72, 296–99; Rosenberg, "Origins of Overkill," 131–34; Etzold and Gaddis, *Containment*, 315–34.
13. Rosenberg, "Origins of Overkill," 137–38; James M. Erdmann, "The WRINGER in Postwar Germany: Its Impact on United States–German Relations and Defense Policies," in Clifford L. Egan and Alexander W. Knott, eds., *Essays in Twentieth Century Diplomatic History Dedicated to Professor Daniel M. Smith* (Washington, D.C., 1982), 159–91.
14. Etzold and Gaddis, *Containment*, 165.
15. Ibid., 167–68.
16. Ibid., 339–43.
17. Ibid., 191.
18. Ibid., 173–221.
19. Acheson, *Present at the Creation*, 344–47; Rearden, *History*, 522–23.
20. Rearden, *History*, 523–24.
21. Ibid., 522–27; Paul Hammond, "NSC-68: Prologue to Rearmament," in Warner R. Schilling et al., *Strategy, Policies and Defense Budgets* (New York, 1962), 267–378.
22. Joseph M. Siracusa, "Paul H. Nitze, NSC 68, and the Soviet Union," in Egan and Knott, *Twentieth Century Diplomatic History*, 194.
23. Etzold and Gaddis, *Containment*, 398–400.
24. Gaddis, *Strategies of Containment*, 93–94.
25. Etzold and Gaddis, *Containment*, 426–29.
26. Ibid., 430.
27. Ibid., 436.
28. Ibid., 435.
29. Fain, *Intelligence Community*, 696–98.
30. Acheson, *Present at the Creation*, 374.
31. Samuel P. Huntington, *The Common Defense: Strategic Programs in National Politics* (New York, 1961), 47–64.
32. Ibid., 53–54.

33. Ibid., 60.
34. Ibid., 60–61.
35. Alan K. Henrikson, "The Creation of the North Atlantic Alliance," reprinted in Reichart and Sturm, *American Defense Policy*, 312–14.
36. Rosenberg, "Origins of Overkill," 137–43.

6. THE SHIFTING SOVIET THREAT OF THE FIFTIES

1. These figures are given in Soviet sources. See USSR, *Bol'shaia sovetskaia entsiklopedia*, vol. 13 (Moscow, 1952), 652–553. See also Thomas W. Wolfe, *Soviet Power and Europe, 1945–1970* (Baltimore, 1970), 9–11.
2. "Rech' N. Khrushcheva," *Pravda*, 15 January 1960.
3. Wolfe, *Soviet Power and Europe*, footnote 6, pp. 10–11; Rearden, *History*, 4–5.
4. Wolfe, *Soviet Power and Europe*, 11.
5. Harriet Fast Scott and William F. Scott, *The Armed Forces of the USSR* (Boulder, 1981), 38–39.
6. Wolfe, *Soviet Power and Europe*, 38–44.
7. *Pravda*, 15 January 1960.
8. Wolfe, *Soviet Power and Europe*, 42–44.
9. Ibid., 44–47, 188–94.
10. Ibid., 47–48, 184–88.
11. David Holloway, *The Soviet Union and the Arms Race* (New Haven, 1983), 15–16.
12. Ibid., 19–20.
13. Ibid., 20–22.
14. Ibid., 23–27.
15. Jerome H. Kahan, *Security in the Nuclear Age: Developing U.S. Strategic Arms Policy* (Washington, D.C., 1975), 48; Robert P. Berman and John C. Baker, *Soviet Strategic Forces: Requirements and Responses* (Washington, D.C., 1982), 38–45.
16. Kahan, *Security in the Nuclear Age*, 30; John Prados, *The Soviet Estimate: U.S. Intelligence Analysis and Russian Military Strength* (New York, 1982), 41–50.
17. Berman and Baker, *Soviet Strategic Forces*, 45–46; Kahan, *Security in the Nuclear Age*, 30–39; Huntington, *Common Defense*, 40–42.
18. Berman and Baker, *Soviet Strategic Forces*, 45–50; Kahan, *Security in the Nuclear Age*, 40–42.
19. Arnold L. Horelick and Myron Rush, *Strategic Power and Soviet Foreign Policy* (Chicago, 1966), 43.
20. Ibid., footnote 7, p. 51.
21. Kahan, *Security in the Nuclear Age*, 41; Gregg Herken, *Counsels of War* (New York, 1985), 112–16.
22. See V.I. Lenin, *Imperialism, the Highest Stage of Capitalism* (New York, 1939); V. Kubalkova and A.A. Cruickshank, *Marxism-Leninism and the Theory of International Relations* (London, 1980); and E.A. Tarabrin, ed., *USSR and Countries of Africa* (Moscow, 1977).
23. Alexander L. George and Richard Smoke, *Deterrence in American Foreign Policy: Theory and Practice* (New York, 1974), 184–234.

24. Ibid., 235–41.

25. Ibid., 266–94.

26. Ibid., 363–89; Kahan, *Security in the Nuclear Age*, 21–23.

27. George C. Herring, *America's Longest War: The United States and Vietnam, 1950–1975* (New York, 1979), 1–26.

28. Ibid., 26–42; George Herring and Richard H. Immerman, "Eisenhower, Dulles, and Dienbienphu: The Day We Didn't Go to War 'Revisited,' " *Journal of American History* 71(September 1984): 343–63.

29. Dwight D. Eisenhower, *Mandate for Change, 1953–1956* (Garden City, 1963), 372.

30. Herring, *America's Longest War*, 443–72.

31. Robert A. Divine, *Eisenhower and the Cold War* (New York, 1981), 71–104; George and Smoke, *Deterrence in American Foreign Policy*, 309–21.

32. George and Smoke, *Deterrence in American Foreign Policy*, footnote 8, p. 313.

33. Ibid., 321–62.

7. MILITARY PLANNING UNDER EISENHOWER

1. Divine, *Eisenhower and the Cold War*, 3–24; Gaddis, *Strategies of Containment*, 127–36.

2. Douglas Kinnard, *President Eisenhower and Strategic Management: A Study in Defense Management* (Lexington, 1976), 1–36.

3. Kahan, *Security in the Nuclear Age*, 11–26.

4. Divine, *Eisenhower and the Cold War*, 16.

5. Gaddis, *Strategies of Containment*, 164–97.

6. Huntington, *Common Defense*, 73–75; Rosenberg, "Origins of Overkill," in Graebner, *National Security*, 141–43.

7. Huntington, *Common Defense*, 73–85; Kahan, *Security in the Nuclear Age*, 26–30.

8. Kahan, *Security in the Nuclear Age*, 12–17.

9. Robert S. McNamara, "The Military Role of Nuclear Weapons" *Foreign Affairs* 62(Fall 1983): 59–80.

10. A.J. Bacevich, *The Pentomic Era: The U.S. Army between Korea and Vietnam* (Washington, D.C., 1986), 7–128; Henry A. Kissinger, *Nuclear Weapons and Foreign Policy* (New York, 1969).

11. Rosenberg, "Origins of Overkill," 144–45.

12. Prados, *Soviet Estimate*, 38–66.

13. Fred Kaplan, *The Wizards of Armageddon* (New York, 1983), 109–32; Kahan, *Security in the Nuclear Age*, 36–38.

14. Kaplan, *Wizards of Armageddon*, 109–32.

15. Ibid., 125–43.

16. Kahan, *Security in the Nuclear Age*, 40–45.

17. Rosenberg, "Origins of Overkill," 173.

18. Huntington, *Common Defense*, 341–46.

19. Ibid.; Bacevich, *Pentomic Era*, 129–57; Maxwell D. Taylor, *The Uncertain Trumpet* (New York, 1959).

8. ARMS CONTROL, 1945-1960

1. For a general discussion of these problems, see John H. Barton and Lawrence D. Weiler, eds., *International Arms Control: Issues and Agreements* (Stanford, 1976), 9–69.

2. Yergin, *Shattered Peace*, 122–37.

3. Herken, *Winning Weapon*, 23–31.

4. Barton and Weiler, *International Arms Control*, 69–70.

5. Ibid., 70.

6. Ibid., 70–71.

7. Herken, *Winning Weapon*, 172–74.

8. A.A. Gromyko and B.N. Ponomarev, eds., *Soviet Foreign Policy, Volume II, 1945–1980* (Moscow, 1980), 89–97.

9. Ibid.; Barton and Weiler, *International Arms Control*, 71–72.

10. Yergin, *Shattered Peace*, 266.

11. Barton and Weiler, *International Arms Control*, 72–74.

12. Ibid., 82; Kahan, *Security in the Nuclear Age*, 54–56.

13. Divine, *Eisenhower and the Cold War*, 120–23.

14. See "Strontium in the Skeleton," in *Readings from Scientific American* (San Francisco, 1973), 83–84.

15. Ibid., 71–77.

16. Ibid., 107–9.

17. Glenn T. Seaborg with the assistance of Benjamin S. Loeb, *Kennedy, Khrushchev and the Test Ban* (Berkeley, 1981), 11; Sir Edward Bullard, "The Detection of Underground Explosions," in *Readings from Scientific American*, 140–50.

18. Seaborg, *Kennedy, Khrushchev and the Test Ban*, 12–13.

19. Ibid., 14–16.

20. Ibid., 16–24.

9. STRATEGIC PLANNING UNDER KENNEDY AND JOHNSON

1. Kahan, *Security in the Nuclear Age*, 35–47.

2. Herken, *Counsels of War*, 138–40; Kaplan, *Wizards of Armageddon*, 268–72.

3. George and Smoke, *Deterrence in American Foreign Policy*, 309–62.

4. Richard Smoke, *National Security and the Nuclear Dilemma: An Introduction to the American Experience* (Menlo Park, Calif., 1984), 88–92.

5. McNamara, "Military Role of Nuclear Weapons," 67–68.

6. Gaddis, *Strategies of Containment*, 217–18, 223–25.

7. See, for example, David Halberstam, *The Best and the Brightest* (New York, 1972).

8. Clark A. Murdock, *Defense Policy Formation: A Comparative Analysis of the McNamara Era* (Albany, 1974), 44–58.

9. Kahan, *Security in the Nuclear Age*, 84–86.

10. Ibid., 86–90.

11. Kaplan, *Wizards of Armageddon*, 268–60.

12. Kahan, *Security in the Nuclear Age*, 74–77.

13. Alain C. Enthoven and K. Wayne Smith, *How Much Is Enough? Shaping the Defense Program, 1961–1969* (New York, 1971), 31–72.

14. Kahan, *Security in the Nuclear Age*, 90–92.
15. Ibid.
16. Herken, *Counsels of War*, 148–56, 162–63; Smoke, *National Security*, 111–15.
17. Kahan, *Security in the Nuclear Age*, 91–94.
18. Kaplan, *Wizards of Armageddon*, 315–17.
19. Enthoven and Smith, *Shaping the Defense Program*, 165–96.
20. William W. Kaufman, "Planning Conventional Forces, 1950–1980," reprinted in Daniel J. Kaufman et al., *U.S. National Security: A Framework for Analysis* (Lexington, 1985), 526–28.
21. Ibid., 528–36.
22. Ibid.
23. William P. Mako, *U.S. Ground Forces and the Defense of Central Europe* (Washington, D.C., 1983), 16–23.
24. McNamara, "Military Role of Nuclear Weapons," 63–65.
25. Ibid.

10. DEFENSE PLANNING AND THE BUDGET

1. Rearden, *History*, 23–146.
2. Paul Y. Hammond, *Organizing for Defense: The American Military Establishment in the Twentieth Century* (Princeton, 1961), 288–370.
3. Huntington, *Common Defense*, 151.
4. Hammond, *Organizing for Defense*, 371–91.
5. Glenn H. Snyder, *Strategy, Politics and Defense Budgets* (New York, 1962), 391.
6. Douglas Kinnard, *The Secretary of Defense* (Lexington, 1980), 44–71.
7. Murdock, *Defense Policy Formation*, 15–16.
8. Taylor, *Uncertain Trumpet*, 123.
9. Enthoven and Smith, *Shaping the Defense Program*, 21–22.
10. Kinnard, *Secretary of Defense*, 77–78.
11. Enthoven and Smith, *Shaping the Defense Program*, 33.
12. Samuel A. Tucker, ed., *A Modern Design for Defense Decisions: A McNamara-Hitch-Enthoven Anthology* (Washington, D.C., 1966), 126–27.
13. Murdock, *Defense Policy Formation*, 51.
14. Enthoven and Smith, *Shaping the Defense Program*, 73–116.
15. Murdock, *Defense Policy Formation*, 74–113.
16. Kinnard, *Secretary of Defense*, 85–90.
17. Enthoven and Smith, *Shaping the Defense Program*, 48–50.
18. Ibid., 50–58.
19. Ibid.
20. Ibid., 165–95.
21. Kahan, *Security in the Nuclear Age*, 94–98.
22. Murdock, *Defense Policy Formation*, 166–67.

11. ARMS CONTROL IN THE SIXTIES

1. Bernard J. Firestone, *The Quest for Nuclear Stability: John F. Kennedy and the Soviet Union* (Westport, Conn., 1982), 45–70.

2. Barton and Weiler, *International Arms Control*, 72–83.
3. Smoke, *National Security*, 103–11.
4. Barton and Weiler, *International Arms Control*, 96–97.
5. Seaborg, *Kennedy, Khrushchev and the Test Ban*, 172–81.
6. Ibid., 200–262.
7. *Readings from Scientific American: Arms Control* (San Francisco, 1973), 151–53.
8. Seaborg, *Kennedy, Khrushchev and the Test Ban*, 269–71.
9. Ibid., 285.
10. Ibid., 286–88.
11. Ibid., 288–90.
12. Barton and Weiler, *International Arms Control*, 288–92.
13. Ibid., 290–91.
14. Ibid., 290–92.
15. Ibid., 295–96.
16. Gaddis, *Strategies of Containment*, 222–23.
17. Barton and Weiler, *International Arms Control*, 296–301.
18. Ibid., 301–9.
19. *Readings from Scientific American: Arms Control*, 154–158.

12. AMERICA'S VIETNAM POLICY

1. David Fromkin and James Chance, "What *Are* the Lessons of Vietnam?" *Foreign Affairs* 64 (Spring 1985): 722.
2. See Cordell Hull, *The Memoirs of Cordell Hull*, vol. 2 (New York, 1948), 1013–15.
3. Herring, *America's Longest War*, 5–6.
4. Ibid., 1–4.
5. Leslie H. Gelb with Richard K. Betts, *The Irony of Vietnam: The System Worked* (Washington, D.C., 1979), 36–42.
6. Ibid., 42.
7. Ibid., 182.
8. Ibid.
9. Ibid., 50–60; Neil Sheehann et al., *The Pentagon Papers as Published by the New York Times* (New York, 1971), 9–10. (Hereafter *Pentagon Papers*.)
10. Herring, *America's Longest War*, 18–19.
11. Ibid., 29.
12. Herring and Immerman, "Eisenhower, Dulles, and Dienbienphu, 343–63.
13. Herring, *America's Longest War*, 36–41; *Pentagon Papers*, 49–53.
14. Gelb, *Irony of Vietnam*, 183.
15. Walter LaFeber, *America, Russia and the Cold War, 1945–1975* (New York, 1976), 167–68.
16. Herring, *America's Longest War*, 45–53.
17. Gelb, *Irony of Vietnam*, 61–68.
18. Herring, *America's Longest War*, 67.
19. *Pentagon Papers*, 76–78.
20. Ibid., 126–27.
21. Herring, *America's Longest War*, 80–84; *Pentagon Papers*, 141–43.

22. Gelb, *Irony of Vietnam*, 78–95.

23. *Pentagon Papers*, 283–85.

24. Gelb, *Irony of Vietnam*, 100–101.

25. Herring, *America's Longest War*, 122–23.

26. Norman A. Graebner, *America as a World Power: A Realist Appraisal from Wilson to Reagan* (Wilmington, 1984), 236–38.

27. For a discussion of U.S. strategy in Vietnam, see Harry G. Summers, Jr., *On Strategy: A Critical Analysis of the Vietnam War* (Novato, Calif., 1982).

28. Gelb, *Irony of Vietnam*, 144–78.

13. EASTERN EUROPE IN THE SIXTIES

1. See Zbigniew K. Brzezinski, *The Soviet Bloc: Unity and Conflict* (Cambridge, 1967); and Christopher D. Jones, *Soviet Influence in Eastern Europe: Political Autonomy and the Warsaw Pact* (New York, 1981), 1–22.

2. A. Ross Johnson, "Has Eastern Europe Become a Liability to the Soviet Union?" in Charles Gati, ed., *The International Politics of Eastern Europe* (New York, 1975), 37–42.

3. Jones, *Soviet Influence*, 111–12.

4. Ibid., 112–13.

5. Johnson, "Eastern Europe," 46.

6. Ibid., 47–52.

7. Jones, *Soviet Influence*, 60–105.

8. Roy E.H. Mellor, *Comecon: Challenge to the West* (New York, 1971), 1–24.

9. Brzezinski, *Soviet Bloc*, 284–89.

10. Michael M. Boll, "Soviet Policy for Eastern Europe: The Complex Integration Plan," *Military Review* 54 (April 1974): 59–72.

11. Mellor, *Comecon*, 92–116; Marie Lavigne, *The Socialist Economies of the Soviet Union and Europe* (White Plains, 1974), 294–331.

12. Stanislav J. Kirschbaum, "Comecon and Political Integration in Eastern Europe," in Roger F. Kanet, ed., *Soviet Foreign Policy and East-West Relations* (New York, 1982), 125–43; Kalman Pecsi, *The Future of Socialist Economic Integration* (Armonk, N.Y., 1981), 3–39.

13. Told to the author by an East German professor while he was attending a summer seminar in Sofia, Bulgaria.

14. Ulrich Scheuner, "Das Problem der Nation und der Verhaeltnisses zur Bundesrepublik Deutschland," in Hans-Adolf Jacobsen, ed., *Drei Jahrzehnte Aussenpolitik der DDR* (Munich, 1980), 85–108.

15. See the chapter entitled "Ostpolitik" in Willy Brandt, *People and Politics: The Years 1960–1975* (Boston, 1978), 166–67; and Werner Kaltefleiter, "Europe and the Nixon Doctrine: A German Point of View," in William R. Kinttner and Richard B. Foster, *National Strategy in a Decade of Change: An Emerging U.S. Policy* (Lexington, 1973), 37–50.

16. Karl E. Birnbaum, *East and West Germany: A Modus Vivendi* (Lexington, 1973), 1–28.

17. Ibid., 34–52.

18. Ibid., 110–11.

19. Ibid., 117–18.

14. STRATEGIC PLANNING UNDER NIXON

1. Robert A. Divine, *Since 1945: Politics and Diplomacy in Recent American History*, 3d ed. (New York, 1985), 168–69; Dan Caldwell, *American-Soviet Relations from 1947 to the Nixon-Kissinger Grand Design* (Westport, Conn., 1981), 78–82.
2. Caldwell, *American-Soviet Relations*, 79.
3. Divine, *Politics and Diplomacy*, 177, 184.
4. Gaddis, *Strategies of Containment*, 296.
5. Henry Kissinger, *American Foreign Policy*, 3d ed. (New York, 1977), 52.
6. Ibid., 53–57.
7. Ibid., 57–58.
8. Ibid., 59–64.
9. Ibid., 65–73.
10. Ibid., 66.
11. Ibid., 85–90, 145–50.
12. Gaddis, *Strategies of Containment*, 305–7; Richard M. Nixon, *U.S. Strategy for the 1970s: A New Strategy for Peace* (Washington, D.C., 1970).
13. Kahan, *Security in the Nuclear Age*, 149.
14. Ibid., 150–53.
15. Ibid., 153–54.
16. Ibid., 154–56.
17. Gaddis, *Strategies of Containment*, 300.
18. Richard M. Nixon, *RN: The Memoirs of Richard Nixon*, vol. 1 (New York, 1978), 484–86.
19. Ibid., 486–88; Henry Kissinger, *White House Years* (Boston, 1979), 223–25.
20. Richard Nixon, "Asia after Viet Nam," *Foreign Affairs* 46(October 1967): 121.
21. Nixon, *Memoirs*, 2:48.
22. Kahan, *Security in the Nuclear Age*, 147–49; Gaddis, *Strategies of Containment*, 297.
23. Kissinger, *White House Years*, 114–30; idem., *American Foreign Policy*, 299–323.
24. Kissinger, *American Foreign Policy*, 141–76.

15. THE FOUNDATIONS OF SOVIET FOREIGN POLICY

1. This discussion of Marxist theories of international relations is derived from the author's twenty years of teaching courses in Soviet history and government, as well as from innumerable Russian language sources. General background on the issues is available in M.M. Bober, *Karl Marx's Interpretation of History* (Cambridge, 1962); Frank Griffiths, "The Sources of American Conflict: Soviet Perspectives and Their Policy Implications," *International Security* 9(Fall 1984): 3–50; Lenin, *Imperialism;* Kubalkova and Cruickshank, *Marxism-Leninism;* Uri Valenta and William Potter, eds., *Soviet Decisionmaking for National Security* (London, 1984); William Zimmerman, *Soviet Perspectives on International Relations, 1956–1967* (Princeton, 1969).
2. For a compendium of Kissinger's views on this problem, see Kissinger, *American Foreign Policy.*

3. Kubalkova and Cruickshank, *Marxism-Leninism*, 139.
4. Ulam, *Expansion and Coexistence*, 745.

16. THE STRATEGIC ARMS LIMITATIONS TALKS

1. Kahan, *Security in the Nuclear Age*, 117–26.
2. Barton and Weiler, *International Arms Control*, 173.
3. Berman and Baker, *Soviet Strategic Forces*, 38–54, 144–46.
4. Kahan, *Security in the Nuclear Age*, 101–5.
5. Raymond L. Garthoff, "BMD and East-West Relations," in Ashton B. Carter and David N. Schwartz, eds., *Ballistic Missile Defense* (Washington, D.C., 1984), 295.
6. Herbert F. York, "Military Technology and the National Security," in *Readings from Scientific American: Arms Control*, 188–200.
7. Kahan, *Security in the Nuclear Age*, 170–89; Barton and Weiler, *International Arms Control*, 172–207.
8. *Readings from Scientific American: Arms Control*, 260–63, 266–73.
9. Ibid. This latter point received considerable debate during the Reagan administration in conjunction with research for the strategic defense initiative. For the issues involved, see Alan B. Sherr, "Sound Legal Reasoning or Policy Expedient? The 'New Interpretation' of the ABM Treaty," *International Security* 11(Winter 1986–87): 71–93.
10. *Readings from Scientific American: Arms Control*, 264–66; Kissinger, *White House Years*, 1202–57. For an excellent account of the SALT I process, see John Newhouse, *Cold Dawn: The Story of SALT* (New York, 1973).
11. Raymond L. Garthoff, *Détente and Confrontation: American-Soviet Relations from Nixon to Reagan* (Washington, D.C., 1984), 158–68.
12. Kahan, *Security in the Nuclear Age*, 126–28; Kissinger, *White House Years*, 540–45.
13. *Readings from Scientific American: Arms Control*, 264–66.
14. Barton and Weiler, *International Arms Control*, 202–7; Berman and Baker, *Soviet Strategic Forces*, 57–59.
15. Smoke, *National Security*, 154–56.
16. Caldwell, *American-Soviet Relations*, 107–41.
17. Barton and Weiler, *International Arms Control*, 383–84; Alexander L. George, "The Basic Principles Agreement of 1972: Origins and Expectations," in idem, *Managing U.S.–Soviet Rivalry: Problems of Crisis Prevention* (Boulder, 1983), 107–17.
18. *Readings from Scientific American: Arms Control*, 270.
19. U.S. Department of State, *Washington Summit: General Secretary Brezhnev's Visit to the United States, June 18–25, 1973* (Washington, D.C., 1973).
20. Garthoff, *Détente and Confrontation*, 166.
21. James Schlesinger, "The Eagle and the Bear," *Foreign Affairs* 63(Summer 1985): 948.
22. Strobe Talbott, *Endgame: The Inside Story of SALT II* (New York, 1980), 26–27.
23. Henry Kissinger, *Years of Upheaval* (Boston, 1982), 256–73.
24. Ibid., 1020–28.
25. Barton and Weiler, *International Arms Control*, 219–20.
26. Ibid., 220–25; Talbott, *Endgame*, 31–36.

27. Talbot, *Endgame*, 52–54.
28. Smoke, *National Security*, 168–69.
29. Berman and Baker, *Soviet Strategic Forces*, 65–67.
30. Smoke, *National Security*, 169.
31. U.S. Department of State, *SALT II Agreement* (Washington, D.C., 1979).
32. For a discussion of the SALT II provisions, see Garthoff, *Détente and Confrontation*, 801–27; and Talbott, *Endgame*, 279–81.
33. Talbott, *Endgame*, 109–19, 275. Technically, the U.S. Minuteman had been tested to seven fractionations during the Ford administration.
34. Department of State, *SALT II Agreement*.
35. Ibid.
36. Ibid.
37. Ibid.; Talbott, *Endgame*, 279–81.

17. DÉTENTE TO DISENCHANTMENT

1. Kissinger, *White House Years*, 1114.
2. Ibid., 1155–61.
3. Ibid.
4. Nixon, *RN*, 2:69.
5. Ibid., 261.
6. Ibid., 433–36; Herring, *America's Longest War*, 255–57.
7. Herring, *America's Longest War*, 258.
8. Ibid., 258–64; Gerald R. Ford, *A Time to Heal* (New York, 1979), 249–58.
9. John M. Collins, *American and Soviet Military Trends since the Cuban Missile Crisis* (Washington, D.C., 1978), 166–288; Gaddis, *Strategies of Containment*, 320–26.
10. Department of State, *Washington Summit*, 30.
11. Kissinger, *Years of Upheaval*, 282.
12. Ibid., 274–86.
13. George W. Breslauer, "Soviet Policy in the Middle East, 1967–1972: Unalterable Antagonism or Collaborative Competition?" in George, *Managing U.S.–Soviet Rivalry*, 65–99.
14. Alexander L. George, "The Arab-Israeli War of October 1973: Origins and Impact," in idem, *Managing U.S.–Soviet Rivalry*, 139–48; Garthoff, *Détente and Confrontation*, 366–68.
15. Garthoff, *Détente and Confrontation*, 368–73.
16. Kissinger, *Years of Upheaval*, 282.
17. Garthoff, *Détente and Confrontation*, 373–98.
18. Larry C. Apper, "The African Terrain and U.S. Soviet Conflict in Angola and Rhodesia: Some Implications for Crisis Prevention"; and Alexander L. George, "Missed Opportunities for Crisis Prevention: The War of Attrition and Angola," in idem, *Managing U.S.–Soviet Rivalry*, 155–86, 187–224.
19. Garthoff, *Détente and Confrontation*, 521.
20. Ibid., 548.
21. Gloria Duffy, "Crisis Prevention in Cuba," in George, *Managing U.S.–Soviet Rivalry*, 285–305.
22. Garthoff, *Détente and Confrontation*, 828–48; Jimmy Carter, *Keeping Faith: Memoirs of a President* (New York, 1982), 262–64.

23. Joseph J. Collins, *The Soviet Invasion of Afghanistan: A Study in the Use of Force in Soviet Foreign Policy* (Lexington, 1985), 1–83.
24. Carter, *Keeping Faith*, 472; *New York Times*, 1 January 1980.
25. Carter, *Keeping Faith*, 483.

18. THE EVOLUTION OF U.S. STRATEGIC DOCTRINE

1. Herken, *Counsels of War*, 18–38; Huntington, *Common Defense*, 25–47.
2. See chapter 5.
3. David Alan Rosenberg, "American Atomic Strategy and the Hydrogen Bomb Decision," *Journal of American History* 66(June 1979): 68–71.
4. Henry S. Rowan, "Formulating Strategic Doctrine," in U.S. Government, *Commission on the Organization of the Government for the Conduct of Foreign Policy, Volume 4, Appendix K: Adequacy of Current Organizations: Defense and Arms Control* (Washington, D.C., 1975): 219–34.
5. David Alan Rosenberg, "U.S. Nuclear War Planning, 1945–1960," in Desmond Ball and Jeffrey Richelson, eds., *Strategic Nuclear Targeting* (Ithaca, 1986), 35–56.
6. Desmond Ball, "The Development of the SIOP, 1960–1983," in Ball and Richelson, *Strategic Nuclear Targeting*, 57–62; Kaplan, *Wizards of Armageddon*, 264–67.
7. Berman and Baker, *Soviet Strategic Forces*, 43.
8. Ibid., 42.
9. Herken, *Counsels of War*, 148–62.
10. Desmond Ball, *Politics and Force Levels: The Strategic Missile Program of the Kennedy Administration* (Berkeley, 1980), 195–200.
11. Ball, "Development of the SIOP," 62–64.
12. Ball, *Politics and Force Levels*, 195–204.
13. Berman and Baker, *Soviet Strategic Forces*, 42.
14. Ball, *Politics and Force Levels*, 70.
15. Kaplan, *Wizards of Armageddon*, 316–20.
16. Ball, "Development of the SIOP," 62–70.
17. Keith B. Payne, *Nuclear Deterrence in U.S.–Soviet Relations* (Boulder, 1982), 11–19.
18. Smoke, *National Security*, 111–12.
19. Berman and Baker, *Soviet Strategic Forces*, 117–19.
20. Herken, *Counsels of War*, 259–66; Kaplan, *Wizards of Armageddon*, 356–60.
21. Leon Sloss and Marc Dean Millot, "U.S. Nuclear Strategy in Evolution," *Strategic Review* (Winter 1984): 22–23.
22. Ibid.; Thomas Powers, "Choosing a Strategy for World War III," *Atlantic Monthly* 250 (November 1982): 82–111.
23. Sloss and Millot, "U.S. Nuclear Strategy," 23–25; Ball, "Development of the SIOP," 75–83.

Notes continue on next page

19. THE SOVIET THREAT OF THE EIGHTIES

1. For yearly assessments of Soviet military might, see the editions of *The Military Balance* published annually by the International Institute for Strategic Studies in London.

2. Vernon V. Aspaturian, "Soviet Global Power and the Correlation of Forces," *Problems of Communism* 29 (May–June 1980): 1–18.

3. Kubalkova and Cruickshank, *Marxism-Leninism*, 63–232.

4. Among many works on Soviet strategy, see Edwina Moreton and George Segal, eds., *Soviet Strategy toward Western Europe* (Boston, 1984); John Bayler and Gerald Segal, eds. *Soviet Strategy* (Montclair, 1981); and Derek Leebaert, ed., *Soviet Military Thinking* (London, 1981).

5. International Institute for Strategic Studies,` *The Military Balance, 1983–1984* (London, 1983), 11–18.

6. Scott and Scott, *Armed Forces of the USSR*, 322–26.

7. Berman and Baker, *Soviet Strategic Forces*, 45–69.

8. International Institute for Strategic Studies, *Military Balance*, 119.

9. Scott and Scott, *Armed Forces of the USSR*, 147–53; Sayre Stevens, "The Soviet BMD Program," in Carter and Schwartz, *Ballistic Missile Defense*, 182–220.

10. International Institute for Strategic Studies, *Military Balance*, 15.

11. Scott and Scott, *Armed Forces of the USSR*, 161–71; Michael MccGwire, "Soviet Naval Doctrine and Strategy," in Leebaert, *Soviet Military Thinking*, 125–81.

12. MccGwire, "Soviet Naval Doctrine," 125–81; International Institute for Strategic Studies, *Military Balance*, 16–18.

13. Scott and Scott, *Armed Forces of the USSR*, 153–61; International Institute for Strategic Studies, *Military Balance*, 18.

14. International Institute for Strategic Studies, *Military Balance*, 14.

15. Garthoff, *Détente and Cofrontation*, 870–86.

16. *The North Atlantic Treaty Organization: Facts and Figures* (Brussels, 1981), 8–81.

17. Garthoff, *Détente and Confrontation*, 849–70.

18 Ibid., 865–66.

19. Fritz Ermarth, "Contrasts in American and Soviet Strategic Thought," in Leebaert, *Soviet Military Thinking*, 51.

20. See Nobutaka Ike, *Japan's Decision for War: Records of the 1941 Policy Conferences* (Stanford, 1967).

21. Derek Leebaert, "The Context of Soviet Military Thinking," in idem, *Soviet Military Thinking*, 3–27; Holloway, *Soviet Union and the Arms Race*, 81–108.

22. Ermarth, "Contrasts," 50–69; Garthoff, *Détente and Confrontation*, 768–85.

20. OFFENSIVE AND DEFENSIVE PLANNING UNDER REAGAN

1. Caspar W. Weinberger, "U.S. Defense Strategy," *Foreign Affairs* 64(Spring 1986): 676–77.

2. Jeffrey Richelson, "PD-59, NSDD-13 and the Reagan Strategic Modernization Program," *Journal of Strategic Studies* (June 1983): 131.

3. Ibid.

4. James K. Oliver and James A. Nathan, "The Reagan Defense Program: Concept, Continuity, and Change," in Stephen J. Cimbala, ed., *The Reagan Defense Program: An Interim Assessment* (Wilmington, 1986), 1–21; Leonard Sullivan, Jr., "The Defense Budget," in George E. Hudson and Joseph Kruzel, eds., *American Defense Annual* (Lexington, 1985), 53–75.

5. Charles R. Gellner with Jeanette Voas, "Arms Control: An Evolving Record of Hope," in Cimbala, *Reagan Defense Program*, 161–85; Walter B. Slocombe, "Strategic Forces," in Hudson and Kruzel, *American Defense Annual*, 77–83.

6. Slocombe, "Strategic Forces," 85–86.

7. Ibid., 83–85.

8. Congressional Quarterly, Inc., *U.S. Defense Policy*, 3d ed. (Washington, D.C., 1983), 72–82; Smoke, *National Security*, 227–31.

9. Slocombe, "Strategic Forces," 83–87.

10. William M. Arkin and Richard W. Fieldhouse, *Nuclear Battlefields: Global Links in the Arms Race* (Cambridge, 1985); Bruce G. Blair, *Strategic Command and Control: Redefining the Nuclear Threat* (Washington, D.C., 1985), 182–303.

11. Blair, *Strategic Command and Control*, 241–80.

12. Weinberger, "U.S. Defense Strategy," 683.

13. Among the many studies of SDI, see James R. Schlesinger, "Rhetoric and Realities in the Star Wars Debate," *International Security* 10(Summer 1985): 3–13; "The Star Warriors," *Newsweek*, 17 July 1985, 34–45; Keith B. Payne, et al., "Forum: The Strategic Defense Initiative," *Orbis* 28(Summer 1984): 215–55; and especially Sidney D. Drell et al., "Preserving the ABM Treaty: A Critique of the Reagan Strategic Defense Initiative," *International Security* 9(Fall 1984): 51–91.

14. Drell, "Preserving the ABM Treaty," 67–76.

15. Ibid., 76–87.

16. Weinberger, "U.S. Defense Strategy," 687.

17. Lawrence J. Korb, "Defense Manpower and the Reagan Record," in Cimbala, *Reagan Defense Program*, 63–79.

18. Ibid., 82–97; Martin Binkin, "Manpower," in Hudson and Kruzel, *American Defense Annual*, 131–44.

19. Strobe Talbott, *Deadly Gambits: The Reagan Administration and the Stalemate in Nuclear Arms Control* (London, 1985), 209–342.

20. Ibid.

21. Alexander Haig, *Caveat—Realism, Reagan and Foreign Policy* (New York, 1984), 229.

22. Gellner, "Arms Control," 164–66.

23. Sullivan, "Defense Budget," 53–60.

24. Ibid., 55.

CONCLUSION

1. For a discussion of the maritime strategy, see Jack Beatty, "In Harm's Way," *Atlantic* 259 (May 1987): 37–53; John J. Mearsheimer, "A Strategic Misstep: The Maritime Strategy and Deterrence in Europe," *International Security* 11 (Fall 1986): 3–57; Linton F. Brooks, "Naval Power and National Security: The Case for the Maritime Strategy," ibid., 58–88.

2. John L. Romjue, *From Active Defense to AirLand Battle: The Development of Army Doctrine, 1973–1982* (Fort Monroe, Va., 1984), 70.

3. Ibid., 71.

4. Samuel P. Huntington, "U.S. Defense Strategy: The Strategic Innovations of the Reagan Years," in Joseph Kruzel, ed., *American Defense Annual, 1987–1988* (Lexington, 1987), 31–35.

5. Ibid., 29.

6. P. Edward Haley, " 'You Could Have Said Yes.' Lessons from Reykjavik," *Orbis* 31(Spring 1987): 75–97; Mikhail Gorbachev, *Once More on Reykjavik* (Moscow, 1986).

7. See the section entitled, "Containment: 40 Years Later," in *Foreign Affairs* 65(Spring 1987): 827–90.

8. E. Primakov, "Novye protivorechiia kapitalitsticheskoi ekonomiki," *Pravda* 25245(September 15, 1987): 4.

9. Quoted in Viktor Yasmann, "The New Political Thinking and the Civilized Class Struggle," *Radio Free Europe Report 292/87* (July 29, 1987): 3.

10. M.S. Gorbachev, "Rech' tovarishcha Gorbacheva M.S.," *Pravda* 25262 (October 2, 1987): 1–3.

Bibliographical Essay

The sources dealing in whole or part with national security planning since the war are too numerous for any single individual to read or list. I have attempted in this bibliographical essay to mention those I have found most useful with respect to the topic at hand. I have followed the general outline of the book in identifying sources, categorizing them as to the various themes discussed.

Basic to an understanding of prewar and wartime planning remains the multivolume series on the war published by the Office of the Chief of Military History, Department of the Army. Among the most useful are Ray S. Cline, *Washington Command Post: The Operations Division* (Washington, D.C., 1951); Stetson Conn and Byron Fairchild, *The Framework of Hemisphere Defense* (Washington, D.C., 1960); Richard M. Leightton and Robert W. Coakley, *Global Logistics and Strategy, 1940–1943* (Washington, D.C., 1955); Maurice Matloff and Edwin M. Snell, *Strategic Planning for Coalition Warfare, 1941–1942 (Washington, D.C., 1953); Maurice Matloff, Strategic Planning for Coalition Warfare, 1943–1944* (Washington, D.C., 1959); and Louis Morton, *Strategy and Command: The First Two Years* (Washington, D.C., 1962). The Office of Air Force History issued a series of volumes edited by Wesley F. Craven and James L. Cate entitled *The Army Air Force in World War II.* The most useful of these are *Plans and Early Operations, January 1939 to August 1942* and *Europe: Torch to Pointblank, August 1942 to December 1943* (Chicago: Univ. of Chicago Press, 1948–49). Naval planning and operations are discussed in Samuel E. Morison, *History of the United States Naval Operations in World War II,* 15 volumes (Boston: Little, Brown and Co., 1947).

Among the more important secondary sources on restricted aspects of prewar and wartime planning and operations, see Omar N. Bradley and Clay Blair, *A General's Life: An Autobiography by General of the Army*

Omar N. Bradley (New York: Simon and Schuster, 1983); Winston Churchill, *The Second World War*, 6 volumes (Boston: Houghton Mifflin, 1948–1953); Robert Divine, *The Illusion of Neutrality* (Chicago: Univ. of Chicago Press, 1962); Dwight D. Eisenhower, *Crusade in Europe* (Garden City: Doubleday and Co., 1948); Kent R. Greenfield, *American Strategy in World War II: A Reconsideration* (Baltimore: Johns Hopkins Univ. Press. 1973); Maurice Matloff, "Prewar Military Plans and Preparations, 1939–41," *United States Naval Institute Proceedings* 79(July 1953): 741–48; Mark A. Stoler, "The 'Pacific-First' Alternative in American World War II Strategy," *International History Review* 2(July 1980): 432–52; and Gerald E. Wheeler, *Prelude to Pearl Harbor: The United States Navy and the Far East, 1921–1931* (Columbia: Univ. of Missouri Press, 1963).

Books and articles dealing with Franklin Roosevelt and his wartime policy are diverse in quality if overwhelming in number. Most important for my conclusions have been James MacGregor Burns, *Roosevelt: Soldier of Freedom* (New York: Harcourt Brace Jovanovich, 1970); Orville H. Bullitt, ed., *For the President: Personal and Secret: Correspondence Between Franklin Roosevelt and William C. Bullitt* (Boston: Houghton Mifflin, 1972); Robert Divine, *Roosevelt and World War II* (Baltimore: Johns Hopkins Univ. Press, 1969); Willard Range, *Franklin Roosevelt's World Order* (Athens: Univ. of George Press, 1959); Samuel I. Rosenman, *Working with Roosevelt* (New York: Harper and Brothers, 1952); and Robert E. Sherwood, *Roosevelt and Hopkins: an Intimate History* (New York: Harper and Brothers, 1948).

The best single study of Roosevelt's wartime diplomacy is Robert Dallek, *Franklin D. Roosevelt and American Foreign Policy, 1932–1945* (New York: Oxford Univ. Press, 1979). Other works to be consulted include Diane S. Clemens, *Yalta* (New York: Oxford Univ. Press, 1970); Herbert Feis, *Churchill-Roosevelt-Stalin: The War They Waged and the Peace They Sought* (Princeton: Princeton Univ. Press, 1967); Gaddis Smith, *American Diplomacy during the Second World War* (New York: John Wiley and Sons, 1965); and Edward R. Stettinius, Jr., *Roosevelt and the Russians* (Garden City: Doubleday and Co., 1949).

For an overall assessment of the Truman presidency, see Barton Bernstein, ed., *Politics and Policies of the Truman Administration* (Chicago: Quadrangle, 1970); and Alonzo L. Hamby, *Beyond the New Deal: Harry S. Truman and American Liberalism* (New York: Columbia Univ. Press, 1973). Certainly, one ought to consult Harry S. Truman, *Memoirs: Year of Decision* (Garden City: Doubleday and Co., 1956); and idem, *Memoirs: Years of Trial and Hope* (Garden City: Doubleday and Co., 1956). Foreign policy in the Truman years is convered in Michael M. Boll, *Cold War in the Balkans: American Foreign Policy and the Emergence of Communist Bulgaria,*

1943–1947 (Lexington: Univ. Press of Kentucky, 1984); Herbert Feis, *Between War and Peace: The Potsdam Conference* (Princeton: Princeton Univ. Press, 1960); Thomas G. Paterson, *On Every Front: The Making of the Cold War* (New York: Norton, 1979); and Daniel Yergin, *Shattered Peace: The Origins of the Cold War and the National Security State* (Boston: Houghton Mifflin, 1983). Soviet policy in postwar Eastern Europe is analyzed in Werner G. Hahn, *Postwar Soviet Politics: The Fall of Zhdanov and the Defeat of Moderation, 1946–53* (Ithaca: Cornell Univ. Press, 1982); William Taubman, *Stalin's American Policy: From Entente to Détente to Cold War* (New York: Norton, 1982); and Thomas W. Wolfe, *Soviet Power and Europe, 1945–1970* (Baltimore: Johns Hopkins Univ. Press, 1970).

For an excellent discussion of the ideas and influence of George Kennan, see John Lewis Gaddis, *Strategies of Containment: A Critical Appraisal of Postwar American National Security Policy* (New York: Oxford Univ. Press, 1982). A recent symposium held at the National War College produced a most useful collection of papers of various aspects of containment in practice. See Terry L. Deibel and John Lewis Gaddis, *Containment: Concept and Policy*, 2 volumes (Washington, D.C.: National Defense Univ. 1986). Kennan's life up through the formulation of the containment doctrine is in George F. Kennan, *Memoirs, 1925–1950* (Boston: Little, Brown and Co., 1967). A selection of Kennan's policy papers can be found in Thomas H. Etzold and John Lewis Gaddis, eds., *Containment: Documents on American Policy and Strategy, 1945–1950* (New York: Columbia Univ. Press, 1978).

For information and interpretation of the Marshall Plan and the Truman Doctrine, see Dean Acheson, *Present at the Creation: My Years in the State Department* (New York: New American Library, 1970); Joseph M. Jones, *The Fifteen Weeks* (New York: Harcourt Brace and World, 1964); Alan S. Milward, *The Reconstruction Of Western Europe, 1945–51* (Berkeley: Univ. of California Press, 1984); Robert A. Pollard, *Economic Security and the Origins of the Cold War, 1945–1950* (New York: Columbia Univ. Press, 1985); and Lawrence S. Wittner, *American Intervention in Greece, 1943–1949* (New York: Columbia Univ. Press, 1982).

Two books central to an understanding of postwar efforts to construct a creditable defense establishment are Paul Y. Hammond, *Organizing for Defense: The American Military Establishment in the Twentieth Century* (Princeton: Princeton Univ. Press, 1961); and Samuel P. Huntington, *The Common Defense: Strategic Programs in National Politics* (New York: Columbia Univ. Press, 1961). A recent work from the History Office of the Office of the Secretary of Defense offers a comprehensive account of the 1947 National Security Act in the formation and development of the National Military Establishment. See Steven L. Rearden, *History of the*

Office of the Secretary of Defense: The Formative Years, 1947–1950 (Washington, D.C.: GPO, 1984). The following works also shed light on this topic: Douglas Kinnard, *The Secretary of Defense* (Lexington: Univ. Press of Kentucky, 1980), and Russell F. Weigley, *History of the United States Army* (Bloomington: Indiana Univ. Press, 1984). Works on the birth and evolution of America's intelligence establishment include Anthony C. Brown, *The Last Hero: Wild Bill Donovan* (New York: Times Books, 1982); Ray S. Cline, *Secrets, Spies, and Scholars: Blueprint of the Essential CIA* (Washington, D.C.: Acropolis Books, 1976); Jeffrey T. Richelson, *The U.S. Intelligence Community* (Cambridge: Ballinger, 1985); and Harry H. Ransom, *The Intelligence Establishment* (Cambridge: Harvard Univ. Press, 1970). The changing nature of the National Security Council is discussed in John E. Endicott, "The National Security Council," in John F. Reichart and Steven R. Sturm, eds., *American Defense Policy*, 5th ed. (Baltimore: Johns Hopkins Univ. Press, 1982), 521–27; Henry M. Jackson, ed., *The National Security Council* (New York: Frederick A. Praeger, 1965); and John Tower et al., *The Tower Commission Report: The Full Text of the President's Special Review Board* (New York: New York Times, 1987).

The postwar efforts to promote Universal Military Training are described in Russell F. Weigley (1984) and Russell F. Weigley, *The American Way of War* (Bloomington: Indiana Univ. Press, 1973). The evolution of strategic military planning directed against the Soviet Union is discussed in Gregg Herken, *The Winning Weapon: The Atomic Bomb in the Cold War, 1945–1950* (New York: Vintage, 1982); David Alan Rosenberg, "The Origins of Overkill: Nuclear Weapons and American Strategy," in Norman A. Graebner, ed., *The National Security: Its Theory and Practice, 1945–1960* (New York: Oxford Univ. Press, 1986), 123–45; Michael S. Sherry, *Preparing for the Next War: American Plans for Postwar Defense, 1941–45* (New Haven: Yale Univ. Press, 1977). A number of postwar war plans, as well as important NSC documents, are reprinted in Etzold and Gaddis (1978).

Paul Nitze and the birth of NSC-68 is covered in Paul Hammond, "NSC-68: Prologue to Rearmament," in Warner R. Schilling et al., *Strategy, Politics and Defense Budgets* (New York: Columbia Univ. Press, 1962); Paul Nitze, "The Development of NSC-68, *International Security* 4(Spring 1980): 170–76; and Joseph M. Siracusa, "Paul H. Nitze, NSC-68 and the Soviet Union," in Clifford L. Egen and Alexander W. Knott, eds., *Essays in Twentieth Century American Diplomatic History Dedicated to Professor Daniel M. Smith* (Washington, D.C.: Univ. Press of America, 1982).

The Soviet military buildup of the fifties is assessed in Arnold L. Horelick and Myron Rush, *Strategic Power and Soviet Foreign Policy* (Chicago: Univ. of Chicago Press, 1966); David Holloway, *The Soviet Union and the Arms Race* (New Haven: Yale Univ. Press, 1983); Harriet Fast Scott and William F. Scott, *The Armed Forces of the USSR* (Boulder: Westview Press, 1981); and Thomas W. Wolfe (1970). The instabilities of the postwar third world and American efforts to prevent communist expansion are described in Alexander L. George and Richard Smoke, *Deterrence in American Foreign Policy: Theory and Practice* (New York: Columbia Univ. Press, 1974). For an evaluation of John Foster Dulles, see Louis Gerson, *John Foster Dulles* (New York: Cooper Square Publishers, 1967); and Michael Guhin, *John Foster Dulles: A Statesman and His Times* (New York: Columbia Univ. Press, 1972).

Military planning in the Eisenhower administration is dealt with in a number of recent works. Among the more useful are A.J. Bacevich, *The Pentomic Era: The U.S. Army between Korea and Vietnam* (Washington, D.C.: National Defense Univ. Press, 1986); John Lewis Gaddis (1982); Jerome H. Kahan, *Security in the Nuclear Age: Developing U.S. Strategic Arms Policy* (Washington, D.C.: Brookings Institution, 1975); Douglas Kinnard, *President Eisenhower and Strategic Management: A Study in Defense Politics* (Lexington: Univ. Press of Kentucky, 1977); and David A. Rosenberg (1986). For a critical evaluation of the efficiency of atomic weapons in regional conflicts, see Robert E. Osgood, *Limited War* (Chicago: Univ. of Chicago Press, 1957); Robert E. Osgood, *NATO: The Entangling Alliance* (Chicago: Univ. of Chicago Press, 1962); and Maxwell D. Taylor, *The Uncertain Trumpet* (New York; Harper and Brothers, 1959).

Arms control during the Truman administration is discussed in Gregg Herken (1982); Joseph I. Lieberman, *The Scorpion and the Tarantula: The Struggle to Control Atomic Weapons 1945–49* (Boston: Houghton Mifflin, 1970); and Daniel Yergin (1977). Eisenhower's efforts toward the same ends are treated in Robert Divine, *Blowing on the Wind: The Nuclear Test Ban Debate, 1954–1960* (New York: Oxford Univ. Press, 1978); and Jerome H. Kahan (1975).

For a general discussion of the Kennedy administration, see Theodore C. Sorenson *Kennedy* (New York: Harper and Row, 1965); and Arthur M. Schlesinger, Jr., *A Thousand Days: John F. Kennedy in the White House* (Boston: Houghton Mifflin, 1965). For Lyndon Johnson see Doris Kearns, *Lyndon Johnson and the American Dream* (New York: Harper and Row, 1976); and Lyndon Baines Johnson, *The Vantage Point: Perspectives on the Presidency, 1963–1969* (New York: Popular Library, 1971). Defense planning in the sixties is covered in Alain C. Enthoven and K. Wayne Smith, *How Much Is Enough? Shaping the Defense Program, 1961–1969* (New York: Harper and Row, 1971); Gregg Herken, *Counsels of War* (New York: Alfred A. Knopf, 1985); Jerome H. Kahan (1975); Fred Kaplan, *The Wiz-*

ards of Armageddon (New York: Simon and Schuster, 1983); William W. Kaufman, "Planning Conventional Forces, 1950–1980," in Daniel J. Kaufman et al., eds., U.S. National Security: A Framework for Analysis (Lexington: Lexington Books, 1985), 525–46; and Robert S. McNamara, "The Military Role of Nuclear Weapons," Foreign Affairs 62(Fall 1983).

The problem of managing the Defense Department is treated in Harold Brown, Thinking about National Security and Foreign Policy in a Dangerous World (Boulder: Westview Press, 1983); Alain C. Enthoven and K. Wayne Smith (1971); Paul Y. Hammond (1961); Samuel P. Huntington (1961); Arnold Kanter, Defense Politics: A Budgetary Perspective (Chicago: Univ. of Chicago Press, 1979); Robert S. McNamara, The Essence of Security: Reflections in Office (New York: Harper and Row, 1968); Clark A Murdock, Defense Policy Formations: A Comparative Analysis of the McNamara Era (Albany: State Univ. of New York Press, 1974); and Samuel A. Tucker, ed., A Modern Design for Defense Decisions: A McNamara-Hitch-Enthoven Anthology (Washington, D.C.: Industrial College of the Armed Forces, 1966).

Arms control in the sixties is assessed in several general studies. See John Barton and Lawrence Weiler, eds., Arms Control: Issues and Agreements (Stanford: Stanford Univ. Press, 1976); and Jerome H. Kahan (1975). Articles dealing with specific aspects of arms control initially published in Scientific American are reprinted in Readings from Scientific American: Arms Control (San Francisco: W.H. Freeman and Co., 1973); and Readings from Scientific American: Progress in Arms Control? (San Francisco: W.H. Freeman and Co., 1979). More specialized studies also include Bernard J. Firestone, The Quest for Nuclear Stability: John F. Kennedy and the Soviet Union (Westport: Greenwood Press, 1982); and Glenn T. Seaborg, Kennedy, Khrushchev and the Test Ban (Berkeley: Univ. of California Press, 1981).

Studies on America's involvement in Vietnam continue to appear with alarming regularity. A representative sample would include Leslie H. Gelb and Richard K. Betts, The Irony of Vietnam: The System Worked (Washington, D.C.: Brookings Institution, 1975); David Halberstam, The Best and the Brightest (New York: Random House, 1972); George C. Herring, America's Longest War: The United States and Vietnam, 1950–1975 (New York: John Wiley and Sons, 1979); Dave R. Palmer, Summons of the Trumpet: U.S.–Vietnam in Perspective (Novato: Presido Press, 1978); and Herbert Y. Schandler, The Unmasking of a President: Lyndon Johnson and Vietnam (Princeton: Princeton Univ. Press, 1977). A sample of the National Security Council discussions as well as other important documents dealing with Vietnam are contained in Neil Sheehan et al., eds., The Pentagon Papers as Published by the New York Times (New York: New York Times,

1971). Harry G. Summers, Jr., *On Strategy: A Critical Analysis of the Vietnam War* (Novato: Presido Press, 1982) gives a critical assessment of America's war strategy.

A good general survey of the changing nature of Soviet control in Eastern Europe is contained in J.F. Brown, *The New Eastern Europe: The Khrushchev Era and After* (New York: Praeger, 1966); and Zbigniew K. Brzezinski, *The Soviet Bloc: Unity and Conflict* (Cambridge: Harvard Univ. Press, 1971). Military and economic developments are covered in Robert W. Clawson and Lawrence S. Kaplan, eds., *The Warsaw Pact: Political Purpose and Military Means* (Wilmington: Scholarly Resources, 1982); Charles Gati, ed., *The International Politics of Eastern Europe* (New York: Praeger, 1975); Christopher D. Jones, *Soviet Influence in Eastern Europe: Political Autonomy and the Warsaw Pact* (New York: Praeger, 1981); and Robin Alison Remington, *The Warsaw Pact: Case Studies in Communist Conflict Resolution* (Cambridge: MIT Press, 1971). For information on the West German *Ostpolitik*, see Karl E. Birnbaum, *East and West Germany; A Modus Vivendi* (Lexington: Saxon House/Lexington Books, 1973). See also Willy Brandt, *People and Politics: The Years 1960–1975* (Boston: Little, Brown and Co., 1978).

Crucial for understanding the policies of the Nixon-Kissinger period are the memoirs of the main participants. See Henry A. Kissinger, *White House Years* (Boston: Little, Brown and Co., 1979); and idem, *Years of Upheaval* (Boston: Little, Brown and Co., 1982); as well as Richard M. Nixon, *R.N.: Memoirs of Richard Nixon*, 2 volumes (New York: Warner Books, 1978). For insight into Kissinger's goals and objectives, see his collected speeches and essays in Henry A. Kissinger, *American Foreign Policy*, 3d ed. (New York: Norton, 1977). A positive assessment of the period is offered in Dan Caldwell, *American-Soviet Relations from 1947 to the Nixon-Kissinger Grand Design* (Westport: Greenwood Press, 1981). A scathing critique is presented in Seymour M. Hersh, *The Price of Power: Kissinger in the Nixon White House* (New York: Summit Books, 1983).

Soviet foreign policy assumptions and perceptions are discussed in the following: M.M. Bober, *Karl Marx's Interpretation of History* (Cambridge: Harvard Univ. Press, 1962); Franklyn Griffiths, "The Sources of American Conduct: Soviet Perspectives and Their Policy Implications," *International Security* 2(Fall 1984): 3–50; V. Kubalkova and A.A. Cruickshank, *Marxism-Leninism and Theory of International Relations* (London: Routledge and Kegan Paul, 1980); and William Zimmerman, *Soviet Perspectives on International Relations, 1956–1967* (Princeton: Princeton Univ. Press, 1969). The processes by which the USSR makes decisions are considered in Jiri Valenta and William Potter, eds., *Soviet Decisionmaking for National Security* (London: George Allen and Unwin, 1984). For an interesting account of Soviet diplomats in action, see Leon Sloss and M. Scott Davis, *A Game for High Stakes: Lessons Learned in Negotiating with the Soviet Union* (Cambridge: Ballinger Publishing Co., 1986).

The SALT negotiations are discussed in the memoirs of the various participants including those of Henry Kissinger and Richard Nixon. See also Harold Brown (1983); Zbigniew Brzezinski, *Power and Principle: Memoirs of a National Security Adviser, 1977–1981* (New York: Farrar, Straus & Giroux, 1983); Jimmy Carter, *Keeping Faith: Memoirs of a President* (New York: Bantam Books, 1982); Gerald Ford, *A Time to Heal* (New York: Harper and Row, 1979); Gerald Smith, *Doubletalk: The Story of the First Strategic Arms Limitation Talks* (New York: Doubleday, 1980); and Cyrus Vance, *Hard Choices: Critical Years in American Foreign Policy* (New York: Simon and Schuster, 1983). An excellent secondary work on SALT I is John Newhouse, *Cold Dawn: The Story of SALT* (New York: Holt, Rinehart and Winston, 1973). For SALT II see Raymond L. Garthoff, *Détente and Confrontation: American-Soviet Relations from Nixon to Reagan* (Washington, D.C.: Brookings Institution, 1985); and Strobe Talbott, *Endgame: The Inside Story of SALT II* (New York: Harper and Row, 1980). See also Alexander L. George, *Managing U.S.–Soviet Rivalry: Problems of Crisis Prevention* (Boulder: Westview Press, 1983).

U.S.–Soviet relations in the seventies are well covered in the memoirs listed above. Among secondary works the best are Raymond L. Garthoff (1985) and Alexander L. George (1983). Soviet military trends are evaluated in John M. Collins, *American and Soviet Military Trends since the Cuban Missile Crisis* (Washington, D.C.: Georgetown Univ. Press, 1978); Steven Rosefielde, "Soviet Arms Buildup or U.S. Arms Decline?" in Helmut Sonnenfeldt, ed., *Soviet Politics in the 1980s* (Boulder: Westview Press, 1985), 99–129. For an account of the invasion of Afghanistan, see Joseph J. Collins, *The Soviet Invasion of Afghanistan: A Study in the Use of Force in Soviet Foreign Policy* (Lexington: Greenwood Press, 1985).

The evolution of American nuclear strategy is discussed in Desmond Ball, *Politics and Force Levels: The Strategic Missile Program of the Kennedy Administration* (Berkeley: Univ. of California Press, 1980); Desmond Ball and Jeffrey Richelson, eds., *Strategic Nuclear Targeting* (Ithaca: Cornell Univ. Press, 1986); Samuel P. Huntington, ed., *The Strategic Imperative: New Policies for American Security* (Cambridge: Ballinger, 1982); Lawrence Martin, ed., *Strategic Thought in the Nuclear Age* (London: Heinemann, 1979); Keith B. Payne, *Nuclear Deterrence in U.S.–Soviet Relations* (Boulder: Westview Press, 1982); and Richard Smoke, *National Security and the Nuclear Dilemma: An Introduction to the American Experience* (Menlo Park: Addison-Wesley, 1984). More recent changes are discussed in journal articles among which the reader may wish to consult

Jeffrey Richelson, "PD-59, NSDD-13 and the Reagan Strategic Moderni-zation Program,"*Journal of Strategic Studies* 6(June 1983): 125–44; Thomas Powers, "Choosing a Strategy for World War III," *The Atlantic* 250(November 1982): 82–111; and Leon Sloss and Marc D. Millot, "U.S. Nuclear Strategy in Evolution," *Strategic Review* 8(Winter 1984): 19–28.

The status of the Soviet military is assessed year by year in the annual *The Military Balance* published by the International Institute of Strategic Studies in London. The growth of Soviet nuclear forces is analyzed in Robert P. Berman and John C. Baker, *Soviet Strategic Forces: Requirements and Responses* (Washington, D.C.: Brookings Institution, 1982); while the shifting balance of ground force in Europe is discussed in William P. Mako, *U.S. Ground Forces and the Defense of Central Europe* (Washington, D.C.: Brookings Institution, 1983). The general structure and strategy of the Soviet military is offered in Harriet Fast Scott (1981). An unflattering picture of the Soviet army is given by Viktor Suvorov, *Inside the Soviet Army* (London: Panther Books, 1984). For Soviet military strategy, see John Baylis and Gerald Segal, eds., *Soviet Strategy* (Monclair: Allanheld, Osmun and Co., 1981); and Derek Leebaert, ed., *Soviet Military Thinking* (London: George Allen and Unwin, 1981).

The efforts of the Reagan administration to revitalize defense are assessed in the yearly George Hudson and Joseph Kruzel, eds., *American Defense Annual* (Lexington: Lexington Books). Stephen S. Cimbala, ed., *The Reagan Defense Program: An Interim Assessment* (Wilmington: Scholarly Resources, 1986) presents a mid-decade analysis. William M. Arkin and Richard W. Fieldhouse, *Global Links in the Arms Race* (Cambridge: Ballinger, 1985); and Bruce G. Blair, *Strategic Command and Control: Redefining the Nuclear Threat* (Washington, D.C.: Brookings Institution, 1985) discuss the difficulties in maintaining command and control during nuclear conflict. For the Reagan administration approach to the problem of arms control, see Strobe Talbolt, *Deadly Gambits: The Reagan Administration and the Stalemate in Nuclear Arms Control* (New York: Alfred A. Knopf, 1984).

The most recent information on specific aspects of the Reagan defense program are contained in journal articles. Among the more important are William Daugherty et al., "The Consequences of 'Limited' Nuclear Attack on the United States," *International Security* 10(Spring 1986): 3–45; Lawrence J. Korb and Linda Brady, "Rearming America: The Reagan Administration Defense Program," *International Security* 9(Winter 1984–85): 3–18; Barry Posen and Stephen Van Evera, "Defense Policy and the Reagan Administration: Departure from Containment," *International Security* 8(Summer 1983): 3–45; Jeffrey Record, "Jousting with Unreality: Reagan's Military Strategy," *International Security* 8(Winter 1983–84); and Caspar

W. Weinberger, "U.S. Defense Strategy," *Foreign Affairs* 64(Spring 1986): 675–97. For the pros and cons of the strategic defense initiative, see Ashton B. Carter and David N. Schwartz, eds., *Ballistic Missile Defenses* (Washington, D.C.: Brookings Institution, 1984); Sidney D. Drell et al., "Preserving the ABM Treaty: A Critique of the Reagan Strategic Defense Initiative," *International Security* 9(Fall 1984): 51–91; Keith B. Payne et al., "Forum: The Strategic Defense Initiative," *Orbis* 28(Summer 1984): 215–55; and James R. Schlesinger, "Rhetoric and Realities in the Star Wars Debate," *International Security* 10(Summer 1985): 3–12.

Index

universal military training: postwar
policy and, 66-68, 71
USSR: violates Yalta accords, 40;
maintains large postwar army, 45, 80;
improves force readiness (1949-1953),
81-83; postwar naval developments
in, 82-83; postwar air force
developments in, 83; develops
atomic bomb, 83-84; explodes
hydrogen bomb, 84; and bomber
gap, 84-85; postwar rocket programs
in, 84-85; launches Sputnik, 85; and
missile gap, 85-86; expands influence
into Third World, 86-94; views on
decolonization, 87-89; signs
Renunciation of Force Agreement
with West Germany, 154; reaches
nuclear parity with US, 156-57;
theory of international relations,
164-72; view of state in diplomacy,
165-66, 169; affirms primacy of class
struggle in international relations,
166-68; expands weapons testing
following SALT 1, 180; retains heavy
ICBMs at Vladivostok, 182; develops
fourth generation ICBMs, 183-84;
builds up military forces in 1970s,
190-91; and Cuban Brigade, 194-95;
military capabilities of, 207-16; global
strategic objectives of, 208-09; army
in, 209; strategic rocket forces in,
209-10; national air defense force in,
210; navy in, 210-11; air force in,
211; deploys SS-20, 211-12; warhead
development in, 212; view of
socialist-capitalist competition,
213-14; strategic doctrine of, 214-16;
shrinking economic power of, 234;
reforms under Gorbachev, 234-36
US strategic doctrine: evolution of,
198-206

Ustinov, Dmitry, 84

Vance, Cyrus: proposes arms cuts to
USSR, 183; response to discovery of
Cuban Brigade, 195
Victory Program, 15-17, 25
Vietnam: Eisenhower and French
crisis in, 91-92; history of US interest
in, 137-44; discussed at Yalta, 138;
offensive of 1972 in, 188-89;
provisions of 1973 armistice, 189-90;
fall of Saigon, 190; US Congress
restricts use of troops in, 190
Vladivostok Accord (1974), 181-82
Volkspolizei, 82

War College: prewar planning in, 9
Warsaw Pact, 148-49
Washington Naval Conference (1921),
6
Washington Naval Treaty (1921), 7
Weapons System Evaluation Group:
under Eisenhower, 100; under
Kennedy, 114
Weinberger, Caspar: discusses US
defense strategy, 217-19; justifies
SDI, 223; gives criteria for applying
military force, 225
West Germany: formation of, 51; signs
Renunciation of Force Agreements
(1970), 154. *See also Ostpolitik*
Wringer, 70

Yalta Conference: discusses Polish
issue, 35; discusses UN, 36-37;
discusses war against Japan, 37;
adopts Declaration of Liberated
Europe, 38; discussion of Vietnam at,
138
Yom Kippur War, 181, 193